Application of Novel Research Methods

Camelia Oprean-Stan (ed.)

Application of Novel Research Methods

The Study of Current Economic Phenomena

PETER LANG
Berlin - Bruxelles - Chennai - Lausanne - New York - Oxford

Library of Congress Cataloging-in-Publication Data
A CIP catalog record for this book has been applied for at the Library of Congress.

Bibliographic information published by the Deutsche Nationalbibliothek
The Deutsche Nationalbibliothek collects this publication in the Deutsche Nationalbibliografie; detailed bibliographic data are available on the Internet at .Nationalbibliografie; detailed bibliographic data are available on the Internet at http://dnb.d-nb.de.

ISBN 978-3-631-90052-9 (Print)
E-ISBN 978-3-631-91677-3 (E-PDF)
E-ISBN 978-3-631-91678-0 (EPUB)
DOI 10.3726/b21691

Published by Peter Lang GmbH, Berlin, Germany

info@peterlang.com - www.peterlang.com

Table of contents

List of contributors

Alina Georgeta Ailincă
3rd Degree Researcher, Ph.D., "Victor Slavescu" Financial and Monetary Research Center, N.I.E.R., Romanian Academy, Romania, E-mail: alinageorgetaailinca@gmail.com

Trupti Bhosale
Assist. Prof., Symbiosis School of Banking and Finance, Symbiosis International (Deemed University), India, E-mail: trupti.bhosale@ssbf.edu.in

Vasile Brătian
Assoc. Prof. Ph.D., Department of Finance and Accounting, Faculty of Economic Sciences, Lucian Blaga University of Sibiu, Romania, E-mail: vasile.bratian@ulbsibiu.ro

Renate Bratu
Assist. Prof. Ph.D., Department of Finance and Accounting, Faculty of Economic Sciences, University Lucian Blaga Sibiu, Romania, E-mail: renate.bratu@ulbsibiu.ro

Amelia Bucur
Assoc. Prof. Ph.D., Department of Mathematics and Informatics, Faculty of Sciences, Lucian Blaga University of Sibiu, Romania, E-mail: amelia.bucur@ulbsibiu.ro

Marian Pompiliu Cristescu
Department of Finance and Accounting, Faculty of Economic Sciences, Lucian Blaga University of Sibiu, Romania

Lia Cornelia Culda
Faculty of Economic Sciences, Lucian Blaga University of Sibiu, Romania

Emil Dinga
Senior Researcher at Centre for Financial and Monetary Research „Victor Slăvescu" – Romanian Academy, Romania

Gabriela-Mariana Ionescu
Ph.D., Romanian Academy, Romania, E-mail: gabrielaionescu13@gmail.com

Nicolae Ionescu
Prof. Ph.D. Eng., Department of Manufacturing Engineering, National University of Science and Technology POLITEHNICA Bucharest, Romania, E-mail: nicolae.ionescu@upb.ro

Dumitru Alexandru Mara
Faculty of Economic Sciences, Lucian Blaga University of Sibiu, Romania, E-mail: dumitrualexandru.mara@ulbsibiu.ro

Bogdan Mârza
Assoc. Prof. Ph.D., Department of Finance and Accounting, Faculty of Economic Sciences, University Lucian Blaga Sibiu, Romania, E-mail: bogdan.marza@ulbsibiu.ro

Raluca Andreea Nerişanu
Faculty of Economic Sciences, Lucian Blaga University of Sibiu, Romania

Camelia Oprean-Stan
Prof. Ph.D., Department of Finance and Accounting, Faculty of Economic Sciences, Lucian Blaga University of Sibiu, Romania, E-mail: camelia.oprean@ulbsibiu.ro

Deepa Pillai
Prof., Symbiosis School of Banking and Finance, Symbiosis International (Deemed University), India, E-mail: deepa.pillai@ssbf.edu.in

Răzvan Şerbu
Prof. Ph.D., Department of Management, Marketing and Business Administration, Faculty of Economic Sciences, University Lucian Blaga Sibiu, Romania, E-mail: razvan.serbu@ulbsibiu.ro

Nadia Sghaier
Assist. Prof., Ph.D., Department of Finance and Accounting, International Finance Group Tunisia, Faculty of Economics and Management of Tunis, University of Tunis El Manar, Tunisia, E-mail: nadia.sghaier@fsegt.utm.tn

Sebastian Emanuel Stan
Faculty of Military Management, "Nicolae Balcescu" Land Forces Academy, Sibiu, Romania, E-mail: office.sstan@gmail.com

Cristina Tănăsescu
Prof. Ph.D., Department of Management, Marketing and Business Administration, Faculty of Economic Sciences, Lucian Blaga University of Sibiu, Romania, E-mail: cristina.tanasescu@ulbsibiu.ro

Iustina Tudor
Ph.D. Student, Department of Manufacturing Engineering, National University of Science and Technology POLITEHNICA Bucharest, Romania, E-mail: tr.iustina@yahoo.com

Foreword

Prof. Ph.D. Camelia Oprean-Stan

Each science creates and employs its own set of tools, methods, and techniques for comprehending reality. Economic research methods are means of studying specific phenomena that are required to determine the economic behavior of society and individual market agents. Economic models assist in the simplified description of reality; they are an abstract generalization of the interrelationships between economic variables.

Phenomena and processes must be studied in a state of constant development and change. This cannot be accomplished without employing a systematic approach to phenomenon analysis. Techniques and tools used in scientific research can be categorized as follows: physical modeling (such as a model), structural modeling (such as a model-analogy), and functional modeling (such as a system of equations); deterministic, probabilistic, fuzzy, and chaotic simulation; falsification (theorem testing). Economic research primarily employs the following approaches to understanding economic phenomena and processes: dialectical method, scientific abstraction, analysis and synthesis, induction and deduction, historical and logical methods, economic experimentation, economic modeling, and so on.

The purpose of this edited collection is to bridge the gap between advanced research methods and models and the main fields of the economic research by providing a collection of articles illustrating the applicability of new research methods to a wide range of current economic topics, such as, but not limited to, mathematical modeling of the financial market behavior: behavioral finance models, news sentiment analysis, options pricing and time series analysis; modeling in corporate finance and management: bankruptcy and failure prediction, decision-making problems and development of co-created products; modeling of macroeconomic issues: social justice, sustainable GDP, natural gas consumption and economic growth, welfare and artificial intelligence. The research papers present novel results from modeling current economic phenomena using a logical, behavioral, institutional, and quantitative approach.

The book emphasizes the key methodologies and their accessible empirical application while focusing on the most crucial problems, models, and techniques for research in all areas of economics. The areas of application have been carefully chosen so that a wide range of methodological approaches are covered, and all of the techniques described are used to address actual problems rather than being presented for their own sake. Each chapter is largely self-contained and contain the essential references for each subject and serve as a reliable manual for further reading.

This book includes empirical and theoretical original papers written by researchers from different countries and universities. All papers have been peer reviewed. Because of its applied profile of research book, based on a series of empirical analyzes, the book is meant to serve as a resource for doctoral candidates, academics, and researchers who are interested in investigating new methodologies in a variety of economic fields, including corporate finance, financial markets, macroeconomics, microeconomics, management, etc. The book will also be helpful for economics researchers and advanced Masters-level students who are writing dissertations, even for students interested in exploring new ideas and paradigms in the functioning of the economic systems, particularly those preparing for an academic career.

Introduction

The goal of this book is to provide the most recent theory and methodology for economic process analysis. It includes real-world research examples as well as quantitative and qualitative methods commonly used in economics. The novel elements of the book provide researchers with useful and practical knowledge, and they have the potential to add value due to the anticipated effect of this approach on literature and practice. The book is a collection of 12 theoretical and empirical research papers that examine economic phenomena while taking into account global problems. These studies are summarized below.

Ailincă investigates the impact of institutional indicators, such as the Corruption Perceptions Index and other indicators of institutional capacity, on indices of welfare, social equity, education, and health in European Union countries using econometric analysis with panel data. The study emphasizes the significance of institutional measures like the Corruption Perceptions Index in understanding and tackling issues including prosperity, poverty, education, and health. The findings imply that a positive perception of corruption and strong institutional capability can help to reduce crime rates, strengthen national and European judicial systems, and improve health and education outcomes. The findings of the article can be used to improve the connection between citizens and institutions in European Union countries.

Ionescu provides a classification of qualitative and quantitative research methods in the field of social justice that can be used to analyze economic and social phenomena such as economic inequality and wealth distribution. The paper emphasizes the importance of using effective research methods to address societal problems and proposes the use of new research methods to analyze social justice functions, such as TRIZ, QFD, and Value Analysis. The paper also suggests future research directions, such as using new research methods to investigate important issues such as the Principle of Difference and connecting classical and current research methods. The paper emphasizes the role and importance of qualitative and quantitative methods in analyzing and proposing solutions to societal problems, as well as their applicability to a wide range of current economic topics.

Dinga and Tănăsescu introduce the concept of Sustainable GDP, a new type of GDP that considers the value of a country's natural, human, and manufactured capital, resulting in a more comprehensive measure of economic well-being. The paper proposes a methodological approach to calculating Sustainable GDP that takes into account economic, social, and moral constraints, in line with the goal of long-term economic growth. To restore the analytical formula for the general case of sustainability coefficients, the paper employs a mathematical approach, specifically the formulation of recurrence relations and the use of a Kalman type filter. In addition, the paper employs the input-output model, specifically the Leontief (1966) input-output model, to analyze the flows between the structural components of a national economy and proposes the use of the fourth quadrant to formalize Sustainable GDP. The mathematical approach and use of the input-output model in the paper provide a framework for analyzing economic flows and calculating sustainable coefficients, providing a practical tool for assessing and monitoring sustainability in economic systems. Alternative indicators, such as the Sustainable GDP, can provide policymakers with a more comprehensive understanding of the economic process and guide decision-making toward sustainable development.

Oprean-Stan and Stan present a comprehensive approach to analyzing variable relationships, taking structural changes into account and capturing the dynamic nature of causal linkages. To model the causal relationship between natural gas consumption and economic growth in Romania, the authors use a bootstrap full-sample Granger causality test based on a residual bootstrap procedure with a modified-LR test. The parameter stability test is used to confirm the presence of structural changes in the variables' relationship. The paper also reexamines the causal relationship between natural gas consumption and economic growth using a bootstrap subsample causality test with a time-varying approach (RB bootstrap-based modified-LR causality test). Rolling-window estimation is used to investigate the causal relationships between variables over different sub-periods while accounting for time-varying parameters. The bootstrap sub-sample rolling window causality method used in the paper can be used to analyze the relationship between variables other than natural gas consumption and economic growth, providing insights into causal linkages in a variety of domains.

Bratu et al. stress the importance of collaboration among AI researchers, legal experts, and policymakers in developing an ethical framework that respects individual rights while encouraging creativity. The authors discuss the evolution of artificial intelligence from science fiction to its current capabilities, as well as the complexities of AI's impact on society and creativity. The paper discusses the global economy's transformation as a result of diverse perspectives and innovations, particularly artificial intelligence (AI), and emphasizes the importance of collaboration, sustainability, and ethical practices in shaping sustainable growth. It emphasizes the importance of understanding the impact of AI on society and creativity, as well as the responsibility of AI researchers, legal experts, and policymakers in developing an ethical framework that respects individual rights while encouraging creativity. Proactively establishing a digital law for AI and embracing a digital rights constitution can lay the groundwork for an inclusive and responsible AI-driven society. Individuals will be empowered, their digital identities will be protected, and creativity will be preserved.

Sghaier employs a Markov Regime Switching model with the maximum likelihood method to examine the impact of the Covid-19 pandemic and the invasion of Ukraine on the global and 11 individual sector stock market returns. The econometric approach allows for the consideration of two distinct regimes, capturing the heterogeneous investor behaviors. Returns are also described in detail to provide insights into the mean reversion trading strategy and the presence of fundamentalists in various sectors. The paper emphasizes the importance of understanding the diverse behaviors of stock market investors, specifically the presence of both fundamentalists and chartists, and how their actions can influence stock market returns. Investors can use this information to strategically diversify their portfolios and potentially mitigate the negative effects of the crises on their investments. The insights provided by this paper can help risk managers better manage their risk, particularly in boom-and-bust markets.

Cristescu et al. conducted sentiment analysis on financial news titles and descriptions using a three-phase methodology. TextBlob, a lexical-based sentiment analysis tool, was initially used to classify text as positive, neutral, or negative based on word polarity. The paper was later upgraded to the BERT model, which is a more sophisticated and context-aware approach to sentiment analysis. The Polygon.io news API was used to collect data, which provided key details such as article titles, publishing times, and short descriptions of the news in JSON format. The paper also highlights the use of Pandas (Python Data Analysis Library) for sentiment analysis and exporting, providing a practical example for researchers and practitioners. The paper offers a step-by-step guide to using free tools to conduct sentiment analysis on financial news, which can help investors and financial professionals make informed decisions based on market sentiment. Integrating sentiment analysis into investment strategies can help investors gain a better understanding of market sentiment and potentially make better trading decisions.

Dinga's study includes conceptualization, formalization, and the development of a method for measuring stability in time series analysis. The concept of the (fundamental) cycle of a generic time series is introduced and formalized in this paper. Based on the concept of economic number, the author proposes a method for ensuring measurement stability in time series. The paper proposes estimating the cycle period of a time series based on the determination of its own intrinsic rhythm and employing the levels of depth suggested by the author. The paper presents a theoretical and methodological framework for considering time series as causally isolated and calculating their intrinsic rhythm, with applications in economics, finance, and social sciences. Understanding the concept of the (fundamental) cycle of a time series can aid in the analysis and prediction of economic phenomena because it reflects the cyclicality of economic agents' behavior. The concept of natural value, which is the mean of a time series that follows its intrinsic rhythm and cycle, can be used to determine equilibrium values and identify attractors in economic systems. This can help assess stability, measure economic variables, and assess the impact of interventions or policies.

Brătian and Oprean-Stan discuss and compare two methods of pricing option derivatives for European-style option prices. The Black-Scholes methodology is used by the authors to obtain explicit solutions for European-type Call and Put options, which are differential equations with second-order random variables. To estimate the value of the underlying asset at maturity, the Feynman-Kac theorem is also used in conjunction with Monte Carlo simulations. These simulations generate potential outcomes based on the asset's stochastic evolution. The DAX stock index is used as the underlying asset for European Call and Put options, and the specific application of these methods is demonstrated. The results indicate that there are no significant differences in European-style option prices when the Black-Scholes methodology or the Feynman-Kac Theorem are used. This means that practitioners can use either method depending on their preference or specific needs, as both produce similar results. Using explicit solutions obtained through the Black-Scholes methodology can provide a more analytical approach to pricing options, whereas using the Feynman-Kac Theorem in conjunction with Monte Carlo simulations provides a more stochastic approach.

Bucur introduces and defines the concept of t-intuitionistic fuzzy relations in order to solve economic decision-making problems. An algorithm is developed to solve decision-making problems related to current economic phenomena using t-intuitionistic fuzzy relations. The concept of crisp sets and their relationship to decision-making is also discussed in the paper. The weight function defined in t-intuitionistic fuzzy relations can provide a more accurate approximation for measuring the effects of internal parameters in current economic phenomena. The use of t-intuitionistic fuzzy relations in economic decision-making can assist in dealing with ambiguity and uncertainty, providing a flexible model for making informed decisions. The paper's example shows how to use t-intuitionistic fuzzy relations to achieve optimal recognition results for economic organizations based on quality characteristics.

Tudor and Ionescu present practical methods and models for the development of co-created products, allowing for greater customer participation in the product design process. These methods include categorizing products based on their suitability for co-creation, involving experts as well as a broader group of users in the co-creation process, and dynamically adapting customer requirements and product characteristics based on evolutionary laws. Averaging customer scores for requirements, determining correlations between requirements and specifications based on customer feedback, and setting target values and acceptable limit values for product specifications are also discussed in the paper. The paper also includes a cost model for co-created products that can be tailored to different product categories and market scenarios.

Pillai and Bhosale propose a novel "reconstructive mixed method" for predicting distress and bankruptcy in commercial banks that integrates quantitative and qualitative data. It combines machine learning techniques with a mixed research approach to improve prediction accuracy and early detection of distress and bankruptcy warning signs, enabling banks to take proactive measures. The methodology includes a thorough review of the literature, an examination of research gaps, an analysis of existing literature characteristics, and the feasibility of using a mixed research design to address the research gaps. The study's findings can help financial industry stakeholders adopt more efficient strategies for predicting and mitigating financial distress, ultimately contributing to the banking sector's stability and sustainability.

Alina Georgeta Ailincă

Chapter 1 The impact of institutional indicators on some indicators of welfare and social equity, education and health

Abstract: The current context, troubled by permanent imbalances and crises, such as the crisis generated by the COVID-19 pandemic, but also previous crises, call into question the role of the state and its capacity for institutional resilience. In this framework, the role of the chapter is to identify, through an econometric study with panel data, at the level of European Union countries, if and how the Corruption Perceptions Index, but also other indicators regarding institutional capacity have influenced important indicators in the field of welfare and reduction poverty, education, health and social equity. The results can indicate the steps to follow, where and how the relationship between citizens and institutions can be improved.

Keywords: corruption, social inequity, poverty, public health, welfare

1. Introduction

The need for well-being and prosperity is global. There is no society that does not want prosperity, no matter what are the elements of prosperity that it selects as valid and beneficial for it. In this context, the citizens of all the countries of the world, as belonging to established democracies or authoritarian regimes, want peace and prosperity. But often, the general need for prosperity often brings citizens into conflict with the state or with the oligopolies dominated in that economy because of corruption phenomenon. Even the Latin term "corruptio" symbolizes this moral degradation, bribery, seduction, falsification, deterioration, degradation, disintegration and inversion of values (Ochulor & Bassey, 2010), therefore the clearly negative character of the term or the flawed way of achieving and sharing prosperity. However, what can be understood by corruption differs from one political system to another, from one country or region to another, that's why there is no single definition accepted by everyone regarding corruption (Rohwer, 2009).

In general, corruption is not a singular element, it is part of a wider cultural system of values, sometimes even historical, that is why the idea of corruption should not be absolutized, being on the border between legal and illegal, between moral and less moral, between tolerable and intolerable, etc. and it must be reported in the economic sphere rather through a possible phenomenon of restriction of prosperity for society as a whole.

In this context, the chapter tries to discern not on the term of corruption, and its measurement methodology, but rather on its social effects at the level of the European Union states. The main indicator is the Corruption Perceptions Index developed by Transparency International but also taken into consideration within the Eurostat methodology. To this indicator, other institutional indicators are being considered in the sustainable development targets and Eurostat methodology.

Thus, in this chapter, at the level of the European Union as a whole, these institutional indicators are related to a set of prosperity and poverty, income distribution, education and health indicators. The results obtained speak clearly about the importance of raising the level of education and health at the level of all the countries of the European Union, but also of raising awareness of the dangers of corruption and the precarious institutional values on the desired sustainable development goals, implicitly on the multiplier beneficial social factors, in particular – education and health.

2. Motivation, literature review and description of the problem

Signed at Runnymede on June 15, 1215, the Magna Carta Libertatum is the predecessor of the most modern constitutions of the world, and especially of Europe. The importance of this work lies in putting the king and his government under the law, granting some freedoms and stipulating some limits, being, with all its medieval shortcomings, the basis of some modern institutional structures (parliament, courts of justice, etc.) and of some political, legal and economic principles still respected today. But not only the firm and clear legislation, but also the manner of its interpretation and application: on the one hand, flexible enough to conform to society's evolution, and on the other sufficiently clear and above all correctly applied, it makes the difference between a strong society and one crushed by corruption.

Corruption, as a terminology, does not have a unanimously and widely accepted definition. Thus, there are natural limits in the formulation of this concept (Heidenheimer et al., 1989; Knack, 2006; UNDP, 2008 etc.) and no single measure of its evaluation. In this sense, the literature indicates several options for measuring corruption through various indices, for example those developed by Transparency International: Corruption Perceptions Index (CPI), the Global Corruption Barometer and Global Integrity's Global Integrity Index or the one developed by the World Bank: Worldwide Governance Indicators (WGI)

(Rohwer, 2009). Corruption Perceptions Index is a composite index based on corruption-related data surveys, which ranks countries in terms of the degree to which corruption is perceived to exist among politicians and public officials (Rohwer, 2009). Its low score indicates a high level of corruption, thus we can say that the index has mainly a positive connotation with the increase of the score.

Numerous empirical works study the link between corruption and democracy, with debatable results regarding the influence of democracy in emerging markets societies on the reduction of corruption (e.g. Paldam, 1999; Goldsmith, 1999; Treisman, 2000).

Corruption and poor public decision-making represent undesirable aspects, affecting economic and social relations, affecting public perception of country risk, the level of private and public investments, leading to the increase of social inequalities. The analysis of the causes of corruption has been treated in numerous studies (de Castro Soares, 2017; Wang & Hui, 2017; Gutierrez-Garcia & Rodríguez, 2016; Bologna, 2016; Stevens, 2016; Yamamura, 2014; Heywood & Meyer-Sahling, 2013; Villoria & Jimenéz, 2012; O'Connor & Fischer, 2012; Faria et al., 2012; Arvate et al., 2010; Quinn, 2008; Adsera et al., 2003; Silva et al., 2001; Treisman, 2000; Andvig et al., 2000). The results generally demonstrating a negative relationship between corruption and economic growth measured by the variation of GDP and with the degrees of economic freedom of a country and with productivity and a positive relationship of corruption with unemployment, with mortality, but also of corruption with the size of the government, with the excessive degree of regulation, as well as with the succession of shocks in the economy, including against the backdrop of natural disasters.

In general, all studies point to the harmful influence of corruption on society, some of which state the need for a reversal of the strategy by reducing corruption through education, in order to reduce not only corruption but also poverty and social inequity and to properly reach the goals of sustainable development (e.g. Hallak & Poisson, 2005; Cheung & Chan, 2008; Pitsoe, 2013; Dirwan, 2019).

3. Methodology and data sources

This chapter investigates the impact of the Corruption Perceptions Index and other indicators regarding institutional capacity on some important indicators in the field of welfare, equity, poverty reduction, education and health at the European Union 27 (EU27) level. The selected indicators reflect the targets of sustainable development and the database is Eurostat. The analysis period is 2012–2022, and the data are panel systematized for the all European Union 27 member states.

The used variables, the notations and data sources are presented in Tab. 1.1.

Where the series lack information, they are extended by extrapolation and where the data are missing, they are interpolated or are used proxies, which is why the results must be viewed with caution.

Tab. 1.1: The description of the variables and data source

Description of Variable	Notation of Variable	Source of Data
Corruption Perceptions Index	*CPIx*	Transparency International, EUROSTAT, SDG_16_50__custom_5235981
Standardized death rate due to homicide by sex	*SDDH*	EUROSTAT, SDG_16_10
Population reporting occurrence of crime, violence or vandalism in their area by poverty status	*Procvv*	EUROSTAT, SDG_16_20
General government total expenditure on law courts	*GGELC*	EUROSTAT, SDG_16_30
Perceived independence of the justice system	*PIJS*	DG COMM, EUROSTAT, SDG_16_40
Population with confidence in EU institutions by institution	*PcEUi*	DG COMM, EUROSTAT, SDG_16_60
Real GDP per capita	*RGDPC*	EUROSTAT, SDG_08_10
In work at-risk-of-poverty rate	*IWARPR*	EUROSTAT, SDG_01_41
Income distribution	*Idistrib*	EUROSTAT, SDG_10_41
Relative median at-risk-of-poverty gap	*RMARPG*	EUROSTAT, SDG_10_30
Early leavers from education and training by sex	*ELET*	EUROSTAT, SDG_04_10
Adult participation in learning in the past four weeks by sex	*APLP4W*	EUROSTAT, SDG_04_60
Healthy life years at birth by sex	*HLYB*	EUROSTAT, SDG_03_11
Self-reported unmet need for medical examination and care by sex	*SRUNMEC*	EUROSTAT, SDG_03_60

Source: Eurostat database; author's selection

The regression models verified in this chapter are presented below:

RGDPC = f(CPIx, SDDH, Procvv, GGELC, PIJS, PcEUi) (1)

IWARPR = f(CPIx, SDDH, Procvv, GGELC, PIJS, PcEUi) (2)

Idistrib = f(CPIx, SDDH, Procvv, GGELC, PIJS, PcEUi) (3)
RMARPG = f(CPIx, SDDH, Procvv, GGELC, PIJS, PcEUi) (4)
ELET = f(CPIx, SDDH, Procvv, GGELC, PIJS, PcEUi) (5)
APLP4W = f(CPIx, SDDH, Procvv, GGELC, PIJS, PcEUi) (6)
HLYB = f(CPIx, SDDH, Procvv, GGELC, PIJS, PcEUi) (7)
SRUNMEC = f(CPIx, SDDH, Procvv, GGELC, PIJS, PcEUi) (8)

The equations are represented as:

$$Y=\alpha+\beta 1x1+\beta 2x2+\beta 3x3+\beta 4x4+\beta 5x5+\beta 6x6+\varepsilon$$

where
Y= the dependent variables chosen successively as: RGDPC – Real GDP per capita; IWARPR – In work at-risk-of-poverty rate; Idistrib -Income distribution; RMARPG – Relative median at-risk-of-poverty gap; ELET – Early leavers from education and training by sex; APLP4W – Adult participation in learning in the past four weeks by sex; HLYB – Healthy life years at birth by sex; SRUNMEC – Self-reported unmet need for medical examination and care by sex.

α= Constant; β1-6=Slope of x1–x6 coefficients; x1–x6= the coefficients of the regression or the independent variables, namely CPIx – Corruption Perceptions Index; SDDH – Standardized death rate due to homicide by sex; Procvv – Population reporting occurrence of crime, violence or vandalism in their area by poverty status; GGELC – General government total expenditure on law courts; PIJS – Perceived independence of the justice system; PcEUi – Population with confidence in EU institutions by institution; ε = error term.

4. Results

Based on the above information, it can be constructed an Augmented Dickey-Fuller (ADF) unit root test (see Tab. 1.2). The Tab. 1.2 demonstrates that the used variables from this investigation are stable at order 0.

In Tab. 1.3 there is presented the descriptive statistics of the models: the mean, the median, the standard deviation, the skewness, as well as kurtosis, and other variables are shown.

The standard deviation shows in some cases close to the average, being below the average for the targeted explanatory indicators, except for GGELC and SRUNMEC. Usually, that the values are grouped around the average, and the median and mean are close to each other in value for the most of the predictive variables investigated, showing a relatively symmetrical distribution.

Considering the Skewness, it can be noticed that the independent variables are some below the value of 1, which indicates that they are less significant and negatively skewed and some above the value of 1, which indicates that they are substantially and positively skewed. The kurtosis is above 3 for the most of these variables, which indicates that the distribution is leptokurtic, producing more values than a normal distribution, except for CPIx, PIJS and PcEUi.

Tab. 1.2: The result of unit root tests

Variables ADF	T-statistic	Mackinnon Critical Value at 5 %	P-value	Order of Integration	Observations
CPIx	−3.6244	−3.4251	0.0294	I(0)	Stationary
SDDH	−4.6404	−3.4251	0.0010	I(0)	Stationary
Procvv	−4.9712	−3.4251	0.0003	I(0)	Stationary
GGELC	−3.4555	−3.4257	0.0363	I(0)	Stationary
PIJS	−3.6792	−3.4251	0.0252	I(0)	Stationary
PcEUi	−6.4287	−3.4251	0.0000	I(0)	Stationary
RGDPC	−4.1478	−3.9894	0.0060	I(0)	Stationary
IWARPR	−4.2335	−3.4251	0.0045	I(0)	Stationary
Idistrib	−4.2560	−3.4251	0.0042	I(0)	Stationary
RMARPG	−4.9462	−3.4251	0.0003	I(0)	Stationary
ELET	−5.2034	−3.4251	0.0001	I(0)	Stationary
APLP4W	−3.6595	−3.4251	0.0267	I(0)	Stationary
HLYB	−3.6847	−3.4251	0.0248	I(0)	Stationary
SRUNMEC	−4.8551	−3.4251	0.0005	I(0)	Stationary

Source: Eurostat database; author's processing

From Tabs. 1.5 to 1.12 there are shown the regression equation results for dependent variables RGDPC, IWARPR, Idistrib, RMARPG, ELET, APLP4W, HLYB, SRUNMEC considering the Least Squares method, and for the equations which showed a higher than 50 % R-squared – for RGDPC and APLP4W – there had been used also a quantile regression method (see Tabs. 1.13 and 1.14).

Tables 1.5–1.12 shows the connection between the predictor variables and the response variable (RGDPC, IWARPR, Idistrib, RMARPG, ELET, APLP4W, HLYB and SRUNMEC) and only for RGDPC and respectively APLP4W the R-squared is quite significant, above 0.50 more exactly 0.6698 and respectively 0.68086 for APLP4W.

The R-squared of 0.234317 for IWARPR, 0.440747 for IDISTRIB, 0.410255 for RMARPG, 0.192038 for ELET, 0.323909 for HLYB and, 0.337830 for SRUNMEC are small but indicate a positive relationship, some of them getting closer to 50 % (e.g. IDISTRIB and RMARPG). Thus, accounting for the above information we can conclude that institutional features – including the perception about justice and EU institutions can determine to some extent the social, educational and health indicators. The F-statistics p-value is less than 5 %, indicating that all the models are acceptable.

Tab. 1.3: Statistics describing the chosen variables

Variable's Notation (Obs.297)	Mean	Median	Maximum	Minimum	Std.dev.	Skewness	Kurtosis	Jarque-Bera	Prob.	Sum	Sum Sq.Dev.
CPIx	63.741	60.000	92.000	36.000	14.427	0.241	1.885	18.263	0.000	18931.0	61609.0
SDDH	1.148	0.820	6.950	0.150	1.028	2.765	11.596	1292.854	0.000	340.9	313.0
Procvv	10.828	10.800	26.900	2.400	4.653	0.640	3.778	27.785	0.000	3216.1	6408.4
GGELC	1561.235	573.000	1433.000	22.000	2662.311	2.960	12.177	1475.899	0.000	463686.8	2.10E + 09
PIJS	54.438	52.000	88.000	17.000	18.400	0.045	1.973	13.157	0.001	16168.0	100211.4
PcEUi	50.747	52.000	80.000	23.000	10.544	-0.186	2.783	2.289	0.318	15072.0	32906.1
RGDPC	26295.180	20770.000	84750.000	5390.000	17125.250	1.519	5.595	197.615	0.000	7809667.0	8.68E + 10
IWARPR	8.125	7.800	19.800	2.700	3.203	0.865	4.037	50.331	0.000	2413.2	3036.2
Idistrib	4.865	4.490	8.320	3.030	1.181	0.756	2.679	29.585	0.000	1445.0	412.9
RMARPG	22.550	21.700	38.200	13.200	5.430	0.502	2.512	15.409	0.000	6697.2	8726.4
ELET	9.272	8.400	24.700	2.200	4.102	0.927	3.822	50.861	0.000	2753.8	4979518.0
APLP4W	11.172	8.500	36.200	0.900	7.900	7.912	3.822	50.861	0.000	2753.8	4979.5
HLYB	61.897	61.780	73.600	51.400	4.786	0.403	2.797	8.543	0.014	18383.4	6780.5
SRUNMEC	2.999	1.800	16.400	0.000	3.253	1.805	5.999	272.621	0.000	890.8	3131.8

Source: Eurostat database; author's processing

Tab. 1.4: The chosen variables correlation matrix

	CPIx	*SDDH*	*Procvv*	*GGELC*	*PIJS*	*PcEUi*	*RGDPC*	*IWARPR*	*Idistrib*	*RMARPG*	*ELET*	*APLP4W*	*HLYB*	*SRUNMEC*
CPIx	1													
SDDH	–.172	1												
Procvv	–.033	–.095	1											
GGELC	.190	–.289	.173	1										
PIJS	.838	–.104	.095	.097	1									
PcEUi	.374	.055	–.195	–.184	.388	1								
RGDPC	.743	–.391	.117	.121	.697	.335	1							
IWARPR	–.369	.115	.192	.161	–.265	–.158	–.17423	1						
Idistrib	–.470	.416	.241	.024	–.370	–.157	–.395	.730	1					
RMARPG	–.592	.181	.051	.043	–.560	–.206	–.475	.699	.760	1				
ELET	–.198	.016	.335	.210	–.160	–.157	–.186	.499	.449	.389	1			
APLP4W	.804	–.140	–.030	–.021	.684	.332	.594	-.333	–.431	-.490	–.137	1		
HLYB	.041	–.430	.385	.230	.108	–.030	.251	.025	–.041	–.144	.211	.095	1	
SRUNMEC	–.249	.538	.065	–.189	–.162	–.129	–.375	.366	.406	.328	.092	–.184	–.312	1

Source: Eurostat database; author's processing

In Tab. 1.5, the p-value is suitable for all independent variables in relation to the dependent variable RGDPC with an attached probability below 0.05. And the coefficients of the independent variables are substantially different from zero. For SDDH – Standardized death rate due to homicide by sex, and GGELC – General government total expenditure on law courts, the coefficients are negative, fact that highlights that crime and its financial implications in the courts of justice negatively affect economic growth.

Tab. 1.5: The regression result for RDGPC

Dependent Variable: RDGPC			
Method: Least Squares		**Observations: 297**	
R-squared	0.6698	Mean dep.var.	26295.18
Adjusted R-squared	0.6629	Akaike inf crit.	21.2703
F-statistic	98.0233	Schwarz crit.	21. 35739
Prob.(F-statistic)	0.0000	Hannan-Quinn crit.	21.3052
Sum sqrd.resid.	2.87E +10	Durbin-Watson stat.	0.7499
Variable	**Coefficient**	**t-Statistic**	**Prob.**
C	−27878.87	−6.537929	0.0000
CPIx	601.5463	7.675582	0.0000
SDDH	−5018.215	−8.442156	0.0000
Procvv	436.7332	3.274800	0.0012
GGELC	−0.554716	−2.308819	0.0217
PIJS	189.3791	3.113742	0.0020
PcEUi	146.1771	2.310612	0.0216

Source: Eurostat database; author's processing

In Tab. 1.6, the p-value is suitable for the most of independent variables in relation to the dependent variable IWARPR – In work at-risk-of-poverty rate, except for PIJS and PcEUi. Thus, these variables can be proposed to be excluded form the model. The coefficients of the independent variables are not substantially different from zero and for CPIx, the coefficient has also a negative sign.

Tab. 1.6: The regression result for IWARPR

Dependent Variable: IWARPR			
Method: Least Squares		**Observations: 297**	
R-squared	0.234317	Mean dep.var.	8.125318
Adjusted R-squared	0.218475	Akaike inf crit.	3.202729
F-statistic	14.79110	Schwarz crit.	4.942663
Prob.(F-statistic)	0.000000	Hannan-Quinn crit.	4.977515
Sum sqrd.resid.	2324.778	Durbin-Watson stat.	0.233032
Variable	**Coefficient**	**t-Statistic**	**Prob.**
C	11.34667	9.344274	0.0000
CPIx	−0.113313	−5.077291	0.0000
SDDH	0.397107	2.345959	0.0197
Procvv	0.097278	2.561490	0.0109
GGELC	0.000325	4.749101	0.0000
PIJS	0.019647	1.134346	0.2576
PcEUi	0.018038	1.001235	0.3175

Source: Eurostat database; author's processing

In Tab. 1.7, the p-value is suitable for the most of independent variables in relation to the dependent variable IDISTRIB – Income distribution, except for PIJS and PcEUi. These variables, according to the p-value, can be excluded from the model. The coefficients of the independent variables are not substantially different from zero and for CPIx and PIJS, the coefficients have also a negative sign.

Tab. 1.7: The regression result for IDISTRIB

Dependent Variable: IDISTRIB			
Method: Least Squares		**Observations: 297**	
R-squared	0.440747	Mean dep.var.	4.865360
Adjusted R-squared	0.429176	Akaike inf crit.	2.633252
F-statistic	38.09141	Schwarz crit.	2.720309
Prob.(F-statistic)	0.000000	Hannan-Quinn crit.	2.668104
Sum sqrd.resid.	230.8963	Durbin-Watson stat.	0.326372

(*continued on next page*)

Tab. 1.4: Continued

Dependent Variable: IDISTRIB			
Variable	**Coefficient**	**t-Statistic**	**Prob.**
C	5.346290	13.970500	0.0000
CPIx	−0.033322	−4.737622	0.0000
SDDH	0.478827	8.975812	0.0000
Procvv	0.064650	5.401663	0.0000
GGELC	8.81E -05	4.086804	0.0001
PIJS	−0.003933	−0.720563	0.4718
PcEUi	0.009260	1.630931	0.1040

Source: Eurostat database; author's processing

For the dependent variable RMARPG – Relative median at-risk-of-poverty gap, in Tab. 1.8, the p-value is suitable for the most of independent variables in relation to the dependent variable, except for Procvv and PcEUi. These variables, according to the p-value, can be excluded from the model. The coefficients of the independent variables are not substantially different from zero, except for SDDH, and for CPIx and PIJS (which have positive connotations) the coefficients have also a negative sign.

Tab. 1.8: The regression result for RMARPG

Dependent Variable: RMARPG			
Method: Least Squares		**Observations: 297**	
R-squared	0.410255	Mean dep.var.	22.54963
Adjusted R-squared	0.359805	Akaike inf crit.	5.737324
F-statistic	33.62295	Schwarz crit.	5.824381
Prob.(F-statistic)	0.000000	Hannan-Quinn crit.	5.772176
Sum sqrd.resid.	5146.338	Durbin-Watson stat.	0.413554
Variable	**Coefficient**	**t-Statistic**	**Prob.**
C	32.34757	17.90443	0.0000
CPIx	−0.163867	−4.934972	0.0000
SDDH	0.729595	2.896922	0. 0041
Procvv	0.065971	1.167533	0.2440
GGELC	0.000398	3.914115	0.0001
PIJS	−0.070875	−2.750408	0.0063
PcEUi	0.045944	1.714064	0.0876

Source: Eurostat database; author's processing

For the dependent variable ELET – Early leavers from education and training, in Tab. 1.9, the p-value is suitable only for Procvv and GGELC in relation to the dependent variable, linking education or rather its abandonment to the idea of crime and its social costs. The coefficients of the independent variables are not substantially different from zero and for CPIx and PIJS, the coefficients have also a negative sign.

Tab. 1.9: The regression result for ELET

Dependent Variable: ELET			
Method: Least Squares		**Observations: 297**	
R-squared	0.192038	Mean dep.var.	9.272054
Adjusted R-squared	0.175321	Akaike inf crit.	5.491131
F-statistic	11.48795	Schwarz crit.	5.578189
Prob.(F-statistic)	0.000000	Hannan-Quinn crit.	5.525984
Sum sqrd.resid.	4023.262	Durbin-Watson stat.	0.364444
Variable	**Coefficient**	**t-Statistic**	**Prob.**
C	8.700592	5.446627	0.0000
CPIx	−0.046270	−1.575980	0.1161
SDDH	0.286036	1.284503	0.2000
Procvv	0.275099	5.506415	0.0000
GGELC	0.000341	3.792243	0.0002
PIJS	−0.017733	−0.778300	0.4370
PcEUi	0.012729	0.537115	0.5916

Source: Eurostat database; author's processing

For the dependent variable APLP4W – Adult participation in learning in the past four weeks by sex, in Tab. 1.10, the p-value is suitable only for CPIx and GGELC in relation to the dependent variable, linking education on the perception over corruption and on the social cost of it. The coefficients of the independent variables are not substantially different from zero, except for CPIx, and only for CPIx and Procvv the coefficients have positive sign.

Tab. 1.10: The regression result for APLP4W

Dependent Variable: APLP4W			
Method: Least Squares		**Observations: 297**	
R-squared	0.680860	Mean dep.var.	11.17239
Adjusted R-squared	0.674257	Akaike inf crit.	5.876253
F-statistic	103.1155	Schwarz crit.	5.963311
Prob.(F-statistic)	0.000000	Hannan-Quinn crit.	5.911105
Sum sqrd.resid.	5913.364	Durbin-Watson stat.	0.739708
Variable	**Coefficient**	**t-Statistic**	**Prob.**
C	−16.9336	−8.743779	0.0000
CPIx	0.464218	13.04207	0.0000
SDDH	−0.390811	−1.447618	0.1488
Procvv	0.046702	0.771061	0.4413
GGELC	−0.000599	−5.491374	0.0000
PIJS	−0.004381	−0.158599	0.8741
PcEUi	−0.007227	−0.251540	0.8016

Source: Eurostat database; author's processing

When considering the dependent variable HLYB – Healthy life years at birth by sex, in Tab. 1.11, the p-value is suitable only for CPIx, SDDH and Procvv in relation to the dependent variable, linking health on the perception over corruption, death rate due to homicide and on the reporting of occurrence of crime, violence or vandalism. The coefficients of the independent variables are not substantially different from zero, except for SDDH, and only for CPIx and SDDH the coefficients have negative sign. Thus, we can consider the Standardized death rate due to homicide to substantially influence life and quality of life from birth for all citizens of the EU27 countries.

Tab. 1.11: The regression result for HLYB

Dependent Variable: HLYB			
Method: Least Squares		**Observations: 297**	
R-squared	0.323909	Mean dep.var.	61.89697
Adjusted R-squared	0.309921	Akaike inf crit.	5.621657
F-statistic	23.156080	Schwarz crit.	5.708715
Prob.(F-statistic)	0.000000	Hannan-Quinn crit.	5.656509
Sum sqrd.resid.	4584.215	Durbin-Watson stat.	0.392763
Variable	**Coefficient**	**t-Statistic**	**Prob.**
C	60.155170	35.27837	0.0000
CPIx	−0.068964	−2.200567	0.0286
SDDH	−1.833536	−7.713669	0.0000
Procvv	0.333244	6.248831	0.0000
GGELC	0.000178	1.848194	0.0656
PIJS	0.043654	1.794895	0.0737
PcEUi	0.039016	1.542256	0.1241

Source: Eurostat database; author's processing

In Tab. 1.12, the p-value is suitable for the independent variables SDDH and PcEUi in relation to the dependent variable SRUNMEC-Self-reported unmet need for medical examination. The coefficients of the independent variables are not substantially different from zero, except for SDDH, and for CPIx, GGELC and PcEUi, the coefficients have also a negative sign, two of them CPIx and PcEUi having positive significance.

Also, to refine the models and provide additional information in the analysis, for the equations that have a high R square, for the clarity of the dependent variables RDGPC and APLP4W, it has been used quantile regressions. For the equation that explains the behavior of the dependent variable RDGPC, we eliminated the variables PROCVV, GGELC and PCEUI, with a p value above 0.05. Similarly, for the dependent variable APLA4W, we eliminated the independent variables PROCVV, PIJS and PCEUI. The quartile results are presented in Tabs. 1.13 and 1.14.

The econometric estimation in Tabs. 1.13 and 1.14 was performed using quantile regression. The conditional and unconditional techniques on quantiles were developed by Koenker (2005), Hao and Naiman (2007) and Firpo et al. (2009), each with specific advantages and disadvantages.

Tab. 1.12: The regression result for SRUNMEC

Dependent Variable: SRUNMEC			
Method: Least Squares		**Observations: 297**	
R-squared	0.337830	Mean dep.var.	2.999327
Adjusted R-squared	0.324130	Akaike inf crit.	4.828408
F-statistic	24.65904	Schwarz crit.	4.915466
Prob.(F-statistic)	0.000000	Hannan-Quinn crit.	4.863261
Sum sqrd.resid.	2073.774	Durbin-Watson stat.	0.299890
Variable	**Coefficient**	**t-Statistic**	**Prob.**
C	4.004984	3.492111	0.0006
CPIx	−0.036090	−1.712153	0.0879
SDDH	1.636564	10.23661	0.0000
Procvv	0.062491	1.742237	0.0825
GGELC	−6.32E − 05	−0.977858	0.3290
PIJS	0.011907	0.727876	0.4673
PcEUi	−0.035665	−2.096061	0.0369

Source: Eurostat database; author's processing

In Tab. 1.13, the dependent variable is Real GDP per capita (RGDPC). The evolution on quantiles 10 %–90 % describes the evolution of the dependent variable from one year to the next, from reduction to increase. The Q50 quantile describes the situation in which the dynamics of the dependent variable (RGDPC) does not register large variations from one year to another, representing the median.

In Tab. 1.13 we can see that the coefficient values of the selected independent variables – CPIx and PIJS are positive, significant and increasing and have a high degree of revelation with an adequate p-value, while the SDDH variable instead has a negative value, due to the significance indicator – Standardized death rate due to homicide by sex.

Regarding the Adult participation in learning in the past four weeks by sex (APLP4W) indicator, using the same method as shown in Tab. 1.13, only the CPIx explanatory variable maintains its positive and significant coefficients and adequate p-value probabilities, while the SDDH and GGELC variables have either negative or inadequate coefficients probabilities (p-value above 5 %), or both situations, proposing their removal from the model or additional refinement of the variables.

Tab. 1.13: The quantile regression result for RDGPC

Explanatory variables		**Q10**	**Q20**	**Q30**	**Q40**	**Q50**	**Q60**	**Q70**	**Q80**	**Q90**
CPIx	coef.	403.64	432.78	490.48	500.35	547.75	555.40	548.45	540.63	760.64
	prob.	0.000	0.000	0.000	0.000	0.000	0.000	0.000	0.000	0.000
SDDH	coef.	−4972.7	−4644.4	−4214.7	−4255.2	−3496.2	−3796.6	−3655.9	−3523.0	−4464.3
	prob.	0.000	0.000	0.000	0.000	0.000	0.000	0.000	0.000	0.000
PIJS	coef.	265.41	242.17	182.69	202.52	175.31	176.91	195.30	213.18	404.86
	prob.	0.000	0.000	0.000	0.000	0.000	0.000	0.000	0.000	0.000
Adjusted R-squared		0.469	0.497	0.510	0.526	0.542	0.543	0.504	0.436	0.359
Pseudo R- squared		0.474	0.491	0.515	0.531	0.547	0.547	0.509	0.442	0.366
Observations		297	297	297	297	297	297	297	297	297

Source: Eurostat database; author’s processing

Tab. 1.14: The quantile regression result for APLP4W

Explanatory variables		**Q10**	**Q20**	**Q30**	**Q40**	**Q50**	**Q60**	**Q70**	**Q80**	**Q90**
CPIx	coef.	0.244	0.348	0.402	0.416	0.453	0.461	0.508	0.534	0.528
	prob.	0.000	0.000	0.000	0.000	0.000	0.000	0.000	0.000	0.000
SDDH	coef.	0.311	−0.008	−0.220	−0.383	−0.361	−0.502	−0.607	−0.666	−0.823
	prob.	0.066	0.963	0.217	0.052	0.074	0.048	0.018	0.028	0.009
GGELC	coef.	0.000	0.000	−0.001	−0.001	−0.001	0.000	−9.27E-05	−6.45E-05	−9.55E -06
	prob.	0.168	0.000	0.000	0.000	0.000	0.496	0.762	0.810	0.975
Adjusted R-squared		0.297	0.347	0.374	0.390	0.419	0.441	0.484	0.521	0.561
Pseudo R-squared		0.304	0.354	0.380	0.397	0.413	0.447	0.489	0.526	0.566
Observations		297	297	297	297	297	297	297	297	297

Source: Eurostat database; author's processing

In the two equations, both the real economic growth per capita and the participation of adults in the learning process are related and evolve in accordance with the axis of the perception of corruption, so that the normal development of a society, including the economic one, makes sense only through the prism of reporting to the mechanisms for reducing corruption and its perception.

The Granger causality test (see Tab. 1.15) with a probability below 0.05, shows that rather the influence comes from education and health indicators on crime and trust in justice, and indicators related to institutions can support each other as evolutions over time. It should be noted that the relationship between indicators is also complex: good perception over corruption (low corruption perceived) leads to greater trust in European institutions, the trust in institutions leads to the reduction of violence and crime, and the reduction of crime has a positive impact on the educational system and public health, on the relationship between equity and inequity in society, a fact that leads to a refueling of confidence in European institutions.

Tab. 1.15: The Granger causality test results in the limit of 5 % probability

Sample: 1297		
Lags: 2		
Obs: 295		
Null Hypothesis:	**F-Statistic**	**Prob.**
CPIX does not Granger Cause PCEUI	3.51987	0.0309
PCEUI does not Granger Cause PROCVV	5.94444	0.0030
PROCVV does not Granger Cause PCEUI	4.20405	0.0159
HLYB does not Granger Cause PROCVV	5.04724	0.0070
APLP4W does not Granger Cause PIJS	3.79494	0.0236

Source: Eurostat database; author's processing

5. Conclusions

Although it seems somewhat detached from economic development in the strict sense, corruption and the perception of this phenomenon play an important role in the development of a society as a whole. In the first phase, the accession to the European Union was linked to the observance of the general principles of democracy, the respect and protection of minorities and the rule of law (formulated under the title of the Copenhagen Criteria). These elements must be respected in other cases as well (including for accessing European funds), and non-compliance can lead to various infringement procedures on the member states. Therefore, the idea of appropriate institutional management, respect for basic democratic principles are also elements of good economic and social practice.

In this sense, through an econometric analysis with panel data, the chapter seeks to see how the Corruption Perceptions Index and other institutional indicators, selected at the European Union level, connect with indicators related to prosperity, health and education.

The results clearly indicate that in the case of economic growth per capita and the participation of adults in the educational process in the last 4 weeks, the links with institutional factors are quite strong. At the same time, even if the connections are not as intense, other indicators of prosperity, poverty, education and health show significant links with various institutional indicators, and thanks to the complex way in which the Corruption perception index is formulated, this indicator is almost indispensable in the explanation the behavior of these social variables.

It should also be mentioned that although the indicators chosen as independent variables show an adequate statistical level regarding the interconnectivity (variance inflation factor or Centred VIF are below 10), in reality, all the indicators are part of a logical system of ontologically interconnected institutional values, which they support each other. For example, a good perception of the level of corruption leads to a low crime rate and a good perception of national and European justice, and implicitly of European institutions. These elements are also supporting factors for health and education, and prosperity, and especially the evolution of economic growth, is directly related to the perception of good institutional functioning. That is why, at the level of the European Union, moral values are a fundamental pillar for its institutions and a reference for the member countries, a real identity root for its prosperity and development in the future.

Bibliography

Adsera, A., Boix, C., & Payne, M. (2003). Are You Being Served? Political Accountability and Quality of Government. The Journal of Law, Economics, and Organization, 19(2), 445–490.

Andvig, J.C., Fjeldstad, O., Amundsen, I., Sissener, T.K., & Søreide, T. (2000). Research on Corruption. A Policy Oriented Survey. https://api.semanticscholar.org/CorpusID:153638980.

Arvate, P., Curi, A.Z., & Sanches, F.M. (2010). Corruption and the Size of Government: Causality Tests for OECD and Latin American Countries. Applied Economics Letters, 17(10), 1013–1017.

Bologna, J. (2016). The Effect of Informal Employment and Corruption on Income Levels in Brazil. Journal of Comparative Economics, 44(3), 657–695.

Cheung, H.Y., & Chan, A.W.H. (2008). Corruption across Countries: Impacts from Education and Cultural Dimensions. The Social Science Journal, 45(2), 223–239, https://doi.org/10.1016/j.soscij.2008.03.002.

de Castro Soares, D. (2017). Fatores econômicos determinantes da corrupção no Brasil: uma análise com dados em painel do Ministério Público Federal. Dissertation presented to the Graduate Program in Economics at the University of Brasília as a partial requirement for obtaining the Master's degree in economics. Online at: http://icts.unb.br/jspui/bitstream/10482/31316/1/2017_DannydeCastroSoares.pdf.

Dirwan, A. (2019). The Effect of Education against Corruption in Indonesia (January 30, 2019). OIDA International Journal of Sustainable Development, 12(01), 53–64. Available at SSRN: https://ssrn.com/abstract=3355214.

Faria, H.J., Morales, D., Pineda, N., & Montesinos, H. (2012). Can Capitalism Restrain Public Perceived Corruption? Some Evidence. Journal of Institutional Economics, 8(4), 511–535.

Firpo, S., Fortin, N.M., & Lemieux, T. (2009). Unconditional Quantile Regressions. Econometrica, 77(3), 953–973.

Goldsmith, A. (1999). Slapping the Grasping Hand: Correlates of Political Corruption in Emerging Markets. American Journal of Economics and Sociology, 58(4), 866–883.

Gutierrez-Garcia, J.O., & Rodríguez, L.F. (2016). Social Determinants of Police Corruption: toward Public Policies for the Prevention of Police Corruption. Policy Studies, 37(3), 216–235.

Hallak, J., & Poisson, M. (2005). Ethics and Corruption in Education: An Overview. Journal of Education for International Development, 1(1). Retrieved from http://equip123.net/JEID/articles/1/1-3.pdf.

Hao, L., & Naiman, D.Q. (2007). Quantile Regression. Thousand Oaks, CA: Sage.

Heidenheimer, A.J., Johnston, M., & LeVine, V.T. (1989). Political Corruption: A Handbook. New Brunswick: Transaction Publishers.

Heywood, P., & Meyer-Sahling, J.-H. (2013). Danger Zones of Corruption: How Management of the Ministerial Bureaucracy Affects Corruption Risks in Poland. Public Administration and Development, 33(3), 191–204.

Knack, S. (2006). Measuring Corruption in Eastern Europe and Central Asia: A Critique of the Cross-country Indicators. World Bank Policy Research Working Paper 3968.

Koenker, R. (2005). Quantile Regression. New York: Cambridge University Press.

Ochulor, C.L., & Bassey, E.P. (2010). Analysis of Corruption from the Ethical and Moral Perspectives. European Journal of Scientific Research, 44(3), 466–476.

O'Connor, S., & Fischer, R. (2012). Predicting Societal Corruption Across Time: Values, Wealth, or Institutions? Journal of Cross-Cultural Psychology, 43(4), 644–659.

Paldam, M. (1999). The Big Pattern of Corruption: Economics, Culture and the Seesaw Dynamics. Working Paper No. 1999-11, Department of Economics, University of Aarhus.

Pitsoe, V.J. (2013). Values Education as a Social Instrument for Reducing Corruption, Poverty and Inequality. Mediterranean Journal of Social Sciences, 4, 745.

Quinn, J.J. (2008). The Effects of Majority State Ownership of Significant Economic Sectors on Corruption: A Cross-regional Comparison. International Interactions, 34(1), 84–128.

Rohwer, A. (2009). Measuring Corruption: A Comparison between the Transparency International's Corruption Perceptions Index and the World Bank's Worldwide Governance Indicators. CESifo DICE Report, ISSN 1613-6373, München, 07(3), 42–52. Online at: https://www.econstor.eu/bitstream/10419/166975/1/ifo-dice-report-v07-y2009-i3-p42-52.pdf.

Silva, M.F.G., Garcia, F., & Bandeira, A.C. (2001). How Does Corruption Hurt Growth? Evidences about the Effects of Corruption on Factors Productivity and Per Capita Income. Textos para discussão, Universidade de São Paulo. https://core.ac.uk/reader/6239429.

Stevens, A. (2016). Configurations of Corruption: A Cross-national Qualitative Comparative Analysis of Levels of Perceived Corruption. International Journal of Comparative Sociology, 57(4), 183–206.

Treisman, D. (2000). The Causes of Corruption: A Cross-national Study. Journal of Public Economics, 76(3), 399–457.

UNDP. (2008). A Users' Guide to Measuring Corruption. Online at: https://www.undp.org/sites/g/files/zskgke326/files/publications/users_guide_measuring_corruption.pdf (accessed 14 June 2023).

Villoria, M., & Jimenéz, F. (2012). Corruption in Spain (2004–2010): Data, Perception and Consequences. Revista Espanola de Investigaciones Sociologicas, 138(1), 109–134.

Yamamura, E. (2014). Impact of Natural Disaster on Public Sector Corruption. Public Choice, 161(3–4), 385–405.

Wang, Y., & Hui, E.C. (2017). Are Local Governments Maximizing Land Revenue? Evidence from China. China Economic Review, 43, April, 196–215.

Gabriela-Mariana Ionescu

Chapter 2 New research methods from the social justice perspective

Abstract: The chapter aims, in its first part, to achieve a classification of research methods that fall into the field of social justice, both qualitatively and quantitatively. Next, two research methods (TRIZ and Value Analysis) will be updated, which will be integrated into the analysis of some current phenomena faced by modern societies in the current period (economic inequality, distribution of wealth, opportunities and privileges). The choice of the two methods had in mind the blurring of the boundaries between the methods used in the analysis of economic phenomena and the methods used in innovation and creativity and bringing these methods into the mainstream of the methods used in order to obtain effective research methods and understand the perspective of justice social in the analysis of current economic phenomena, in order to obtain well-founded results. The presentation of the two methods will also be accompanied by an example of how they can be applied in an integrated manner.

Keywords: social justice, research methods, TRIZ, fairness, capability, entitlement

1. Introduction

The current economic conditions generated by the two major events of recent years, namely the COVID-19 pandemic and the war in Ukraine, have made us witnesses of shocks that have destabilized the growth prospects of the European economies and beyond. The analysis of the negative phenomena (stagflation, the increase in debt costs, the impact of climate change, the food crisis, the energy crisis, etc.) that these events generated led both to the refinement of the research methods used in the economic sciences and to the emergence of some new research methods to analyze the interesting details of the changes that happen so quickly.

Social justice, as we will show in this chapter, is based on values such as fairness, entitlement, merit, desert (Smilansky, 1996), etc. These values are more important than ever as we face the consequences of the crises mentioned in the previous paragraph. Economic insecurity, austerity, ongoing conflicts at global, zonal, societal levels have led to growing economic and social polarization. Refining and updating new research methods is useful to observe economic, social, environmental phenomena in times of despair and conflict, times when it is necessary to pay attention to the importance and the way our democratic societies function, the obligations that every citizen he has them towards law and truth. The analysis tools from this chapter that have either been presented briefly or have been presented in detail show the role and importance of qualitative and quantitative methods available to researchers to analyze and propose solutions to solve the problems that have arisen in our societies in the current period.

In this chapter they will be presented in detail some theoretical aspects of the theory of social justice (Barry, 2015) in order to integrate the two methods TRIZ and Value Analysis in the field of social justice but also to emphasize the applicability of some research methods to a wide range of current economic topics. Also considering the influence of artificial intelligence, we can say that until today there has not been a better time in which we have effective means to collect and analyze information.

2. Some general considerations about social justice

We will begin this brief presentation of some theoretical aspects of the concept of social justice by emphasizing the fact that the distribution of material resources in a society (based on criteria of social equity, equal opportunities, etc.) can leads to situations of professional, social, and family risk for a category of individuals vulnerable to the accelerated pace of changes occurring in the economy and society. The two components of social justice, commutative justice (which is based on the principle of contribution) and distributive justice (which is based on the principle of solidarity) (Olsaretti, 2018), can ensure a fair distribution in the process of distribution of the economic product, within a society, only if this distribution is based on positive law. The area of interest of social justice includes the following three concepts:

1. *the concept of social* – social aspects, especially those of a material nature, more concretely those expressed in monetary form, respectively current income and economic wealth;
2. *the concept of justice* – which describes the just state of a system, namely the result reached and which is necessary to be in accordance with the observance of a positive norm (law);
3. *the concept of social justice* – the result (mechanism, procedure, institution, etc.) obtained must express the property of social justice.

We thus say that social justice provides that institutional/normative framework with the help of which the social and economic inequalities that individuals feel as a result of the polarization of society in terms of asset ownership are monitored and controlled, in an effort to ensure a balance between necessity and merit in the distribution of the economic product in society, taking into account the crises that societies have gone through and will still go through, we are referring here to the crisis in the field of health (the COVID-19 pandemic), the regional military conflict (the war of aggression launched by Russia against Ukraine), food crisis (destabilization of supply chains, unprecedented increases in food and fertilizer prices, significant labor shortage, increase in extreme weather events), climate crisis (global warming produces extreme events with damages significant, climate lockdown, fires, drought, etc.) and last but not least the energy crisis (delays in the distribution chain, higher costs for handling and transportation, increased demand for natural gas and electricity, decreased production, reduced stocks, climate conditions), financial crisis (inflation, high interest rates, reduced economic growth, higher borrowing costs, tight monetary policies).

Thus, social justice assigns some institutions within society rights and duties that allow individuals to have access to basic benefits, we are referring here to social assistance services, public health, education, non-discriminatory access to the labor market, income taxation with the aim of fair distribution of the economic product of society based on equal opportunities.

From another point of view, in arguing the importance of social justice, which we consider an axiom of generating the basic structure of society, the theory of social justice will be analyzed from three perspectives, which we find in the literature of specialty, namely:

(a) the approach based on fairness;
(b) the capability-based approach;
(c) the entitlement-based approach.

(a) In the case of the approach based on fairness, the most important author of this orientation is John Rawls who in his reference work "*A Theory of Justice*" published in 1999 considers that the determining element, from the point of view of the structure, of a theory of *social justice* is that of *social fairness*, and the determined element, from the point of view of the cause, is the basic structure of society, which means the set of axioms/principles that underpin the normative framework (formal and informal) of society. The approach of social justice theory based on equity has its origin in the basic structure of society, the basic principles of the functioning of society contained in the social contract. Otherwise, in an original position, the members of the future society agree, under the conditions of the veil of ignorance (the concept of the veil of ignorance refers to the fact that in the original position, the participating individuals do not know the position they will have in the future society and ignore any interests idiosyncratic principles to follow in "negotiating" the basic principles of the future society), to choose certain principles (called basic principles) to underpin the organization and functioning of the future society they wish to shape. It is assumed that if the basic principles are correct, then the results of their application are also correct, the Rawlsian theory (Rawls, 1999) being known as a theory of justice of fairness.

The main features of the Rawlsian approach are:

1. *deductive character* – the results of the allocations of social position, income/ assets, access to the benefits of social cooperation (mutualism) for the individuals of the future society are certain. In other words, social equity is not subject to uncertainty or risk, it has a necessary character, not a contingent one;
2. *self-regulatory character* – the choice of basic principles is established, in the Rawlsian theory, by the Constitution – we recall that the Rawlsian theory of justice has four stages, ordered logically and chronologically;
3. *incompleteness* – refers to the fact that there may be desirable results that citizens are interested in within social cooperation, but which cannot be ensured by the principles chosen in the original position, Rawls proposing that the inconsistencies be examined by society after the conclusion of the social contract.

(b) The capability-based approach is an outcome-based approach and is defined by each individual's choice to focus on the moral significance of their ability to achieve the kind of life they have reason to value. The main representatives of this orientation are Amartya Sen and Martha C. Nussbaum. Capability theory is presented by Sen in his work "Equality of What?" published in 1979 in which he states that well-being must be examined from the perspective of functionality and basic capabilities, less from the point of view of utilitarianism, an idea taken up and developed by the author in his other works (Sen, 1979). However, Nussbaum starts from ethical considerations in his work "Frontiers of Justice. Disability, Nationality, Species Membership" formulates a list of ten capabilities that he discusses in detail, specifying that he does not discuss their functioning and does not condition the acceptance of the list of capabilities on their functioning in society. In the author's opinion, updating the potential of capabilities (Nussbaum, 2007) is up to individuals, preserving their freedom of choice.

The main characteristics of this type of approach to social justice theory are the following:

1. *inductive nature*: rejecting the procedural nature of social justice, the capabilities approach avoids the deductive potential that generates generality,

continuity and homogeneity in the application and functioning of social justice;
2. *non-regulatory character*: by proposing that, in the original position of concluding the social contract, the principles that would possibly provide, procedurally, the basic capabilities for the individuals of the future society, should be chosen directly, but those necessary capabilities should be chosen directly the functioning of people's lives;
3. *completeness character*: claiming to be provided, right from the start, with a complete list of basic capabilities, this approach to social justice has a completeness, in the sense that no novelty in the matter of the list of basic capabilities can appear (precisely through the absence of the procedural nature of the offer of capabilities).

(c) The justification-based approach was introduced to the literature by Robert Nozick. In his work "Anarchy, State and Utopia" Nozick positions himself equidistantly from both the procedural theory and the result-based theory in the matter of social justice. The basic idea of Nozick's proposal (Nozick, 1997) can be formulated as follows: the individual/citizen should not suffer injustice. If they accidentally suffer such injustices, they must be redressed (Sen, 2009).

An important problem of the theory of social justice is the problem of the bases of social justice and as can be seen in the following figure (Fig. 2.1) we have two criteria with which we analyze this problem, according to the type of social justice and according to the basis of social justice. The two types of social justice are:

- procedural social justice: establishes the basic principles on which the functioning of society is founded, it starts from the assumption that the potential of the principles (Nozick, 1993) to produce the expected results is a sufficient guarantee that those results will be obtained;
- social justice of result (of final state): the desirable results (or final states) are established directly, in accordance with the status of the human being. Through an extraordinary conceptualization effort made in this sense and through an active presence in the scientific debate of the concept, it stands out, in this type of social justice, Martha C. Nussbaum (2007) who developed a list of ten basic capabilities that social justice must or should ensure to each individual, regardless of their state of normality vs. disability, not to mention other possible discrimination criteria.

The typology of social justice according to its basis – according to the most primitive justification of the realization of social justice includes four elements:

- fairness – refers to the fundamental assurance of each individual's access to primary goods;
- entitlement – refers to the assurance of each individual, what the normative framework of society provides, formally and explicitly, that he must be assured;
- merit – refers to ensuring access (to positions and benefits of social cooperation) of each individual depending on and in proportion to the effective contribution to the results of social cooperation;
- desert – refers to ensuring the access of each individual to the positions and benefits of social cooperation in the same way as the entitlement, with the difference that, in the case of the right, the existence of a positive norm in this sense is no longer a sufficient condition.

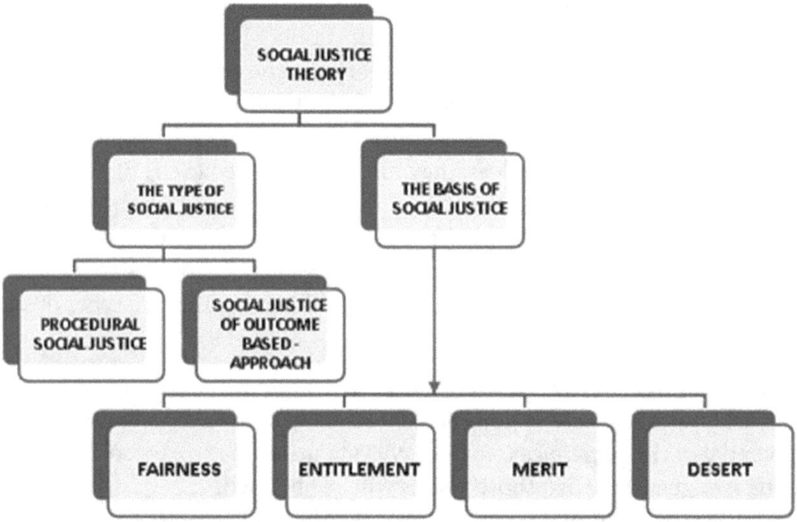

Fig. 2.1: Social justice theory
Source: Created by the author

3. Overview of TRIZ methods and value analysis

The Theory of Inventive Problem Solving – TRIZ is a collection of techniques that can be used, regardless of the field, which has proven its effectiveness in numerous applications. Each technique consists of a number of guidelines, rules and principles that indicate how to solve a certain problem or situation.

Compared to other methods used in data processing in the economic field, TRIZ offers a systematic methodology for innovative – conceptual design.

The TRIZ philosophy is based on the fact that the evolution of a phenomenon (technical, economic or from any other field of study) is not a random process but is subject to certain laws/influences. The major discovery underlying the TRIZ method highlighted the origin of the inventive problem: the contradiction (Mazur, 2001; Salamatov, 1999). When a researcher encounters a contradiction that cannot be resolved by redesigning the entire system, or part of it, by a known method, he can approach two ways of solving it: by finding a compromise between the two parameters in conflict or by eliminating the contradiction. The TRIZ method aims to solve the problem by removing the contradiction. In the specialized literature (Mazur, 2001), the solutions were ranked on 5 levels according to the degree of innovation required:

- ***Level I:*** routine problems at the level of a system, solved only by a few attempts, based on the researcher's own knowledge, using well-known methods in the field for which there is no need to search for innovative solutions.
- ***Level II:*** minor improvements to the existing system by methods known in the field where a minimum level of innovation is needed to find compromises. Several tens of attempts are needed based on knowledge of the field in which the researcher works, available at the organization for which he works.
- ***Level III:*** fundamental improvements of the existing system, by extrapolating and adapting some methods taken from other fields, which require an average degree of innovation to solve contradictions and a relatively large number of attempts, in the order of hundreds.
- ***Level IV:*** a new generation of systems that uses totally new principles, by clarifying some effects and phenomena that were less understood until that time, to reach the main functions of the system that require a very high level of innovation corroborated with extensive scientific research carried out during more many years of searching and thousands of attempts.
- ***Level V:*** a rare scientific discovery that can lead to the realization of new, revolutionary systems that require the highest degree of innovation, in most cases based on scientific accumulations that transcend several generations, by overcoming the known boundaries of science.

In the specialized literature (Choulier & Drăghici, 1999) it is considered that in order to apply the TRIZ method, it is necessary to go through five stages: Identification/documentation of the problem, Formulation of the problem, Development of generic concepts using TRIZ methods, techniques and tools, Interpretation of generic solutions and Evaluation of solutions.

As shown in numerous case studies that have used the TRIZ method in various fields, it helps to considerably accelerate the new product development process by rapidly generating new problem-solving concepts. This is possible due to the following advantages of the TRIZ methodology:

- It is an intensive cognitive process and its success depends on how quickly the necessary knowledge can be found. TRIZ solves this requirement by organizing a rapid search for the required knowledge, currently aided by dedicated software programs.
- TRIZ provides systematic access to the previous experience of many generations of researchers. This experience is generalized and presented in the form of rules and directions of action.
- In some cases, it may be quite clear what function is required, but it is unclear what principle can be used to materialize this function. Specific methods based on database access are used to organize and guide the search for appropriate principles.
- TRIZ does not replace human creativity but restructures the thinking process of a researcher and provides quick access to the necessary knowledge, but does not solve the problem without the intervention of the researcher.
- No prior specialist skills are required to effectively solve new problems creatively.

On the other hand, there are some disadvantages of using TRIZ mainly related to the formulation of contradictions, the identification of conflicting parameters, the interpretation and customization of the generic solutions found for the studied system, etc.

Although there are results regarding the adaptation of TRIZ to non-technical fields as well as the combination of this methodology with other methods (QFD, FMEA, etc.), from the study of the specialized literature (Blosiu & Kowalick, 1996; Domb & Kowalick, 1997) it can be established that on a global level these problems are still in their infancy and their effective application, especially in the economic field, is still a wish. The adaptation of TRIZ in the economic field is a strictly current and particularly controversial issue. Are the 40 principles universally valid? Which methods associated with TRIZ can be adopted or adapted for the economic field? Are other methods and tools needed? Why is the technical TRIZ matrix asymmetric and the one specific to the economic domain is symmetric? [Thesis 1] There are only a few questions that troubled the scientific world worldwide, especially in the USA (Domb & Kowalick, 1997), England (Fey et al., 1994), Ireland (Şerban et al., 2004), Japan (Nakagawa et al., 2009), France (Cavallucci, 2001), Belgium, Israel, etc.

Another established method is the Value Analysis (VA) method, which, however, is poorly represented in the field of social justice. In the current context, the Value Analysis Method (MAV) is generally applied for:

(a) The assimilation of new cost-effective and high-quality products and the revitalization of existing ones in production, through redesigns and modernizations in order to satisfy social needs;
(b) Replacing raw materials and deficient materials with newer and cheaper ones and reducing material, energy and labor consumption;
(c) Application of the value analysis method in order to increase manufacturing flexibility;
(d) Applying the value analysis method to technological processes, organizational structures, investment objectives, services, etc.

In the specialized literature the delimitation between value engineering and value analysis indicates the stage at which each variant is applied: value engineering is generally applied in the design/development phase of a system and the analysis values in the improvement phase of an existing system. Value analysis is a technique for reducing the costs of an existing system without affecting its quality level by studying the function-cost correlation. In this case, reducing the cost for a certain level of quality is possible by eliminating unjustified costs for the performance of system functions (or the socio-institutional construct, in the case of social justice), respectively by rationalizing the costs necessary for these functions.

In the existing approaches it is mentioned that the main objective of the AV method is to maximize the ratio between the use value of the product V_u, and the direct and indirect costs it generates, C_t:

$$\frac{V_u}{C_t} = max \tag{1}$$

The relation (1) results from the maximization of the same ratio for each individual function:

$$\frac{\sum_{i=1}^{n} F_i}{\sum_{i=1}^{n} C_i} = \text{max}, \quad (\text{i} = 1,2,\ldots,\text{n}) \tag{2}$$

where F_i represents the product functaions; C_i – the cost corresponding to the F_i function and n – the number of product functions.

In value analysis studies, three basic notions are used: value, use value and function. Regarding the function concept studied through value analysis, the system is a sum of elementary functions that give it the intended use value. Functions are the elementary characteristics of a system and, taken as a whole, constitute complete, useful utility values. Taken separately, functions are partial use-values that contribute to the realization of the total use-value. They result from the social need they must satisfy and are supported by parts of the system (sub-systems).

In the specialized literature the functions are classified according to importance (main functions, which correspond to the main purpose of the studied objective and auxiliary functions that serve to achieve the main functions and are determined especially by the adopted solution), according to the contribution to the use value (necessary functions and useless functions), according to the time of the analysis (existing functions and new functions), according to the way of perception by the user (utilitarian functions and aesthetic functions) and according to the possibility of measurement (measurable functions and unmeasurable functions).

4. Research methods applied in the field of the social justice

The qualitative and quantitative research methods applicable in the field of social justice are very numerous, we will only choose a few to make a summary classification of them considering that through the working tools they use qualitative research methods generate theories and quantitative research methods verify theories (Runcan, 2023). If we analyze the influence that AI systems have today in data processing, we notice that in addition to the fact that they are very interesting for the economic field (Bickley et al., 2022), they have in their composition powerful algorithms for solving problems and for the procedural rationality that they have in mind (Machine Learning, Big Data, Expert Systems, Neural Networks, and others). As shown in Fig. 2.2, the qualitative research methods we chose for this classification use working tools that build theoretical models that explain phenomena of interest from the direct perspective of the participants (fundamental theory), interviews that create models and trends for identifying the particularities of economic/social phenomena that have not been addressed in specialized literature (phenomenological research), the presentation of complex processes as they naturally occur within groups or systems (descriptive, exploratory, explanatory case studies), software programs NVIVO, ATLAS.ti, MAXQDA, Dedoose.

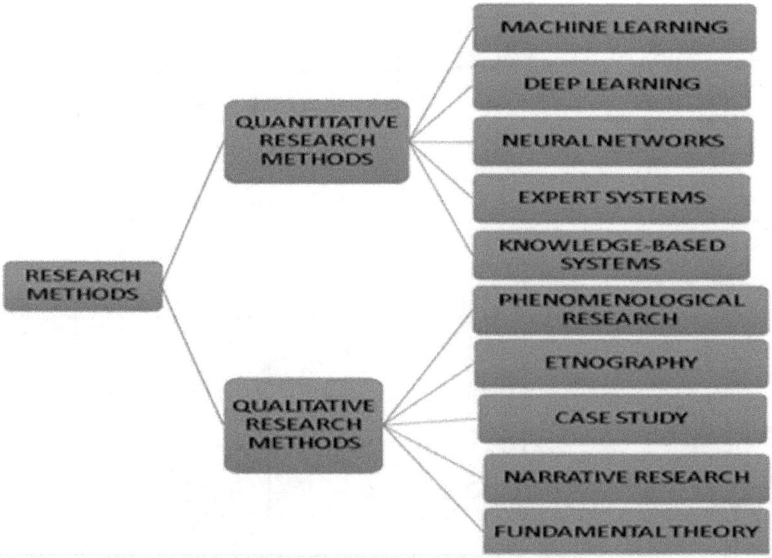

Fig. 2.2: Research methods with applicability in the field of social justice
Source: Created by the author

Another category of research methods that can be applied in the field of social justice are shown in Fig. 2.3. It should be highlighted that being such a fundamental artefact (at a fundamental level, it is the very basic structure of society – it is a free and democratic society) and being institutional in nature, social justice has the general structure of any institutional social construct. It should be mentioned that social justice is not part of any of the powers in the generic state (legislative, executive, juridical), but is rather of the nature of 'properties' of any of the three powers, which ensure the full functioning of the human individual and the social groups spontaneously constituted in that society. It is considered that the methods presented below can also be a good element for designing and analyzing the various situations in which social justice can and must intervene.

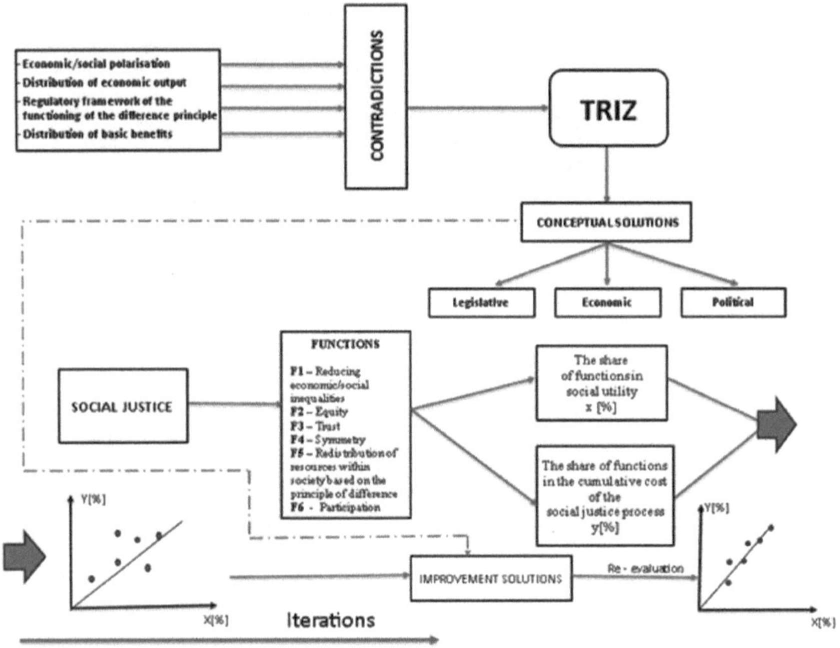

Fig. 2.3: Mechanism of functioning of TRIZ, QFD and value analysis methods
Source: Created by the author

4.1. Application of the Value Analysis (VA) method in social justice

New methods adapted and extrapolated from other fields such as product development, economic analysis, creativity and innovation etc. are proposed for the study of social justice. One of these methods is the value analysis and engineering method. For this, the AV methodology was adapted as follows.

4.1.1. Establishing social justice functions

Based on the specialized literature several functions of social justice can be synthesized, the most important of which are considered to be the following:

F1. Reducing economic/social inequalities; can be measured by the percentage of the population that was below the poverty line;
F2. Equity that aggregates values: income, social welfare, opportunities, freedom; it is proposed to be measured as a percentage of the active population with incomes above the minimum wage for the economy;

F3. Trust – the degree to which individuals agree to freely surrender some of their rights or interests to the state; it is proposed to be measured as a percentage of the majority population which gives this trust to the state;
F4. Symmetry; the degree to which individuals have access to society's positive externalities (education, justice, health, etc.); it is proposed to be measured as a percentage of the total population that has access to positive externalities;
F5. Redistribution of resources within society based on the principle of difference; it is proposed to be measured as a percentage of the total population who benefit from this redistribution;
F6. Participation: the degree and quality in which individuals have the opportunity to take part in public decision-making; it is proposed to be measured as a percentage of the voting population that gets involved in decision-making.

4.1.2. *Establishing the weight of the functions in the value of social utility*

Determining the weight of the functions in the value of social utility (Spader, 1987) is achieved by assigning an importance note to each function by experts and calculating the weight x with the relationship

$$x_{F_k} = \frac{N_{F_k}}{\sum_{k=1}^{n} N_{F_k}} \cdot 100[\%] \quad (3)$$

where x_{F_k} is the weight of the function F_k, k = 1,2,..., n, where N_{F_k} is the function grade F_k and n represents the number of functions.

4.1.3. *Establishing the share of functions in the total cost of social justice*

The realization of social justice at the level of a state involves a total cost C_t, borne largely by allocations from public funds. For this, the structure of social justice (Dinga & Ionescu, 2020) made up of several modules must be taken into account: the institutional module, the functional module, the collaborative/communicative module and the resolutive/regulatory module.

The cost of each function is determined by analyzing the degree of participation of each function in each of the four modules and determining the partial costs C_{ij}, by summing which the CF_k costs corresponding to each function are obtained (Tab. 2.1).

The share of each function in the total cost is then determined using the relationship:

$$y_{F_k} = \frac{C_{F_k}}{\sum_{k=1}^{n} C_{F_k}} * 100 \quad (4)$$

After plotting each function in coordinates (x_{F_k}, y_{F_k}) the regression line is determined using the least squares method (Fig. 2.4). The functions above the regression line are oversized and cost reduction solutions must be sought at the level of each module.

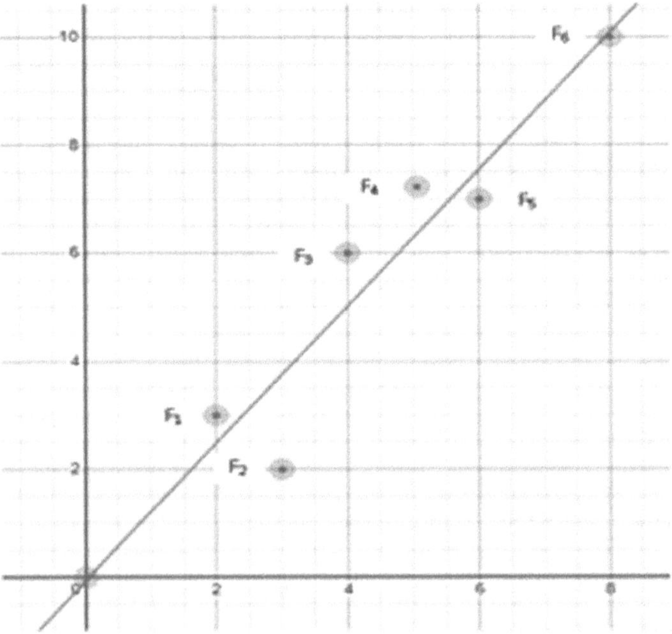

Fig. 2.4: Regression line

Source: Created by the author

4.2. Application of the TRIZ method in social justice

Launched first in the technical field, the TRIZ method has been developed and adapted in various other fields, among which we can mention IT, economics, business and management, medicine, construction, the food field, etc.

One of the most important philosophical pillars of TRIZ is the reference to ideality, i.e. fixing as a target the ideal values of some characteristics, even if in

Tab. 2.1: Distribution of functions by costs

	1. Institutional Module	**2. Functional Module**	**3. The Collaborative/ Communicative Module**	**4. The Resolutive/ Regulatory Module**	**Costs by Function**
F1. Reducing inequalities and mitigating poverty	C_{11}	C_{12}	C_{13}	C_{14}	$C_{F_1} = \sum_{j=1}^{4} C_{1j}$
F2. Equity that aggregates values	C_{21}	C_{22}	C_{23}	C_{24}	$C_{F_2} = \sum_{j=1}^{4} C_{2j}$
F3. Trust	C_{31}	C_{32}	C_{33}	C_{34}	$C_{F_3} = \sum_{j=1}^{4} C_{3j}$
F4. Symmetry	C_{41}	C_{42}	C_{43}	C_{44}	$C_{F_4} = \sum_{j=1}^{4} C_{4j}$
F5. Redistribution of resources within society	C_{51}	C_{52}	C_{53}	C_{54}	$C_{F_5} = \sum_{j=1}^{4} C_{5j}$
F6. Contribution	C_{61}	C_{62}	C_{63}	C_{64}	$C_{F_6} = \sum_{j=1}^{4} C_{6j}$

Source: Created by the author

some cases they are utopian or impossible to achieve. Only by setting ideal values as a target do we have a chance to get closer and closer to these values.

For example, regarding some defining functions and elements of social justice, the philosophy based on ideality can be applied as follows.

1. Reducing economic/social inequalities ⇒ Target: elimination of inequalities and poverty so that every member of society benefits from the best allocation scheme.
2. Equity that aggregates values ⇒ Target: perfect equity in the distribution of income and social welfare;
3. Trust ⇒ Target: all individuals agree to freely surrender any rights or interests deemed necessary for the good running of society;
4. Symmetry ⇒ Target: All individuals have full access to society's positive externalities;
5. Redistribution of resources within society ⇒ Target: all individuals considered to be in difficulty benefit from aid from the state based on the principle of difference and the common good that is essential for the proper functioning of a society
6. Participation ⇒ Target: all individuals have the opportunity to take part in public decision-making.

5. Conclusions

The main conclusions of this chapter concern both the three perspectives from which we have looked at social justice, namely the fairness – based approach, the capability – based approach and the entitlement – based approach, as well as highlighting some research methods whose tools can help to analyze the economic and social phenomena that concern us today. A first attempt has been made to update some of the research methods that are known and successfully used in different fields. The importance of artificial intelligence and the methods it has generated was also highlighted. Classifications of qualitative and quantitative research methods were made and social justice functions were identified that can be analyzed with methods such as TRIZ, QFD, Value Analysis.

Future research directions will include the application of new research methods to the study of the Principle of Difference, a particularly important issue that has not been given due attention in this study, as well as making connections between classical and current research methods.

Bibliography

Barry, B. (2015). *Why Social Justice Matters* (2015th ed.). Polity Press.

Bickley S.J., Chan, H.F., & Torgler, B. (2022). Artificial Intelligence in the Feld of Economics. *Scientometrics*, 127, 2055–2084.

Blosiu, J., & Kowalick, J. (1996). TRIZ and Business Survival. TRIZ Journal, November 1996, https://the-trizjournal.com/triz-business-survival/.

Cavallucci, D. (2001). Integrating Altshuller's Development Laws for Technical Systems into the Design Process. *Annals of the CIRP*, 50(1).

Choulier, D., & Drăghici, G. (1999). *TRIZ: une approche de rezolution des problemes d'innovation dans la conception de produits.* https://www.academia.edu/16591989/TRIZ_une_approche_de_r%C3%A9solution_des_probl%C3%A8mes_d_innovation_dans_la_conception_de_produits.

Dinga, E., & Ionescu, G.M. (2020). *Social Justice – Vehicle of Social Welfare, Research Work Carried Out for the Institute for Quality of Life Research of the Romanian Academy*, 44–46.

Domb, E., & Kowalick, J. (1997). How to Bring TRIZ into Your Organization. *TRIZ Journal*, 10. https://the-trizjournal.com/bring-triz-organization/.

Fey, V.R., Rivin, E.I., & Vertkin, I.M. (1994). Application of the Theory of Inventive Problem Solving to Design and Manufacturing Systems. *CIRP Annals*, 43/1, 107–110.

Mazur, G. (2001). *Theory of Inventive Problem Solving (TRIZ).* Available online: https://www.qfdi.org/intro-to-triz-glenn-mazur-lecture-series

Nakagawa, T., Itoh, T., & Tsukamoto, M. (2009). *How to Prevent Cords and Cables from Getting Entangled: A Study of Systematic Classification of Various Solutions.* Proceedings of the TRIZ Future Conference, Timişoara Romania, November 4th–6th, 2009, Ed. POLITEHNICA, Timişoara-2009, ISBN 978-973-625-969-2, 131-137.

Nozick, R. (1993). *The Nature of Rationality*. Princeton University Press.

Nozick, R. (1997). *Anarchy, State and Utopia* (in Romanian: *Anarhie, stat şi utopie).* Ed. Humanitas.

Nussbaum, M.C. (2007). *Frontiers of Justice. Disability, Nationality, Species Membership*. The Belknap Press of Harvard University Press.

Olsaretti S. (2018). *The Oxford Handbook of Distributive Justice and the Difference Principle*. Scholarly Research Reviews, Oxford University Press.

Rawls, J. (1999). *A Theory of Justice*. The Belknap Press of Harvard University Press.

Sen, A. (1979). *Equality of What?* Stanford University: Tanner Lectures on Human Values. https://www.ophi.org.uk/wp-content/uploads/Sen-1979_Equality-of-What.pdf.

Sen, A. (2009). *The Idea of Justice* (1st ed.). Belknap Press of Harvard University Press.

Runcan, R. (2023). *Research Methodology in the Social Sciences: Qualitative Research*. University course support, Presa Universitară Clujeană, Cluj. https://www.researchgate.net/publication/370073653_METODOLOGIA_CERCETARII_IN_STIINTELE_SOCIALE_CERCETAREA_CALITATIVA_Suport_de_curs_universitar.

Salamatov, Y. (1999). *TRIZ: The Right Solution at the Right Time*. Insytec B.V., ISBN 90-804680-1-0.

Serban, D., Man, E., Ionescu, N., & Roche, T. (2004). *A TRIZ Approach to Design for Environment*. In D. Talabă & T. Roche (eds.), *Product Engineering*. Dordrecht: Springer. https://doi.org/10.1007/1-4020-2933-0_6.

Smilansky, S. (1996). Responsibility and Desert: Defending the Connection. *Mind*, New Series 105, no. 417, 157–163. https://doi.org/10.1093/mind/105.417.157.

Spader, D.J. (1987). Individual Rights vs. Social Utility: The Search for the Golden Zigzag between Conflicting Fundamental Values. *Journal of Criminal Justice*, 15(2), 121–136.

Emil Dinga and Cristina Tănăsescu

Chapter 3 Conceptual and methodological issues to calculate the sustainable GDP

Abstract: Economists currently instrumentalize three kinds of GDP: actual GDP, optimal GDP, and potential GDP. However, the new economic conditions (including the globalization process) require a new kind of GDP which have features and behavior impossible to be accomplished by the three mentioned concepts – namely the sustainable GDP. The sustainable GDP is that GDP which, by its own functioning (production – distribution – consumption – re-production) ensures its replication, both quantitatively and structurally. The study uses the fourth sector of the Leontief input-output table in order to find the algebraic condition for the sustainable GDP. To this end, in fact, a sui generis matrix of structural coefficients of input-output relationships is generated, based on the replication of the input through the intermediation of output – just the conceptual essence of the macroeconomic sustainability. Finally, the paper formalizes the "sustainability tunnel" of the GDP so it becomes a sustainable GDP. The results of the paper could be used to introduce the concept of sustainable GDP into the economic methodology, including the replacing of the potential GDP (which, in fact, is not a potential one, especially if its calculation is filters-based) with the sustainable GDP. Another consequence could be the revisiting of the input-output macroeconomic model by including the fourth sector where is located the sustainable GDP formation.

Keywords: GDP, sustainability, sustainable GDP, sustainable tunnel

1. Introduction

> *"Distinctions must be kept in mind between quantity and quality of growth, between its costs and return, and between the short and the long run. Goals for more growth should specify more growth of what and for what." –Simon Kuznets, 1962*

There is almost general agreement that Gross Domestic Product (GDP) is not a perfect metric for economic welfare, prosperity and progress in living standards of citizens, the ultimate goal of the macroeconomic policies. However, as Simon Kuznets (1962) observed while designing GDP, "for those not intimately acquainted with [systems of national accounts] it is difficult to realize the degree to which estimates of national income have been and must be affected by explicit or implicit value judgments" (Kuznets et al., 1941, 5). This concern has fueled efforts to develop aggregate well-being metrics as either alternatives or complements to the GDP. Here are some alternative tools and concepts that have gained prominence as alternatives or complements to GDP for measuring growth, along with some of the organizations and researchers associated with these ideas:

- Genuine Progress Indicator (GPI) (Cobb et al., 1995) – a modification of the Index of Sustainable Economic Welfare (ISEW) developed by Daly and Cobb Jr. (1989), and some assessments of its theoretical and empirical foundations (e.g. Atkinson, 1995; Neumayer, 1999, 2000; Lawn, 2005), GPI attempts to measure economic growth while also accounting for negative externalities such as environmental degradation, income inequality, and the value of unpaid household labor. It's designed to provide a more holistic view of economic welfare.
- Human Development Index (HDI): Developed by the United Nations, HDI takes into account factors beyond economic output, such as life expectancy, education, and income. It aims to capture overall human well-being and development.
- Ecological Footprint: This metric measures the environmental impact of human activities in terms of the amount of biologically productive land and water required to support those activities and absorb their waste. It helps assess whether human consumption is within the planet's ecological capacity.
- Happy Planet Index (HPI): HPI combines well-being indicators, life satisfaction, life expectancy, and ecological footprint to gauge the sustainable well-being of a country's citizens.
- Inclusive Wealth Index (IWI): developed by the United Nations Environment Programme, IWI factors in the value of a country's natural, human, and manufactured capital to provide a more comprehensive measure of economic well-being.
- Social Progress Index (SPI): SPI evaluates social and environmental indicators to provide a broader view of a country's development, going beyond economic metrics.
- Bhutan's Gross National Happiness (GNH): Bhutan's unique approach to development emphasizes well-being and happiness over purely economic indicators. It includes indicators related to psychological well-being, health, education, culture, and good governance.
- OECD Better Life Index: This index allows people to compare well-being across countries based on a range of dimensions, including income, housing,

jobs, education, environment, governance, health, life satisfaction, safety, and work-life balance.

- Green GDP (Liu, 2006) – green GDP is the final result of economic activities of a country or region after considering natural resources and environmental factors. It is the total, speed and composition of GDP after deducting environmental costs and resource costs under the current productivity and social development level in accordance with the requirements of sustainable development.
- Gross National Happiness (Ura & Galay, 2004; Veenhoven, 2008), and some of its initial approaches as relationship between happiness and GPD or income and happiness (Easterlin, 1974, 1995, 2001, 2005).

But none of these new measures are still without limitations or weaknesses (Parris & Kates, 2003; Costanza et al., 2009), including: lack of consensus on how to value items that are not regularly reported in monetary terms, lack of consensus on how to quantify the costs of depleting natural resources, data (reliability, availability, timeliness, scope and scale) and methodology issues (standardization issues and the values implied by what is actually measured) are barriers to the use of these in place of GDP.

Rather, a new growth model is needed, a new paradigm to approach GDP in order to reach a long run sustainable economic growth.

This study makes an attempt to rethink the economic growth model, introducing a new kind of GDP – namely the Sustainable GDP. The Sustainable GDP is that GDP which, by its own functioning (production – distribution – consumption – re-production) ensures its replication, both quantitatively and structurally. As a tool, an input-output analysis was used. The Leontief model has been widely implemented to evaluate linkages between industries (economic sectors) and to estimate the relevant multipliers. The paper uses the fourth sector of the Leontief input-output table in order to find the algebraic condition for the Sustainable GDP. To this end, in fact, a sui generis matrix of structural coefficients of input-output relationships is generated, based on the replication of the input through the intermediation of output – just the conceptual essence of the macroeconomic sustainability. A result of the study could be the revisiting of the input-output macroeconomic model by including the fourth sector where is located the Sustainable GDP formation.

Sustainable GDP (SGDP) must be understood as that accounting GDP (AGDP) having the structural capacity of self-replication, over a certain numerical range of variation and over a certain pre-established time interval. From examining the calculation methods of AGDP, one may see that the production method and the income method refer to outputs, whereas the expenditure method refer to inputs. Therefore, the condition for replicability, which seems to contain the essence of the concept of sustainability, must be analyzed within the margin of the input, respectively the output of AGDP. We will say, therefore, that SGDP is that AGDP ensuring (of course, non-punctual) the replication of the input through the output.

Based on the calculation methods of the AGDP above, we may say that the AGDP becomes SGDP if and only if there is an equilibrium (which ensures the replicability) between the inputs, represented by the expenditure structure of the AGDP, and the outputs, represented by the income structure of the AGDP. This hypothesis shall be the basis of the methodological and formal proposal for calculating the SGDP, which will be addressed in the final part of the study. Fig. 3.1 tries to suggest the concept of sustainable GDP in the vision described above.

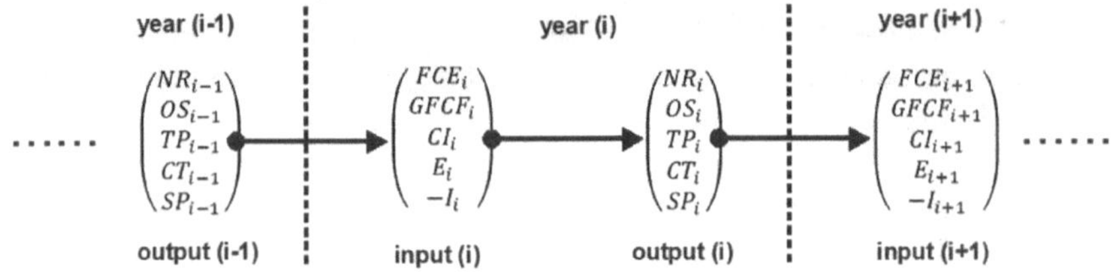

Fig. 3.1: The continuous input-output chain in ensuring SGDP
Source: Created by the authors

Where: NR: net remuneration of employees; OS: operational surplus and mixed income, gross; TP: taxes on production; CT: customs taxes; SP: subsidies on production; FCE: final consumption expenditures; GFCF: gross fixed capital formation; CI: changes in inventories; E: exports; I: imports

2. Meaning of sustainable GDP concept

SGDP (sustainable GDP) is that AGDP (accounting GDP) providing structural conditions (we shall see below that these structural conditions refer to the structure of the *input*, respectively of the *output*, at the macroeconomic level, as these structures are generated by AGDP dynamics) for the latter to oscillate within an economically, socially and morally acceptable tunnel (Dinga, 2018). We mention that, in this study, the concept of SGDP has no (possibly moral) value connotation, but only concerns the technical aspect of the reproducibility, at least conservative, of the AGDP from the previous year. In general, the economic and social significance of SGDP may be described as follows:

- that AGDP (more specifically, that structure of AGDP) not entering a downward (self-sustained) curve of the monetary size of AGDP that would affect the living standard and the quality of life;
- that AGDP not entering an upward (self-sustained) curve (this is obviously the case of a positive, self-escalating feed-back) of the monetary size of the AGDP that would affect the conservation or reproduction of the economic resources for supporting economic activity;
- that AGDP not submitting to the extremizing commands, commands that do not, in fact, respond to the long-term economic and social interest, but only to the short-term ones;
- that AGDP corresponding, based on the variations appearing in the structure of the input components, respectively the output, of the structure and dynamics of the economic demand; in this context, SGDP seems to be "natural" AGDP. The preoccupations of the economic theory and methodology for identifying and calculating certain natural economic quantities have been based, until now, on economic equilibrium considerations (either static or dynamic) or on economic optimum considerations. Our opinion is that if it is desired to calculate such natural rates (natural inflation, natural interest rate, natural unemployment etc.), it should start from sustainability considerations.

3. Qualitative analysis of sustainable GDP concept

In this paragraph we will systematize the main qualitative aspects regarding Sustainable GDP, and in the next chapter we will propose a formalism and a method for quantitative determination of Sustainable GDP.

We consider that the main qualitative characteristics of Sustainable GDP are the following:

- it introduces the concept of stability at the macroeconomic level, sustainability referring to both the stability of the real economy and the stability of the nominal economy (As a rule, the interest of current economic policies (not associated with the concept of sustainable GDP) is to ensure the financial stability, which concerns, above all, the nominal economy);
- it verifies both the economic efficacy criteria, and ethics criteria;
- it indicates a solution regarding the assessment of economic cyclicality: economic cycle it refers to those oscillations of the AGDP checking the matrix of sustainability structural coefficients; therefore, there

will be "natural" economic cycles, which conserve GDP sustainability and pathological economic cycles, which do not conserve GDP sustainability;

- it introduces a special type of crisis (which we propose to call, for example, *orbital crisis*) which refers to the case where the matrix of sustainability structural coefficients comes out of the acceptable (predetermined) margin for ensuring GDP sustainability;
- there are two further special *gaps* in GDP: the difference between accounting (current) GDP and sustainable GDP, respectively the difference between sustainable GDP and potential GDP (These two new categories of *gaps* of GDP should be studied and examined from the perspective of economic significance and, in particular, from the perspective of macroeconomic adjustment policy);
- sustainable GDP responds to the new demands for representativeness and relevance of economic dynamics from the perspective of well-being, quality of life and inter-generational ethics;
- the use of sustainable GDP will lead to the internalization of aspects that now are not included in the calculation of the accounting GDP (e.g., non-market activity);
- from a formal point of view, a *sui generis* variant for the balance of the connections between sectors (input-output model) may be developed, which shall include our proposal from this study on the matrix evaluation of sustainable GDP;
- from a formal sustainable (mathematical) point of view, sustainable GDP is best suited to the use complexity theory (chaos theory) in modeling macroeconomic dynamics, since the sustainable character of GDP is equivalent to identifying an attractor that shall maintain the accounting value of GDP in its area, given by the accepted (or acceptable) values of $\tilde{\alpha}$, respectively for $\tilde{\beta}$;
- calculating and using sustainable GDP will also lead to the renunciation of punctual optimization (possibility/extremization) and the shift to the calculation of possibility/acceptability of the values of the macroeconomic variables;
- sustainable GDP will entail the recalculation of a series of values (so-called natural) that, thus, are better founded (i.e. not based on economic equilibrium, as at present, but on sustainability considerations): natural inflation, natural unemployment, natural interest rate, natural rate of budget deficit, natural rate of public debt etc.;
- sustainable GDP could generate a *sui generis* formalism, including in the direction of inventing mathematical functions of sustainability, analogous to the present optimization functions.

The general relationships among Accounting GDP (AGDP), Potential GDP (PGDP), and Sustainable GDP (SGDP) are shown in Fig. 3.2.

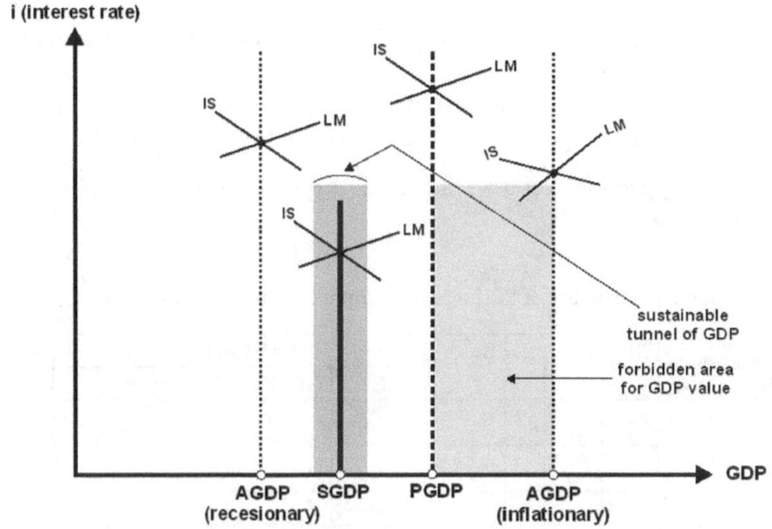

Fig. 3.2: Reciprocal positioning among AGDP, PGDP, and SGDP
Source: Created by the authors

4. A formal proposal for determining the conditions for the sustainability of GDP

4.1. A sui-generis matrix for sustainable GDP assessment

As it is known, at the macroeconomic level, a matrix (double entry table) can be constructed describing, at static equilibrium, the flows (inputs, respectively outputs) between the structural components of a national economy. The best-known of these matrices is the input-output model introduced in the economic analysis by Wassily Leontief. The model operates with four quadrants (of which only three are used for the analysis of static macroeconomic equilibrium – quadrants I, II and III):

- quadrant I: systematizes the intermediate consumption from the national economy, in the form of technological coefficients between the sectors: e is a monetary value from the output of the sector i is consumed in the sector j, reported to the total value produced in the sector j;

- quadrant II: systematizes the monetary value of the gross added value produced in the national economy, by intended uses (final use); this is the newly produced output;
- quadrant III: systematizes the monetary value of the entries in the production process from the national economy, based on input sources; this is the newly entered input;
- quadrant IV: is not usually used. In fact, our study will make a proposal to use precisely the fourth quadrant for the purpose of formalizing SGDP.

Figure 3.3 gives a synoptic image of the classical input-output balance (Leontief).

Fig. 3.3: Standard structure of the balance of connections between sectors

To / From		**B1**	**B2**	…	**Bn**	**End Use (U)**				**TOTAL**
						FCE	**GFCF**	**CI**	**E**	
B1		F_{11}	F_{12}	…	F_{1n}	FCE_1	$GFCF_1$	CI_1	E_1	$\boldsymbol{T_1}$
B2		F_{21}	F_{22}	…	F_{2n}	FCE_2	$GFCF_2$	CI_2	E_2	$\boldsymbol{T_2}$
…		…	…	…	…	…	…	…	…	…
Bn		F_{n1}	F_{n2}	…	F_{nn}	FCE_n	$GFCF_n$	CI_n	E_n	$\boldsymbol{T_n}$
GAV (R)	**GRE**	RS_1	RS_2	…	RS_n					
	D	A_1	A_2	…	A_n					
	I	I_1	I_2	…	I_n					
Total		$\boldsymbol{T_1}$	$\boldsymbol{T_2}$	…	$\boldsymbol{T_n}$					$\boldsymbol{T}$

Source: Created by the authors

Where: Bi: economic sector i; GAV: gross added value; GRE: gross remuneration of employees; D: fixed capital depreciation; I: imports; FCE: final consumption expenditures; GFCF: gross fixed capital formation; CI: changes in inventories; E: exports; R: resources; U: uses; F_{ij}: economic flows from sector i to sector j; T_i: total (value) of sector i $\left(T = \sum_{i=1}^{n} T_i\right)$

Noting

$$k_{ij} = \frac{F_{ij}}{T_j}, \quad \text{for } i, \tag{1}$$

results

$$F_{ij} = k_{ij} \cdot T_j \tag{2}$$

and if we form the matrix

$$A = \begin{pmatrix} k_{11} & k_{12} & \dots & k_{1n} \\ k_{21} & k_{22} & \dots & k_{2n} \\ \dots & \dots & \dots & \dots \\ k_{n1} & k_{n2} & \dots & k_{nn} \end{pmatrix} \tag{3}$$

the vectors:

$$FCE = \begin{pmatrix} FCE_1 \\ FCE_2 \\ \dots \\ FCE_n \end{pmatrix} \tag{4}$$

$$GFCF = \begin{pmatrix} GFCF_1 \\ GFCF_2 \\ \dots \\ GFCF_n \end{pmatrix}$$

$$CI = \begin{pmatrix} CI_1 \\ CI_2 \\ \dots \\ CI_n \end{pmatrix}$$

$$E = \begin{pmatrix} E_1 \\ E_2 \\ \dots \\ E_n \end{pmatrix}$$

$$GRE = \begin{pmatrix} GRE_1 & GRE_2 & \dots & GRE_n \end{pmatrix} \tag{5}$$

$$A = \begin{pmatrix} A_1 & A_2 & \dots & A_n \end{pmatrix}$$

$$I = \begin{pmatrix} I_1 & I_2 & \dots & I_n \end{pmatrix}$$

$$T = \begin{pmatrix} T_1 & T_2 & \dots & T_n \end{pmatrix}$$

as well as relationships

$$U = FCE + GFCF + CI + E \tag{6}$$

$$R = GRE + D + I \tag{7}$$

then one may write the well-known (static equilibrium) balance equations:

$$A \cdot T + U = T \tag{8}$$

respectively

$$A \cdot T + R = T \tag{9}$$

from which the following equality results immediately

$$U = R \tag{10}$$

that is exactly the idea of replicating the *input* by the *output*, which we have introduced above.

Based on the standard Input-Output model, we will now develop our own proposal to use the fourth quadrant of this model for the purpose of extracting certain conditions regarding the sustainability of GDP .

Let us make some preliminary clarifications.

- regarding R: we have the following resources (*input*):

NR: net remuneration of employees

PIT: personal income tax of employees (We also include here the other taxes related to the individual: on property, on capital gains etc.)

NI: net income of non-employees

OIT: non-wage income tax

NFNI: net income of private non-financial organizations – the essential part of VAB which remains after deducting the salary expenses. We also include here the state private domain (companies, authorities etc. with full state capital).

FNI: net income of private financial organizations – both banking and non-banking financial organizations (IFN).

CPI: corporate profit tax

PT: product tax (i.e. indirect taxes) – it includes value added tax, customs duty, excise duty.

D: depreciation of fixed capital in the private sector

I: import of goods and services – no distinction shall be made between intra-Community imports (or exports) and imports (or exports) involving countries outside the EU, but any goods or services transiting the economic frontier shall be considered as imports (respectively exports).

PS: product subsidies (this quantity shall enter with a negative algebraic sign, in order to maintain the expression of the monetary value of AGDP in the market price).

- regarding U: we have the following end uses (*output*):

FPrMC: market final consumption of private sector

FPrnMC: non-market final consumption of private sector

FPC: final consumption of public sector

GPI: gross public investment

GPrI: gross private investments

PNS: net saving of public sector – net saving is the positive difference between saving and investments (if the difference is negative, we can use the name of net investment, but not in the established sense, i.e. not as the difference between gross investment and depreciation).

PrNS: net saving of private sector

VSGS: variation of goods and services stock

CSC: variation of currency stock: It refers to the variation of the monetary base in the economy (the variation of the balance of current and deposit accounts in commercial banks, the variation of the existing cash at the central bank, the variation of the existing cash in the population).

E: export of goods and services

We will organize the two categories of variables in a matrix, so we will, in fact, complete the fourth quadrant of the standard model of connections balance between sectors (Fig. 3.4).

To / From	*FPrMC*	*FPrnMC*	*FPC*	*GPI*	*GPrI*	*PNS*	*PrNS*	*VSGS*	*CSC*	*E*	**TOTAL**
NR	$F_{1.1}$	~~$F_{1.2}$~~	$F_{1.3}$	~~$F_{1.4}$~~	$F_{1.5}$	$F_{1.6}$	$F_{1.7}$	~~$F_{1.8}$~~	$F_{1.9}$	~~$F_{1.10}$~~	$\boldsymbol{R_1}$
PIT	~~$F_{2.1}$~~	~~$F_{2.2}$~~	$F_{2.3}$	$F_{2.4}$	~~$F_{2.5}$~~	$F_{2.6}$	~~$F_{2.7}$~~	~~$F_{2.8}$~~	$F_{2.9}$	~~$F_{2.10}$~~	$\boldsymbol{R_2}$
NI	$F_{3.1}$	$F_{3.2}$	~~$F_{3.3}$~~	~~$F_{3.4}$~~	$F_{3.5}$	~~$F_{3.6}$~~	$F_{3.7}$	~~$F_{3.8}$~~	$F_{3.9}$	~~$F_{3.10}$~~	$\boldsymbol{R_3}$
OIT	~~$F_{4.1}$~~	~~$F_{4.2}$~~	$F_{4.3}$	~~$F_{4.4}$~~	$F_{4.5}$	$F_{4.6}$	$F_{4.7}$	~~$F_{4.8}$~~	$F_{4.9}$	~~$F_{4.10}$~~	$\boldsymbol{R_4}$
NFNI	~~$F_{5.1}$~~	~~$F_{5.2}$~~	~~$F_{5.3}$~~	~~$F_{5.4}$~~	$F_{5.5}$	~~$F_{5.6}$~~	$F_{5.7}$	$F_{5.8}$	$F_{5.9}$	$F_{5.10}$	$\boldsymbol{R_5}$
FNI	~~$F_{6.1}$~~	~~$F_{6.2}$~~	~~$F_{6.3}$~~	~~$F_{6.4}$~~	$F_{6.5}$	~~$F_{6.6}$~~	$F_{6.7}$	$F_{6.8}$	$F_{6.9}$	$F_{6.10}$	$\boldsymbol{R_6}$
CPI	~~$F_{7.1}$~~	~~$F_{7.2}$~~	$F_{7.3}$	$F_{7.4}$	~~$F_{7.5}$~~	$F_{7.6}$	~~$F_{7.7}$~~	~~$F_{7.8}$~~	$F_{7.9}$	~~$F_{7.10}$~~	$\boldsymbol{R_7}$
PT	$F_{8.1}$	$F_{8.2}$	$F_{8.3}$	$F_{8.4}$	$F_{8.5}$	$F_{8.6}$	~~$F_{8.7}$~~	~~$F_{8.8}$~~	$F_{8.9}$	$F_{8.10}$	$\boldsymbol{R_8}$
D	~~$F_{9.1}$~~	~~$F_{9.2}$~~	~~$F_{9.3}$~~	~~$F_{9.4}$~~	$F_{9.5}$	~~$F_{9.6}$~~	$F_{9.7}$	~~$F_{9.8}$~~	$F_{9.9}$	~~$F_{9.10}$~~	$\boldsymbol{R_9}$
I	$F_{10.1}$	~~$F_{10.2}$~~	$F_{10.3}$	$F_{10.4}$	$F_{10.5}$	$F_{01.6}$	$F_{10.7}$	$F_{10.8}$	$F_{10.9}$	$F_{10.10}$	$\boldsymbol{R_{10}}$
−PS	~~$F_{11.1}$~~	~~$F_{11.2}$~~	~~$F_{11.3}$~~	~~$F_{11.4}$~~	~~$F_{11.5}$~~	$F_{11.6}$	~~$F_{11.7}$~~	~~$F_{11.8}$~~	$F_{11.9}$	~~$F_{11.10}$~~	$\boldsymbol{R_{11}}$
TOTAL	$\boldsymbol{U_1}$	$\boldsymbol{U_2}$	$\boldsymbol{U_3}$	$\boldsymbol{U_4}$	$\boldsymbol{U_5}$	$\boldsymbol{U_6}$	$\boldsymbol{U_7}$	$\boldsymbol{U_8}$	$\boldsymbol{U_9}$	$\boldsymbol{U_{10}}$	$\boldsymbol{X}$

Fig. 3.4: Matrix model of correlating the input with the output at macroeconomic level for SGDP

Source: Created by the authors

Where with F_{ij} was noted the flow from the *input* „i“ which, from a value point of view, contributes to the formation of the *output* „j“, where

$$\sum_{j=1}^{10} U_j = \sum_{i=1}^{11} R_i = 1 \tag{11}$$

Of course, not every *input* contributes, from the point of view of transmission mechanisms at the macroeconomic level, to the formation of any *output*.

In the table above, we have excluded the formation of *input-output* flows, based on theoretical and methodological considerations (more precisely based on definition considerations). These exclusions were indicated by a cancellation sign. Therefore, only the *input-output* flows highlighted by hatching remain, which means 56 flows from *inputs* to *outpus* (51 % of the total theoretically possible flows).

Therefore, when we calculate the "technological coefficients" in question, some of them will have zero value (and, in the case of subsidies on the product, a negative value).

We will note, therefore,

$$\xi_{ij} = \frac{F_{ij}}{U_j} \tag{12}$$

with $i = 1,2,3,\ldots 11$, and $j = 1,2,3,..10$ which we will call the structural coefficient of GDP sustainability.

Of course:

$$\sum_{j=1}^{10} \xi_{ij} = 1 \tag{13}$$

for $i = 1,2,\ldots,11$.

These coefficients are as follows (Fig. 3.5):

To / From	*FPrMC*	*FPrnMC*	*FPC*	*GPI*	*GPrI*	*PNS*	*PrNS*	*VSGS*	*CSC*	*E*	**TOTAL**
NR	$\xi_{1.1}$		$\xi_{1.3}$		$\xi_{1.5}$	$\xi_{1.6}$	$\xi_{1.7}$		$\xi_{1.9}$		$\boldsymbol{R_1}$
PIT			$\xi_{2.3}$	$\xi_{2.4}$		$\xi_{2.6}$			$\xi_{2.9}$		$\boldsymbol{R_2}$
NI	$\xi_{3.1}$	$\xi_{3.2}$			$\xi_{3.5}$		$\xi_{3.7}$		$\xi_{3.9}$		$\boldsymbol{R_3}$
OIT			$\xi_{4.3}$		$\xi_{4.5}$	$\xi_{4.6}$	$\xi_{4.7}$		$\xi_{4.9}$		$\boldsymbol{R_4}$
NFNI					$\xi_{5.5}$		$\xi_{5.7}$	$\xi_{5.8}$	$\xi_{5.9}$	$\xi_{5.10}$	$\boldsymbol{R_5}$
FNI					$\xi_{6.5}$		$\xi_{6.7}$	$\xi_{6.8}$	$\xi_{6.9}$	$\xi_{6.10}$	$\boldsymbol{R_6}$
CPI			$\xi_{7.3}$	$\xi_{7.4}$		$\xi_{7.6}$			$\xi_{7.9}$		$\boldsymbol{R_7}$
PT	$\xi_{8.1}$	$\xi_{8.2}$	$\xi_{8.3}$	$\xi_{8.4}$	$\xi_{8.5}$	$\xi_{8.6}$			$\xi_{8.9}$	$\xi_{8.10}$	$\boldsymbol{R_8}$
D					$\xi_{9.5}$		$\xi_{9.7}$		$\xi_{9.9}$		$\boldsymbol{R_9}$
I	$\xi_{10.1}$		$\xi_{10.3}$	$\xi_{10.4}$	$\xi_{10.5}$	$\xi_{10.6}$	$\xi_{10.7}$	$\xi_{10.8}$	$\xi_{10.9}$	$\xi_{10.10}$	$\boldsymbol{R_{10}}$
−PS						$\xi_{11.6}$			$\xi_{11.9}$		$\boldsymbol{R_{11}}$
Total	$\boldsymbol{U_1}$	$\boldsymbol{U_2}$	$\boldsymbol{U_3}$	$\boldsymbol{U_4}$	$\boldsymbol{U_5}$	$\boldsymbol{U_6}$	$\boldsymbol{U_7}$	$\boldsymbol{U_8}$	$\boldsymbol{U_9}$	$\boldsymbol{U_{10}}$	$\boldsymbol{X}$

Fig. 3.5: Structural coefficient of GDP sustainability

Source: created by the authors

4.2. Formal conditions regarding the calculation of sustainable GDP

We will set the general condition of stationarity, that is, punctual replication of AGDP. Let us build the matrix of sustainability structural coefficients .

$$E=\begin{pmatrix}
\xi_{1.1} & 0 & \xi_{1.3} & 0 & \xi_{1.5} & \xi_{1.6} & \xi_{1.7} & 0 & \xi_{1.9} & 0\\
0 & 0 & \xi_{2.3} & \xi_{2.4} & 0 & \xi_{2.6} & 0 & 0 & \xi_{2.9} & 0\\
\xi_{3.1} & \xi_{3.2} & 0 & 0 & \xi_{3.5} & 0 & \xi_{3.7} & 0 & \xi_{3.9} & 0\\
0 & 0 & \xi_{4.3} & 0 & \xi_{4.5} & \xi_{4.6} & \xi_{4.7} & 0 & \xi_{4.9} & 0\\
0 & 0 & 0 & 0 & \xi_{5.5} & 0 & \xi_{5.7} & \xi_{5.8} & \xi_{5.9} & \xi_{5.10}\\
0 & 0 & 0 & 0 & \xi_{6.5} & 0 & \xi_{6.7} & \xi_{6.8} & \xi_{6.9} & \xi_{6.10}\\
0 & 0 & \xi_{7.3} & \xi_{7.4} & 0 & \xi_{7.6} & 0 & 0 & \xi_{7.9} & 0\\
\xi_{8.1} & \xi_{8.2} & \xi_{8.3} & \xi_{8.4} & \xi_{8.5} & \xi_{8.6} & 0 & 0 & \xi_{8.9} & \xi_{8.10}\\
0 & 0 & 0 & 0 & \xi_{9.5} & 0 & \xi_{9.7} & 0 & \xi_{9.9} & 0\\
\xi_{10.1} & 0 & \xi_{10.3} & \xi_{10.4} & \xi_{10.5} & \xi_{10.6} & \xi_{10.7} & \xi_{10.8} & \xi_{10.9} & \xi_{10.10}\\
0 & 0 & 0 & 0 & 0 & \xi_{11.6} & 0 & 0 & \xi_{11.9} & 0
\end{pmatrix} \quad (14)$$

Let there be two consecutive moments of time (usually two years), t, respectively $t+1$. This leads to two matrices of sustainability structural coefficients, E^t, respectively E^{t+1}:

$$E^t=\begin{pmatrix}
\xi^t_{1.1} & 0 & \xi^t_{1.3} & 0 & \xi^t_{1.5} & \xi^t_{1.6} & \xi^t_{1.7} & 0 & \xi^t_{1.9} & 0\\
0 & 0 & \xi_{2.3} & \xi_{2.4} & 0 & \xi_{2.6} & 0 & 0 & \xi_{2.9} & 0\\
\xi^t_{3.1} & \xi^t_{3.2} & 0 & 0 & \xi^t_{3.5} & 0 & \xi^t_{3.7} & 0 & \xi^t_{3.9} & 0\\
0 & 0 & \xi^t_{4.3} & 0 & \xi^t_{4.5} & \xi^t_{4.6} & \xi^t_{4.7} & 0 & \xi^t_{4.9} & 0\\
0 & 0 & 0 & 0 & \xi^t_{5.5} & 0 & \xi^t_{5.7} & \xi^t_{5.8} & \xi^t_{5.9} & \xi^t_{5.10}\\
0 & 0 & 0 & 0 & \xi^t_{6.5} & 0 & \xi^t_{6.7} & \xi^t_{6.8} & \xi^t_{6.9} & \xi^t_{6.10}\\
0 & 0 & \xi^t_{7.3} & \xi^t_{7.4} & 0 & \xi^t_{7.6} & 0 & 0 & \xi^t_{7.9} & 0\\
\xi^t_{8.1} & \xi^t_{8.2} & \xi^t_{8.3} & \xi^t_{8.4} & \xi^t_{8.5} & \xi^t_{8.6} & 0 & 0 & \xi^t_{8.9} & \xi^t_{8.10}\\
0 & 0 & 0 & 0 & \xi^t_{9.5} & 0 & \xi^t_{9.7} & 0 & \xi^t_{9.9} & 0\\
\xi^t_{10.1} & 0 & \xi^t_{10.3} & \xi^t_{10.4} & \xi^t_{10.5} & \xi^t_{10.6} & \xi^t_{10.7} & \xi^t_{10.8} & \xi^t_{10.9} & \xi^t_{10.10}\\
0 & 0 & 0 & 0 & 0 & \xi^t_{11.6} & 0 & 0 & \xi^t_{11.9} & 0
\end{pmatrix} \quad (15)$$

$$E^{t+1}=\begin{pmatrix}
\xi_{1.1}^{t+1} & 0 & \xi_{1.3}^{t+1} & 0 & \xi_{1.5}^{t+1} & \xi_{1.6}^{t+1} & \xi_{1.7}^{t+1} & 0 & \xi_{1.9}^{t+1} & 0\\
0 & 0 & \xi_{2.3}^{t+1} & \xi_{2.4}^{t+1} & 0 & \xi_{2.6}^{t+1} & 0 & 0 & \xi_{2.9}^{t+1} & 0\\
\xi_{3.1}^{t+1} & \xi_{3.2}^{t+1} & 0 & 0 & \xi_{3.5}^{t+1} & 0 & \xi_{3.7}^{t+1} & 0 & \xi_{3.9}^{t+1} & 0\\
0 & 0 & \xi_{4.3}^{t+1} & 0 & \xi_{4.5}^{t+1} & \xi_{4.6}^{t+1} & \xi_{4.7}^{t+1} & 0 & \xi_{4.9}^{t+1} & 0\\
0 & 0 & 0 & 0 & \xi_{5.5}^{t+1} & 0 & \xi_{5.7}^{t+1} & \xi_{5.8}^{t+1} & \xi_{5.9}^{t+1} & \xi_{5.10}^{t+1}\\
0 & 0 & 0 & 0 & \xi_{6.5}^{t+1} & 0 & \xi_{6.7}^{t+1} & \xi_{6.8}^{t+1} & \xi_{6.9}^{t+1} & \xi_{6.10}^{t+1}\\
0 & 0 & \xi_{7.3}^{t+1} & \xi_{7.4}^{t+1} & 0 & \xi_{7.6}^{t+1} & 0 & 0 & \xi_{7.9}^{t+1} & 0\\
\xi_{8.1}^{t+1} & \xi_{8.2}^{t+1} & \xi_{8.3}^{t+1} & \xi_{8.4}^{t+1} & \xi_{8.5}^{t+1} & \xi_{8.6}^{t+1} & 0 & 0 & \xi_{8.9}^{t+1} & \xi_{8.10}^{t+1}\\
0 & 0 & 0 & 0 & \xi_{9.5}^{t+1} & 0 & \xi_{9.7}^{t+1} & 0 & \xi_{9.9}^{t+1} & 0\\
\xi_{10.1}^{t+1} & 0 & \xi_{10.3}^{t+1} & \xi_{10.4}^{t+1} & \xi_{10.5}^{t+1} & \xi_{10.6}^{t+1} & \xi_{10.7}^{t+1} & \xi_{10.8}^{t+1} & \xi_{10.9}^{t+1} & \xi_{10.10}^{t+1}\\
0 & 0 & 0 & 0 & 0 & \xi_{11.6}^{t+1} & 0 & 0 & \xi_{11.9}^{t+1} & 0
\end{pmatrix} \qquad (16)$$

As stated above, the structure of the *input* at a given time (e.g., at the moment $t+1$) should not differ from the structure of the *input* at the moment t by more than an acceptable, predetermined margin, $\alpha^{t,t+1}$). Let us move from changing the relative structure of AGDP *input* (respectively *output*) components to changing the structural coefficients of sustainability, as introduced above.

Therefore, we know we have

$$S_i=\left(c_1^i,c_2^i,\ldots,c_n^i\right) \qquad (17)$$

Adapting the relation to AGDP *input* there results that, at the moments t, respectively $t+1$, we have respectively:

$$\begin{aligned} S^t &= \left(NR^t,PIT^t,NI^t,OIT^t,NFNI^t,FNI^t,CPI^t,PT^t,D^t,I^t,-PS^t\right)\equiv \\ &\equiv\left(R_1^t,R_2^t,R_3^t,R_4^t,R_5^t,R_6^t,R_7^t,R_8^t,R_9^t,R_{10}^t,R_{11}^t\right) \end{aligned} \qquad (18)$$

$$\begin{aligned} &S^{t+1}=(NR^{t+1},PIT^{t+1},NI^{t+1},OIT^{t+1},NFNI^{t+1},FNI^{t+1},\\ &CPI^{t+1},PT^{t+1},D^{t+1},I^{t+1},-PS^{t+1})\equiv\begin{pmatrix} R_1^{t+1},R_2^{t+1},R_3^{t+1},R_4^{t+1},R_5^{t+1},R_6^{t+1},\\ R_7^{t+1},R_8^{t+1},R_9^{t+1},R_{10}^{t+1},R_{11}^{t+1}\end{pmatrix} \end{aligned} \qquad (19)$$

With the conditions:

$$\begin{cases} |NR^{t+1} - NR^{t}| \leq \alpha_1^{t,t+1} \\ |PIT^{t+1} - PIT^{t}| \leq \alpha_2^{t,t+1} \\ |NI^{t+1} - NI^{t}| \leq \alpha_3^{t,t+1} \\ |OIT^{t+1} - OIT^{t}| \leq \alpha_4^{t,t+1} \\ |NFNI^{t+1} - NFNI^{t}| \leq \alpha_5^{t,t+1} \\ |FNI^{t+1} - FNI^{t}| \leq \alpha_6^{t,t+1} \\ |CPI^{t+1} - CPI^{t}| \leq \alpha_7^{t,t+1} \\ |PT^{t+1} - PT^{t}| \leq \alpha_8^{t,t+1} \\ |D^{t+1} - D^{t}| \leq \alpha_9^{t,t+1} \\ |I^{t+1} - I^{t}| \leq \alpha_{10}^{t,t+1} \\ |PS^{t} - PS^{t+1}| \leq \alpha_{11}^{t,t+1} \end{cases}$$

Taking into account the way in which the structural coefficients of sustainability have been defined, we can successively write the following:

$$\xi_{ij} = \frac{F_{ij}}{U_j},\ F_{ij} = \xi_{ij} \cdot U_j \tag{20}$$

If we form the matrix (respectively the vectors):

$$F = \begin{pmatrix} F_{1.1} & F_{1.2} & F_{1.3} & F_{1.4} & F_{1.5} & F_{1.6} & F_{1.7} & F_{1.8} & F_{1.9} & F_{1.10} \\ F_{2.1} & F_{2.2} & F_{2.3} & F_{2.4} & F_{2.5} & F_{2.6} & F_{2.7} & F_{2.8} & F_{2.9} & F_{2.10} \\ F_{3.1} & F_{3.2} & F_{3.3} & F_{3.4} & F_{3.5} & F_{3.6} & F_{3.7} & F_{3.8} & F_{3.9} & F_{3.10} \\ F_{4.1} & F_{4.2} & F_{4.3} & F_{4.4} & F_{4.5} & F_{4.6} & F_{4.7} & F_{4.8} & F_{4.9} & F_{4.10} \\ F_{5.1} & F_{5.2} & F_{5.3} & F_{5.4} & F_{5.5} & F_{5.6} & F_{5.7} & F_{5.8} & F_{5.9} & F_{5.10} \\ F_{6.1} & F_{6.2} & F_{6.3} & F_{6.4} & F_{6.5} & F_{6.6} & F_{6.7} & F_{6.8} & F_{6.9} & F_{6.10} \\ F_{7.1} & F_{7.2} & F_{7.3} & F_{7.4} & F_{7.5} & F_{7.6} & F_{7.7} & F_{7.8} & F_{7.9} & F_{7.10} \\ F_{8.1} & F_{8.2} & F_{8.3} & F_{8.4} & F_{8.5} & F_{8.6} & F_{8.7} & F_{8.8} & F_{8.9} & F_{8.10} \\ F_{9.1} & F_{9.2} & F_{9.3} & F_{9.4} & F_{9.5} & F_{9.6} & F_{9.7} & F_{9.8} & F_{9.9} & F_{9.10} \\ F_{10.1} & F_{10.2} & F_{10.3} & F_{10.4} & F_{10.5} & F_{10.6} & F_{10.7} & F_{10.8} & F_{10.9} & F_{10.10} \\ F_{11.1} & F_{11.2} & F_{11.3} & F_{11.4} & F_{11.5} & F_{11.6} & F_{11.7} & F_{11.8} & F_{11.9} & F_{11.10} \end{pmatrix} \tag{21}$$

$$U = (U_1, U_2, U_3, U_4, U_5, U_6, U_7, U_8, U_9, U_{10}) \tag{22}$$

$$R = \begin{pmatrix} R_1 \\ R_2 \\ R_3 \\ R_4 \\ R_5 \\ R_6 \\ R_7 \\ R_8 \\ R_9 \\ R_{10} \\ R_{11} \end{pmatrix} \tag{23}$$

There can be written, successively (A' means the transpose of the matrix A, and A^{-1} means the reverse of the matrix A):

$$E' \cdot R = U' \tag{24}$$

$$E \cdot U' = R \tag{25}$$

$$U = \left(R' \cdot E\right) \tag{26}$$

This result can be interpreted as follows: if a structure of the *input* is given, related to a certain time interval, one may determine, based on the matrix of sustainability structural coefficients, the *output* structure of that time interval. The input of a given time interval must be considered to be available at the beginning of that interval (e.g., at the beginning of the calendar or fiscal year, as appropriate), and the output of a given time interval must be considered to be available at the end of that interval (e.g., at the end of the calendar or fiscal year, as appropriate). This static (synchronous, transverse) relationship can be developed in a dynamic (diachronic, longitudinal) way, as follows:

- *moment 1:*

$$R^1 = E^0 \cdot \left(U^0\right)' \tag{27}$$

$$U^1 = \left(R^1\right)' \cdot E^1 \tag{28}$$

- *moment 2:*

$$R^2 = E^1 \cdot \left(U^1\right)' = E^1 \cdot \left(E^1\right)' \cdot R^1 \tag{29}$$

$$U^2 = \left(R^2\right)' \cdot E^2 = \left(R^1\right)' \cdot E^1 \cdot \left(E^1\right)' \cdot E^2 \tag{30}$$

- *moment 3:*

$$R^3 = E^2 \cdot \left(U^2\right)' = E^2 \cdot \left(E^2\right)' \cdot E^1 \cdot \left(E^1\right)' \cdot R^1 \tag{31}$$

$$U^3 = \left(R^3\right)' \cdot E^3 = \left(R^1\right)' \cdot E^1 \cdot \left(E^1\right)' \cdot E^2 \cdot \left(E^2\right)' \cdot E^3 \tag{32}$$

- *moment 4:*

$$R^4 = E^3 \cdot \left(U^3\right)' = E^3 \cdot \left(E^3\right)' \cdot E^2 \cdot \left(E^2\right)' \cdot E^1 \cdot \left(E^1\right)' \cdot R^1 \tag{33}$$

$$U^4 = \left(R^4\right)' \cdot E^4 = \left(R^1\right)' \cdot E^1 \cdot \left(E^1\right)' \cdot E^2 \left(E^2\right)' \cdot E^3 \cdot \left(E^3\right)' \cdot E^4 \tag{34}$$

...

- *general moment k:*

$$R^k = \prod_{i=1}^{k-1} \left[E^{k-i} \cdot \left(E^{k-i}\right)' \right] \cdot E^0 \cdot \left(U^0\right)' \tag{35}$$

$$U^k = U^0 \cdot \left(E^0\right)' \cdot \prod_{i=1}^{k-1} \left[E^i \cdot \left(E^i\right)' \right] \cdot E^k \tag{36}$$

Nota bene: the vector R^0 will be considered as a unitary vector, i.e., ., $(R^0)'$ = (1,1,1,1,1,1,1,1,1,1,1), transforming, somewhat, the concrete values to obtain this initial vector.

Restoring the analytical formula (in this way of formulating recurrence relations, we have the mathematical conditions for using a Kalman type filter.) for the general case (k), we obtain successively (We will take into account two of the rules for transposing the matrix product: (1) the transpose of the matrix product is equal to the product of the transpose of matrices taken in the reverse order $(A_1 \cdot A_2 \cdot \ldots A_{n-1} \cdot A_n)' = (A_n)' \cdot (A_{n-1})' \cdot \ldots \cdot (A_2)' \cdot (A_1)'$; (2) the transpose of the transpose of a matrix is the matrix itself $(A')' = A$).

Therefore, both for *input*, vector and for *output* vector, we have obtained recursive analytical formula based only on the original terms of *input* (R^0), respectively on the matrices of sustainability structural coefficients associated to all the previous moments with respect to the moment for which the two vectors of interest are calculated, R, respectively U.

Of course, we now have to set the condition that the matrix of sustainability structural coefficients, as it has been defined (introduced), ensure that the structure of the output shall not deviate beyond the values considered as "delivering" a sustainable GDP (SGDP). We will make the following assumptions.

Let us resume the relative structure by components of the *input* (X), respectively the *output* (Y) AGDP in a certain period (year):

$$X^t = \begin{pmatrix} x_1^t \\ x_2^t \\ x_3^t \\ x_4^t \\ x_5^t \\ x_6^t \\ x_7^t \\ x_8^t \\ x_9^t \\ x_{10}^t \\ x_{11}^t \end{pmatrix} = \begin{pmatrix} NR^t/X^t \\ PIT^t/X^t \\ NI^t/X^t \\ OIT^t/X^t \\ NFNI^t/X^t \\ FNI^t/X^t \\ CPI^t/X^t \\ PT^t/X^t \\ D^t/X^t \\ I^t/X^t \\ -PS^t/X^t \end{pmatrix} = \begin{pmatrix} R_1^t/X^t \\ R_2^t/X^t \\ R_3^t/X^t \\ R_4^t/X^t \\ R_5^t/X^t \\ R_6^t/X^t \\ R_7^t/X^t \\ R_8^t/X^t \\ R_9^t/X^t \\ R_{10}^t/X^t \\ R_{11}^t/X^t \end{pmatrix} \tag{37}$$

$$Y^t = \begin{pmatrix} y_1^t \\ y_2^t \\ y_3^t \\ y_4^t \\ y_5^t \\ y_6^t \\ y_7^t \\ y_8^t \\ y_9^t \\ y_{10}^t \end{pmatrix}' = \begin{pmatrix} FPrMC^t/X^t \\ FPrnMC^t/X^t \\ FPC^t/X^t \\ GPI^t/X^t \\ GPrI^t/X^t \\ PNS^t/X^t \\ PrNS^t/X^t \\ VSGS^t/X^t \\ CSC^t/X^t \\ E^t/X^t \end{pmatrix}' = \begin{pmatrix} U_1^t/X^t \\ U_2^t/X^t \\ U_3^t/X^t \\ U_4^t/X^t \\ U_5^t/X^t \\ U_6^t/X^t \\ U_7^t/X^t \\ U_8^t/X^t \\ U_9^t/X^t \\ U_{10}^t/X^t \end{pmatrix}' \quad (38)$$

with the obvious condition:

$$\sum_{i=1}^{10} y_i^t = \sum_{j=1}^{11} x_j^t = 1 \quad (39)$$

Let us introduce the acceptability margin of the variation of the *input* structure for AGDP following the *output* of AGDP, so as to ensure the sustainability of AGDP, i.e. to obtain SGDP.

Let us note with:

$$\tilde{x}_i^t = x_i^t - \tilde{\alpha}_i^t \quad (40)$$

$$\tilde{y}_j^t = y_j^t - \tilde{\beta}_j^t \quad (41)$$

where $\tilde{x}_i^t \left(i = 1,2,\ldots,11\right)$ means the value of the weight of component i of the *input*, at the moment t, providing the sustainability of AGDP, $\tilde{\alpha}_i^t$ means absolute deviation of the weight of component i of the *input* in the total of the *input* (It is not necessary to use the module (i.e. absolute value), since it is assumed that either a decrease or an increase (with the same absolute rate) of the weight of that component still ensures the sustainability of AGDP. It is true that a very important methodological problem arises here, but which we are not prepared to examine here: is the effect in the variation of the weight of input concerned on the sustainability of the AGDP? The problem is particularly difficult, because it means examining the analytical behavioral function of each input on the subsequent output, in order to determine both the possible asymmetry with the initial value of the weight in question, and the possible thresholds or even substitution rates between input (sui generis indifference curves), so that AGDP sustainability is still ensured.), at moment t, a deviation generated by the *output* of the previous year, $(t-1)$. Similarly, $\tilde{y}_j^t$ (and $j=1,2,\ldots,10$) means the value of the weight of component j, at moment t, providing sustainability of AGDP, $\tilde{\beta}_i^t$ means absolute deviation of the weight of component j of the *output* in the total of the *output*, at moment t, a deviation generated by the *input* of the previous year, $(t-1)$.

Let us remember that for each $i=1,2,\ldots,11$ and $j=1,2,\ldots,10$:

$$\xi_{ij} = \frac{F_{ij}}{U_j} = \frac{F_{ij}}{y_j} \tag{42}$$

$$F_{ij} = \xi_{ij} \cdot U_j \tag{43}$$

$$y_j = \frac{F_{ij}}{\xi_{ij}} \tag{44}$$

We will pass, for simplification of writing, to the coefficients:

$$\tilde{x}_i^t = \tilde{\varepsilon}_i^t \cdot x_i^t \tag{45}$$

respectively:

$$\tilde{y}_j^t = \tilde{\tau}_j^t \cdot y_j^t \tag{46}$$

where:

$$\tilde{\varepsilon}_i^t = 1 - \frac{\tilde{\alpha}_i^t}{x_i^t} \tag{47}$$

respectively:

$$\tilde{\tau}_j^t = 1 - \frac{\tilde{\beta}_j^t}{y_j^t} \tag{48}$$

If one considers that the numerical values $\tilde{\alpha}_i^t$, respectively $\tilde{\beta}_j^t$ are given, they can be established by experts or on econometric basis from previous AGDP series. Our opinion is that these empirical values shall be set in such a way that the weightings in question do not exceed (either on the "left", or on the "right") 2 % of the reference value. This means that the values for $\tilde{\varepsilon}_i^t$, respectively $\tilde{\tau}_j^t$, would vary between 0.98 and 1.02. Of course, here comes the crucial problem of accumulation, which demands a maximum limit both on the "left" and on the "right" that constitutes a threshold beyond which sustainability is compromised. On a purely intuitive basis, we suggest that this threshold be 5 % (equal to the value taken into account for the nominal GDP variation in establishing the nominal economic convergence criteria of the Maastricht Treaty), then the values for $\tilde{\varepsilon}_i^t$, respectively $\tilde{\tau}_j^t$ are also given.

Therefore, the question arises only of the transition from $\tilde{\varepsilon}_i^t$, respectively $\tilde{\tau}_j^t$ to ξ_{ij}.

Now:

$$y_j = \frac{F_{ij}}{\xi_{ij}} \tag{49}$$

$$\tilde{y}_j^t = \tilde{\tau}_j^t \cdot y_j^t \tag{50}$$

there results:

$$\tilde{y}_j^t = \tilde{\tau}_j^t \cdot \frac{F_{ij}}{\tilde{\xi}_{ij}} \tag{51}$$

where from:

$$\tilde{\xi}_{ij} = \frac{\tilde{\tau}_j^t \cdot F_{ij}}{\tilde{y}_j^t} \tag{52}$$

As all the values to the right of the above equation are given, it turns out that we may determine the matrices of sustainability structural coefficients, so we can construct the statistical series for both the past (post-diction) and the future (prediction) for SGDP.

5. Conclusions

The adoption of alternative measures of GDP can vary by country and region, and there's ongoing debate about the strengths and limitations of each approach.

Additionally, the field of alternative indicators is constantly evolving as researchers refine existing measures and develop new ones to better capture the complexities of economic growth, well-being, and sustainability.

The sustainable values of the economic variables are not yet approached in the scientific literature; at most on the potential values of such variables there are some approaches (especially on the potential PIB – but, in our opinion, in a wrong way based on filters which do not provide potential value but only the long term value, which is not the same with the potential one).

Even the natural values well known in the literature (natural rate of unemployment, natural rate of inflation, natural rate of interest) are determined based on equilibrium (or optimal) condition; in our opinion, all these natural values should be determined based on sustainability condition; unfortunately, mathematically, such a condition is not yet provided.

The Sustainable GDP is the most appropriate macroeconomic value, which could incorporate not only economic considerations, but also social and even moral constraints, which is much more closed to the final purpose of the economic process (e.g., in which way should the economy grow? Perhaps, it is better it be sustainable).

The paper provides a methodological way to calculate an input-output matrix of sustainable coefficients of a kind of Leontieff macroeconomic balance, so the economy gets the sustainable GDP, based on the macroeconomic circuit of flows. The next stage of our research is to test empirically our methodological proposals to calculate the sustainable GDP.

Bibliography

Atkinson, G. (1995). *Measuring Sustainable Economic Welfare: A Critique of the UK ISEW*. Center for Social and Economic Research on the Global Environment Working Paper. Norwich and London, 95–08.

Cobb, C., Halstead, T., & Rowe, J. (1995). *The Genuine Progress Indicator*. Redefining Progress, San Francisco, CA.

Costanza, R., Hart, M., Talberth, J., & Posner, S. (2009). *Beyond GDP: The Need for New Measures of Progress*. The Pardee Papers No. 4 (Boston, Boston University). Available at: https://pdxscholar.library.pdx.edu/cgi/viewcontent.cgi?article=1010&context=iss_pub.pdx.edu/cgi/viewcontent.cgi?article=1010&context=iss_pub.

Daly, H.E., & Cobb, Jr. J.B. (1989). *For the Common Good: Redirecting the Economy Toward Community, the Environment, and a Sustainable Future*. Boston: Beacon Press.

Dinga, E. (2018). *Economic Theory and Modelling Studies* (in Romanian: *Studii de Teorie si Modelare Economica).* Bucharest: Ed. Academiei Romane.

Easterlin, R.A. (1974). Does Economic Growth Improve the Human Lot? Some Empirical Evidence. In *Nations and Households in Economic Growth: Essays in Honor of Moses Abramowitz,* by Paul A. David and Melvin W. Reder. New York: Academic Press, Inc.

Easterlin, R.A. (1995). Will Raising the Incomes of All Increase the Happiness of All? *Journal of Economic Behavior and Organization,* 27(1), 35–48.

Easterlin, R.A. (2001). Income and Happiness: Towards a Unified Theory. *The Economic Journal,* 111(47), 465–484.

Easterlin, R.A. (2005). Feeding the Illusion of Growth and Happiness: A Reply to Hagerty and Veenhoven. *Social Indicators Research,* 74(3), 429–443.

Kuznets, S., Epstein, L., & Jenks, E. (1941). *National Income and Its Composition, 1919–1938,* Volume 1. New York: National Bureau of Economic Research.

Kuznets, S. (1962) About rethinking the system of national accounting. In: *The New Republic,* vol. 147 by Croly, H. D. (eds.). Republic Publishing Company, 1962, p. 29.

Lawn, P. A. (2005). An Assessment of the Valuation Methods Used to Calculate the Index of Sustainable Economic Welfare (ISEW), Genuine Progress Indicator (GPI), and Sustainable Net Benefit Index (SNB). *Environment, Development, and Sustainability,* 7(2), 185–208.

Leontief, W. (1966). *Input-Output Economics.* New York: Oxford University.

Liu, J. (2006). *China Releases Green GDP Index, Tests New Development Path.* Worldwatch Institute: Online Features: China Watch: 28 September 2006.

Neumayer, E. (1999). The ISEW – Not an Index of Sustainable Economic Welfare. *Social Indicators Research,* 48(1), 77–101.

Neumayer, E. (2000). On the Methodology of ISEW, GPI and Related Measures: Some Constructive Suggestions and Some Doubt on the 'threshold' Hypothesis. *Ecological Economics,* 34(3), 347–361.

Parris, T.M., & Kates, R.W. (2003). Characterizing and Measuring Sustainable Development. *Annual Review of Environment and Resources,* 28(13), 559–586.

Ura, K., & Galay, K. (eds.). (2004). *Gross National Happiness and Development.* First International Seminar on Operationalization of Gross National Happiness, Thimphu, Bhutan: The Centre for Bhutan Studies.

Vanham, D., Leip, A., Galli, A., Kastner, T., Bruckner, M., Uwizeye, A., et al. (2019). Environmental Footprint Family to Address Local to Planetary Sustainability and Deliver on the SDGs. *Science of the Total Environment,* 693, 133642.

Veenhoven, R. (2008). World Database of Happiness: Continuous Register of Scientific Research on Subjective Appreciation of Life. Erasmus University Rotterdam. Retrieved from http://hdl.handle.net/1765/8683.

Camelia Oprean-Stan and Sebastian Emanuel Stan

Chapter 4 A bootstrap subsample rolling window causality method for analyzing the relationship between natural gas consumption and economic growth

Abstract: This chapter's objective is to illustrate the application of the bootstrap sub-sample rolling window causality method for analyzing the relationship between two variables. In contrast to the full-sample causality test, the rolling-window estimation method used in this study to investigate the causal relationships between Romania's natural gas consumption and economic development takes structural changes into consideration. In the calculated vector autoregressive models, we find that the link between natural gas consumption and economic development over the short term is unstable. We review the dynamic causal connection in the rolling window's sub-sample causality test using a time-varying methodology (RB bootstrap-based modified-LR causality test), and we find that economic development has small negative effects on natural gas consumption in only a few sub-periods, although the usage of natural gas has a detrimental impact on economic growth in the majority of statistically significant periods. Rolling-window estimation tests produce more accurate results regarding the causal linkages between two variables when time-varying parameters are accounted for.

Keywords: Granger causal relation, sub-sample, natural gas consumption, economic growth

Jelcodes: C32, O13

1. Introduction

Examining the causal relationship between two variables is essential because it enables us to comprehend the nature and direction of their interaction. By determining causality, it is possible to determine which variable influences the other and to what amount. This information is essential for making informed decisions and building effective strategies in a variety of sectors, including economics, finance, and healthcare. In general, studying causality helps us get a clearer understanding of the intricate relationships between factors and their effects on various phenomena, as well as to construct cause-and-effect relationships and validate hypotheses.

The full-sample test has traditionally been used in empirical research that examines the causal link between two variables. The parameters of the VAR model used for testing are often assumed to be constant across time by full-sample Granger causality tests, which implies that a single causality is true for each period of time. But according to Balcilar and Ozdemir (2013), when there are structural changes in the whole data sample, the results of causality tests applied to the whole sample are no longer correct. To address this shortcoming of the causality tests, we use the causality technique applied on the sub-sample rolling window. The rolling window method yields more precise causality results than the full-sample causality test.

In order to demonstrate the empirical application of the bootstrap sub-sample rolling window causality method, this study's goal is to investigate the causal link between natural gas consumption and economic growth. The causal link between energy usage and GDP has been investigated in the research literature on the energy-growth nexus, but the findings have been confusing and inconsistent (Destek, 2016). However, recent studies have shown that there is a two-way causal link between electricity consumption and economic growth, suggesting that energy use both requires and promotes economic growth (Pandelara et al., 2021; Li et al., 2019). Studies indicate that natural gas consumption favorably affects GDP growth on long-term (Emirmahmutoglu et al., 2021). This association holds true for both OECD countries and China, where natural gas has a significant impact on economic growth, according to Chauhan et al. (2020).

The organization of this chapter is as follows. The methodology is introduced in Section 2. The relevant data are presented in Section 3 together with the empirical findings. The study is concluded in Section 4.

2. Methodology

In the context of a bivariate VAR(p) model put forth by Balcilar et al. (2010), we first employ a bootstrap full-sample Granger causality test, which is based on a residual bootstrap approach with a modified-LR test, to model the causal relationship between natural gas consumption and economic growth in Romania. The existence of structural changes is then verified using the parameter stability test. We review the causal link using the bootstrap subsample causality test. Here, the fundamentals of the parameter stability test, the subsample rolling window test, and the bootstrap full-sample causality test are presented.

2.1. Bootstrap full-sample Granger causality test

The causal relationship between natural gas consumption and Romanian economic development is examined in this article using the Granger causality test, which is based on the bivariate Vector Autoregression (VAR) model. Given that the choice of the sample period tends to affect the results of Granger causality tests (Ghysels et al., 2016), we cannot assume that natural gas consumption and economic growth in Romania are permanently correlated. Contrarily, we refer to Granger causality as being "temporary," which implies that it is only valid for certain time periods (Balcilar & Ozdemir, 2013; Baum et al., 2021).

According to Sysoev and Sysoeva (2015), in the VAR framework it is considered that the time series are stationary. But in the case that they are not stationary (because of structural changes), the commonly used test statistics will lead to erroneous results. To address the issue, Toda and Yamamoto (1995) and Dolado and Lütkepohl (1996) suggest a modified Wald test that generates a standard asymptotic distribution by building an augmented VAR model.

Even though the standard vector auto-regressive (VAR) approach may be used to analyze the correlation between time series, the variables and the VAR process must follow the normal distribution (Sims, 1980, 2003). However, if this distribution cannot be complied with, the standard VAR approach's robustness may be diminished proportionally (Qin et al., 2022).

The residual-based bootstrap (RB) approach was created by Shukur and Mantalos (1997) to overcome this problem and may be used with Granger causality statistics that do not follow standard normal distributions. The so-called 'bootstrap' is a method to ensure the accuracy of the test results by multiple sampling (generally more than 1,000 times, allowing repeated sampling) and it can greatly increase the reliability of the outcomes, particularly in the test of small samples, which is also based on the use of rolling causality tests of subsamples (Shukur & Mantalos, 2000; Su et al., 2022). When determining the Granger causality between nonstationary variables, the residual-based bootstrap (RB) approach can boost the power and magnitude of the critical values, proving its validity (Mantalos & Shukur, 1998; Mantalos, 2000; Hacker & Hatemi-J, 2006; Balcilar et al., 2010; Richard, 2019). Using the residual-based bootstrap (RB) method and a modified likelihood ratio (LR) test, we examine the Granger causality link between natural gas consumption and economic development in Romania.

For the RB-based modified-LR causality test, the following bivariate VAR(p) process will be applied:

$$y_t = \varphi_0 + \varphi_1 y_{t-1} + \ldots + \varphi_p y_{t-p} + \varepsilon_t \quad (1)$$

$$t = 1,2,\ldots,T,$$

where $\varepsilon_t = (\varepsilon_{1t}, \varepsilon_{2t})'$ is a zero-mean, independent, white noise process with non-singular covariance matrix, and p is the optimal lag length which is specified by the Schwarz Information Criteria (SIC) (Qin et al., 2023). In this study, we examine the causal link between natural gas consumption (GAS) and economic growth (GDP) in Romania. The aforementioned equation may be expressed as follows by dividing y_t into two sub-vectors, $(y_{1,t}, y_{2,t})'$:

$$\begin{bmatrix} y_{1,t} \\ y_{2,t} \end{bmatrix} = \begin{bmatrix} \varphi_{10} \\ \varphi_{20} \end{bmatrix} + \begin{bmatrix} \varphi_{11}(L) & \varphi_{12}(L) \\ \varphi_{21}(L) & \varphi_{22}(L) \end{bmatrix} \begin{bmatrix} y_{1,t} \\ y_{2,t} \end{bmatrix} + \begin{bmatrix} \varepsilon_{1,t} \\ \varepsilon_{2,t} \end{bmatrix} \quad (2)$$

where $\varphi_{ij}(L) = \sum_{k=1}^{p+1} \varphi_{ij,k} L^k$, *i,j = 1, 2* and L is the lag operator $(L^k x_t = x_{t-k})$.

By applying the restriction where $\varphi_{12,k} = 0$ for k = 1, 2, 3, ..., p, we investigated the null hypothesis that GDP does not Granger cause GAS based on the aforementioned VAR (p) process.

If the null hypothesis is rejected, then GDP Granger cause GAS significantly. This implies that GDP may anticipate changes in GAS. This implies that GDP may anticipate changes in GAS. Analogously, the restriction $\varphi_{21,k} = 0$ for k = 1, 2, 3, ..., p can be used to test the null hypothesis that GAS does not Granger cause GDP. There is a significant statistical causality relating the GAS to GDP if the second null hypothesis is rejected.

2.2. Methodology for testing parameter stability

The parameters of the VAR model are considered to be constant across time in the full-sample causality tests, showing that the link between GDP and GAS is unaltered over the sample period. In addition, prior research has assumed that the variables don't change structurally, and only the full-sample causal link is examined (Balcilar & Ozdemir, 2013). Consequently, if the variables undergo structural changes, the full-sample causality tests based on the assumption of constant parameters are no longer accurate, and the causal linkages between two variables are unstable (Zeileis et al., 2005). Structural instability is a challenging problem for empirical investigations, according to Granger and Ding (1996).

Consequently, the full-sample approach is not appropriate, and more advanced techniques are required to capture this dynamic correlation. In order to assess if the analyzed series displays significant structural changes, we test for the parameter stability on short and long-run.

Accordingly to Andrews (1993) and Andrews and Ploberger (1994) We used the Sup-F, Mean-F, and Exp-F tests to evaluate the stability of the short-term parameters. These tests all have the same null hypothesis, but different alternative hypotheses (Andrew & Ploberger, 1994). We utilize the Lc test developed by Nyblom (1989) and Hansen (1992) to determine whether parameters are stable over time. The tests, which compare the stability of parameters against the possibility of a single structural break, are produced using a series of LR statistics.

The critical values and p-values are computed in this article in accordance with Andrews (1993) and Andrews and Ploberger (1994), utilizing asymptotic distributions created by Monte Carlo simulations. We used 10,000 samples obtained from a VAR model. The Sup-F, Mean-F, and Exp-F tests (Andrews, 1993) need 15 % trimming from both ends of the sample, therefore samples in the range of (0.15, 0.85) are employed in the tests.

2.3. Subsample rolling-window causality estimation methodology

In the case that the examined series display substantial structural changes, to study the causal relationship between GDP and GAS, we employ the rolling-window bootstrap method as in Balcilar et al. (2010). A rolling technique is unstable in various subsamples because of structural changes. Fixed-size subsamples that roll sequentially from the start to the end of the full sample are used in rolling window approaches (Balcilar et al., 2010).

This paper assumes that the size of the total sample is T and sets a fixed-size rolling window with i observations. According to this width, the full-sample is devided into T-i sub-samples and the end of each small section is i, $i+1$, ……, T. As a result, rather of calculating a single causality test for the entire sample, the RB-based modified-LR causality test might be examined in each sub-sample. By computing the bootstrap p-values across T-i sub-samples, it may be possible to determine the possible time-varying causality between the GDP and GAS. To reach a large number of estimation, we use the bootstrap method and the effect of GDP on GAS is calculated as the average of the bootstrap estimations of $N_b^{-1}\sum_{k=1}^{p}\widehat{\varphi_{12,k}^{*}}$, where N_b^{-1} indicates the number of bootstrap repetitions. In a similar manner, the following formula is used to quantify the effect of the GAS on GDP: $N_b^{-1}\sum_{k=1}^{p}\widehat{\varphi_{21,k}^{*}}$. Both $\widehat{\varphi_{12,k}^{*}}$ and $\widehat{\varphi_{21,k}^{*}}$ are bootstrap estimates in Equation

(2). In addition, based on Balcilar et al. (2010), this exploration performs the 90 % confidence interval with lower (the 5th quantile of $\widehat{\varphi^{*}_{12,k}}$ and $\widehat{\varphi^{*}_{21,k}}$) and upper (the 95th quantile of $\widehat{\varphi^{*}_{12,k}}$ and $\widehat{\varphi^{*}_{21,k}}$) bounds (Su et al., 2020).

The accuracy of the model estimates and the method's representativeness across the subsample period are two competing goals in the use of rolling-window estimation. The window size, which is the number of observations, determines the precision of the estimate.

The estimation becomes more accurate as the window size increases. However, if the window size is too big, the representativeness suffers and a lot of changes could be included into the same window sample. According to Pesaran and Timmermann (2005), the square root mean square error's indication of the proper window size depends on the magnitude and persistence of the break. Therefore, we must choose an appropriate window size to ensure representativeness and accuracy. Considering this and the two conflicting requirements, we chose the 18-month size (six quarters).

3. Empirical data and analysis

3.1. Data sources

We use Eurostat's monthly statistics for the period 2008 – M1 to 2023 – M3 for the total consumption of natural gas in Romania. For economic growth, we utilize quarterly GDP data for the same time, as given by the Romanian National Institute of Statistics. Due to the quarterly reporting of GDP data, in order to standardize the database, monthly values for total natural gas consumption have been transformed into quarterly values, yielding the following timeframe for the data series: 2008 Q1 – 2023 Q1. The study is carried out utilizing the E-Views 10 and R programming language (for parameter stability test).

3.2. Stationarity test application

Sims et al. (1990) point out that utilizing non-stationary series variables when evaluating real-world problems with VAR models might offer statistical inference issues because standard statistical tests and statistical inference require all series to be stationary.

To evaluate data using the Vector Autoregression (VAR) technique, examining the data's stationarity is the first step. If a variable exhibits non-stationarity, exemplified by a unit root process (meaning it has a stochastic trend), this can result in spurious regression, in which two independent non-stationary variables show considerable evidence when none exists. In order to use the causality test, the data must be stable, and if they are not stable, they must first be differentiated and transformed into a stable series.

To verify the reliability of the VAR system used to conduct the full-sample Granger causality test and parameter stability tests, we begin our study by checking for the unit root of each sampled variable (Balcilar et al., 2010). Here, the unit root tests ADF (Dickey & Fuller, 1981) and PP (Phillips & Perron, 1988) are used. The tests' null hypothesis is that because the series has a unit root, it is not stationary. Here, the unit root tests ADF (Dickey & Fuller, 1981) and PP (Phillips & Perron, 1988) are used. The tests' null hypothesis is that because the series has a unit root, it is not stationary. The Schwarz Information Criterion (SIC), up to a maximum of 10 lags, is used to automatically calculate the number of lags used in the test since the lag length in ADF is set to zero. The PP test statistic is calculated based on the difference between the time series data and its lagged values.

The null hypothesis of non-stationarity for GAS at level is rejected by the ADF and PP tests, but they fail to reject the null hypothesis that GDP is not stationary. However, when the GDP series are in their first differences, they reject the null hypothesis. Overall, our findings imply that either the level or the first difference of the time series is stable. In other words, it appears that GDP and GAS follow a stationary process, which validates the use of the VAR system. As a result, we may continue our research using the full-sample Granger causality test and the rolling window Bootstrap Granger causality test.

Testing for the long-term stability of the parameters needs the sampled variables in the vector autoregression model to be integrated or cointegrated (see Balcilar et al., 2010; Shahzad et al., 2017). Testing for at least one cointegrating connection is thus a necessary prerequisite. Next, to test if a cointegration connection exists, we use the linear cointegration approach developed by Johansen (1991, 1995). Table 4.1 displays the results of the Johansen cointegration test. The Unrestricted Cointegration Rank Test is used to determine whether or not cointegration exists. The Trace test and the Maximum Eigenvalue test are carried out. At the 0.05 level of significance, one cointegrating equation may be seen by both the Trace test and the Maximum Eigenvalue test. The Unrestricted Cointegrating Coefficients indicate a positive link between GDP and GAS on long-term. We reject the null hypothesis that there are no cointegration vectors in favor of the alternative hypothesis that there is at least one vector based on the test results.

Tab. 4.1: Johansen cointegration test results

Unrestricted Cointegration Rank Test (Trace)				
Hypothesized		Trace	0.05	
No. of CE(s)	Eigenvalue	Statistic	Critical Value	Prob.**
None *	0.453406	36.61695	15.49471	0.0000
At most 1	0.026909	1.582105	3.841466	0.2085

Trace test indicates 1 cointegrating eqn(s) at the 0.05 level
* Denotes rejection of the hypothesis at the 0.05 level
**MacKinnon-Haug-Michelis (1999) *p*-values

Unrestricted Cointegration Rank Test (Maximum Eigenvalue)				
Hypothesized		Max-Eigen	0.05	
No. of CE(s)	Eigenvalue	Statistic	Critical Value	Prob.**
None *	0.453406	35.03485	14.26460	0.0000
At most 1	0.026909	1.582105	3.841466	0.2085

Max-eigenvalue test indicates 1 cointegrating eqn(s) at the 0.05 level
* denotes rejection of the hypothesis at the 0.05 level
**MacKinnon-Haug-Michelis (1999) *p*-values

Source: Authors' calculation

Since we are interested in examining the causal relationship between economic development and natural gas use in Romania, bivariate VAR models consisting of the first-differenced log-levels of both the GDP and GAS are constructed, as shown in equation (3). The equation (2) may be expressed as follows by dividing y_t into two sub-vectors $(y_{GDP,t}, y_{GAS,t})$':

$$\begin{bmatrix} y_{GDP,t} \\ y_{GAS,t} \end{bmatrix} = \begin{bmatrix} \varphi_{10} \\ \varphi_{20} \end{bmatrix} + \begin{bmatrix} \varphi_{GDP,GDP}(L) & \varphi_{GDP,GAS}(L) \\ \varphi_{GAS,GDP}(L) & \varphi_{GAS,GAS}(L) \end{bmatrix} \begin{bmatrix} y_{GDP,t} \\ y_{GAS,t} \end{bmatrix} + \begin{bmatrix} \varepsilon_{GDP,t} \\ \varepsilon_{GAS,t} \end{bmatrix} \quad (3)$$

where $y_{GDP,t}$ is GDP and $y_{GAS,t}$ is GAS.

Because GDP and GAS are I(1), we examine the full-sample causal relationship between GDP and GAS. The optimal lag length must be determined using the Vector Autoregression (VAR) approach. Table 4.2 displays the outcomes of the Lag Length test. The ideal lag lengths are 3, according to the sequential modified LR test statistic and the Hannan-Quinn information criteria.

Tab. 4.2: The test's results for lag length

VAR Lag Order Selection Criteria **Endogenous variables: GDP GAS** **Exogenous variables: C** **Date: 08/03/23 Time: 17:26** **Sample: 2008Q1 2023Q1** **Included observations: 55**						
Lag	**LogL**	**LR**	**FPE**	**AIC**	**SC**	**HQ**
0	149.5824	NA	1.60e-05	-5.366634	-5.293640*	-5.338406
1	154.9428	10.13605	1.52e-05	-5.416103	-5.197121	-5.331421
2	161.0953	11.18629	1.41e-05	-5.494374	-5.129405	-5.353238
3	**168.5710**	**13.04857***	**1.25e-05**	**-5.620765**	**-5.109808**	**-5.423174***
4	173.8871	8.892388	1.19e-05*	-5.668623*	-5.011678	-5.414577
5	176.9399	4.884352	1.24e-05	-5.634177	-4.831244	-5.323676

* Indicates lag order selected by the criterion
LR: sequential modified LR test statistic (each test at 5 % level)
FPE: Final prediction error
AIC: Akaike information criterion
SC: Schwarz information criterion
HQ: Hannan-Quinn information criterion

Source: Authors' calculation

By applying the RB-based modified-LR causality tests, we present the full-sample causality results of Bootstrap (Likelihood Ratio) LR tests in Tab. 4.3. The table reports the statistics and *p*-values for each test. The first test shows a statistic of 2.79 and a *p*-value of 0.3, that implies there is weak evidence to reject the null hypothesis that GDP does not Granger cause GAS. The second test shows a statistic of 3.76 and a *p*-value of 0.14, which means that there is weak evidence to reject the null hypothesis that GAS does not Granger cause GDP. These findings suggest that there is no causal connection between these two factors.

Tab. 4.3: Full-sample Granger causality tests

Tests	H0: GDP Does Not Granger Cause GAS		H0: GAS Does Not Granger Cause GDP	
	Statistics	*p*-values	Statistics	*p*-values
Bootstrap LR test	2.7902	0.30	3.7644	0.14

Source: Authors' calculation

3.3. Parameter stability test

Since it presumes constant parameters during the whole sample period, full-sample estimate is not always correct (Zeileis et al., 2005). Moreover, in this instance, the structural shift in the economy that was disregarded by the full-sample test could have an impact on the natural gas consumption. Due to the aforementioned causes, we evaluate the parameter stability and look for structural alterations in the full-sample. As previously stated, the Sup-F, Ave-F, and Exp-F tests are used to examine the short-run stability of parameters in the aforementioned GDP and GAS-formed VAR models. The long-term stability of each and every parameter in the entire VAR system is also estimated using the Lc test. The stability study of parameters results are shown in detail in Tabs. 4.4 and 4.5.

Tab. 4.4: Short-run parameter stability tests

Tests	GDP Equation		GAS Equation		VAR Process	
	Statistics	Bootstrap *p*-value	Statistics	Bootstrap *p*-value	Statistics	Bootstrap *p*-value
Sup-F	198.471***	0.000	2559.078***	0.000	26.956	0.166
Ave-F	34.089***	0.000	83.025***	0.000	22.784**	0.027
Exp-F	95.498***	0.000	Inf	NA	12.080*	0.079
Lc					4.407***	0.005

Notes: 2,000 bootstrap repeats are used in this study to compute the *p*-values.
*, **, *** denote significance at 10, 5 and 1 %, respectively.
Hansen-Nyblom (L_C) parameter stability test for testing all parameters in the VAR jointly.

Source: Authors' calculation

In the first row of Tab. 4.4, there are presented the Sup-F tests for the null hypothesis of constant parameters vs a sudden rapid change in parameters. Results indicate that, at the 1 % level, the GDP and GAS equations undergo a sudden structural mutation. It suggests that GDP and GAS can reject the null hypothesis that the model's parameters are stable throughout time and have a sudden structural mutation at the 1 % level. The Ave-F test indicates that the GDP, GAS, and VAR (p) processes can alter gradually over time at 1 % and 5 %, respectively. The Exp-F test demonstrates that GDP and VAR (p) process may reject the null hypothesis that the parameters follow a martingale at a 1 % significance level. The results imply that the GDP, GAS, and VAR equations may change gradually over time. In addition, the Lc statistics approach indicates that the null hypothesis of the VAR (p) process conforming to random walk (Granger, 1996) can be rejected at a 1 % level, indicating that the calculated VAR model parameters are inconsistent.

In order to evaluate the long-run relationship's parameter stability, the bootstrap *p*-values in Tab. 4.5 show that Lc statistics reject the null hypothesis of cointegration at 10 %. The Sup-F, Mean-F, and Exp-F tests cannot identify the cointegration equation's gradual parameter shifting, but there is strong support for the assumption that the long-run relationship has had a single, important shift. As a result, these tests cannot provide a valid estimate of the cointegration between Romania's GDP and GAS.

Tab. 4.5: Long-run parameter stability tests

	Sup-F	**Mean-F**	**Exp-F**	**L_C**
GDP=α+β*GAS	0.890	0.325	0.167	0.085*
Bootstrap *p*-value	1.000	1.000	1.000	0.853

Notes: 2,000 bootstrap repetitions are used in this study to compute the *p*-values.
* Denote significance at 10 %.

Source: Authors' calculation

These results offer strong evidence that structural changes cause short-run instability in the anticipated VAR model parameters based on the complete sample. It indicates that the results indicating a lack of full-sample causality between Romania's GDP and GAS are inaccurate. Furthermore, parameter stability tests reveal that there is no valid cointegration between the GDP and GAS. The results show that it is not reasonable to infer a full-sample causal relationship between GDP and GAS.

We use rolling window estimates to investigate the causal link between GDP and GAS in order to account for structural changes. This method is favored over the full-sample causality test for examining the causal relationship between two variables because of the time-varying nature of the subsamples. This is a big deviation from the present research since the rolling-window estimation used accounts for structural changes and allows causal links between variables to be time-varying across different subsamples.

3.4. Sub-sample rolling window causality test

In the sub-sample rolling window causality test, we use the RB based modified-LR causality tests to investigate the causal relationship between GDP and GAS. The tests' null hypothesis is that neither GDP nor GAS can be said to be Granger caused by the other. The rolling sub-sample data containing six quarters (18-month) of observations can be used to estimate the bootstrap p-values of the LR-statistics from the VAR models in Equation (3). Furthermore, the results of an investigation into the causal relationship between GDP and GAS in Romania are presented utilizing the RB-based modified-LR causality test methodology. Figures 4.1–4.2 show all of the rolling estimates for each sub-sample. The estimates shift from 2008 Q1 to 2023 Q1 after removing the first six quarters (18-month) of observations.

Panels A of Figs. 4.1 and 4.2 show the rolling bootstrap p-values of LR-statistics using GDP and GAS as dependent variables. At a 10 % probability, the null hypothesis that one variable does not Granger-cause the other may be disproved. To guard against results with poor descriptive power, *p*-values larger than 10 % (the region above the black horizontal line) are disregarded.

Figures 4.1 and 4.2's Panels B display the impact's magnitudes using GDP and GAS as the dependent variables. When the rolling bootstrap of the *p*-values is less than 10 %, null hypotheses can be strongly rejected in Panels A of Figs. 4.1 and 4.2.

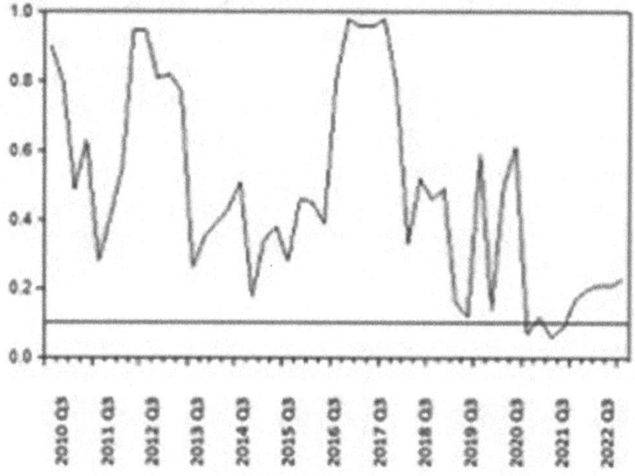

Panel A

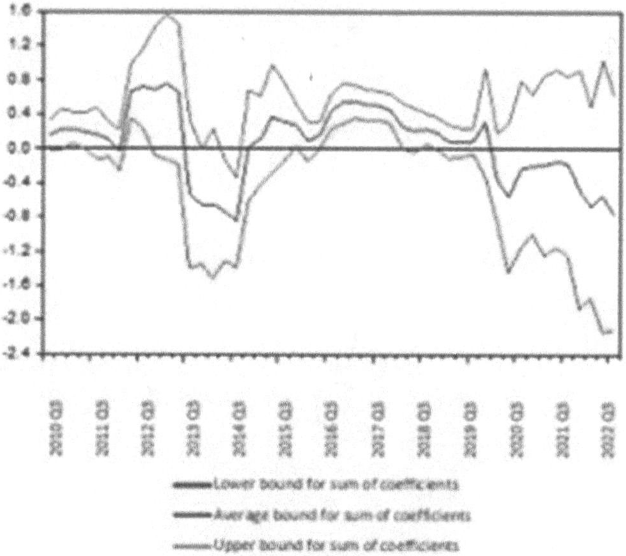

Panel B

Fig. 4.1: Panel A: Bootstrap *p*-values of rolling test statistic testing the null that the GDP does not Granger-cause the GAS in Romania. Panel B: Bootstrap estimates of the sum of the rolling window coefficients for the impact of GDP on GAS in Romania

Source: Authors' calculation

Panel A of Fig. 4.1 illustrates how the null hypothesis is substantially rejected in several sub-periods (2020 Q2–Q4, 2021 Q1–Q2). In other words, GDP influences GAS. The findings suggest that economic growth only influences the direction of gas consumption during specific sub-periods, suggesting that there are temporally variable causal relationships between GDP and GAS. The bootstrap estimates of the rolling window coefficients' sum for the effect of GDP on GAS are shown in Panel B of Fig. 4.1. Only negative effects exist from GDP to GAS.

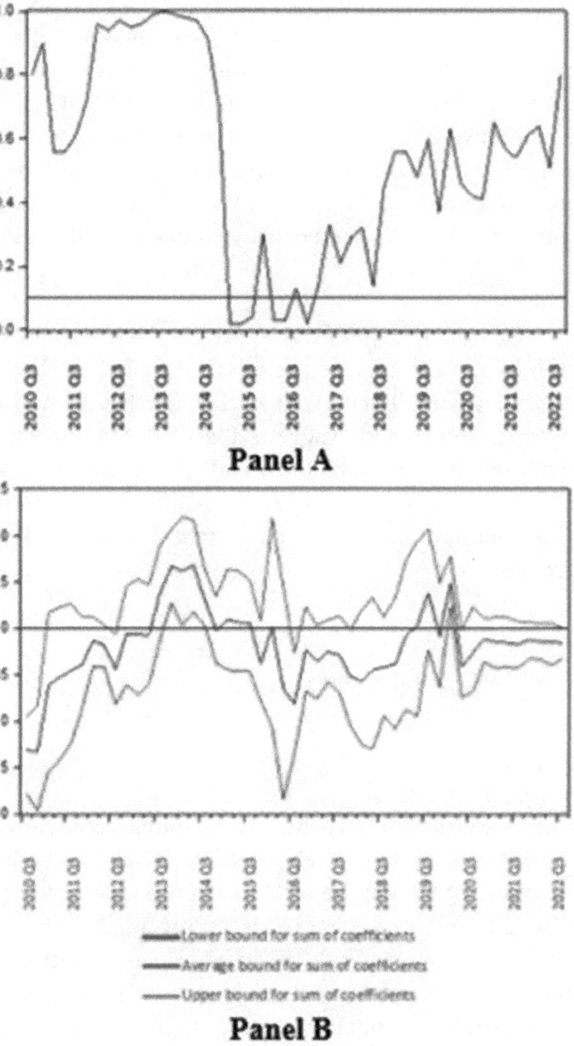

Fig. 4.2: Panel A: Bootstrap p-values of rolling test statistic testing the null that the GAS does not Granger-cause the GDP in Romania. Panel B: Bootstrap estimates of the sum of the rolling window coefficients for the impact of GAS on GDP in Romania

Source: Authors' calculation

In relation to the causal relationship between GDP and GAS, Fig. 4.2's Panel A demonstrates that, in several sub-periods (2015 Q3 – 2016 Q1, 2016 Q3 – 2017 Q1, and 2017 Q1 – 2017 Q3), the null hypothesis is severely rejected. In other words, GAS affects GDP. The findings suggest that only specific sub-periods of the economy are influenced by gas consumption, which suggests that there are temporally variable causal relationships between GAS and GDP. Figure 4.2's Panel B demonstrates that for the majority of the times when the effect is statistically significant, the GAS has a negative impact on GDP (2016 Q3 – 2017 Q1, 2017 Q1 – 2017 Q3), except for 2015 Q3 – 2016 Q1, during which the effect is positive.

Relationship structural changes exist, as seen in Figs. 4.1 and 4.2. The result exposes the time-varying nature of the entire sample, which is a significant departure from the full-sample causality test. The fact that the causal relationship is limited to specific sub-periods suggests that variations in one variable are not entirely explicable by variations in the other. We find that GAS has more detrimental than beneficial effects on GDP. Stated differently, there are times when variations in the amount of natural gas consumed increase the unpredictability of economic growth.

4. Conclusions

In general, empirical research on causal relationships uses the full-sample test. Full-sample Granger causality tests assume that the VAR model parameters are constant over time, assuming a single causality in each time period. However, structural changes in full-sample data may break this assumption. This would invalidate full-sample causality tests and cause variable causal links to fluctuate. Since it can identify the time-varying causal link, the bootstrap sub-sample rolling window causality test can be used to examine the relationship between the variables. The full-sample causality test is less precise than the rolling window technique. The aim of this study is to investigate the causative relationship between Romania's economic development and natural gas consumption, in order to demonstrate the bootstrap sub-sample rolling window causality technique.

Bibliography

Andrews, D. W. K. (1993). Tests for Parameter Instability and Structural Change with Unknown Change Point. *Econometrica*, *61*(4), 821–856, doi: 10.2307/2951764.

Andrews, D. W. K., & Ploberger, W. (1994). Optimal Tests When a Nuisance Parameter Is Present Only Under the Alternative. *Econometrica, 62*(6), 1383–1414, doi: 10.2307/2951753.

Balcilar, M., & Ozdemir, Z. A. (2013). The Export-Output Growth Nexus in Japan: A Bootstrap Rolling Window Approach. *Empirical Economics, 44*(2), 639–660, doi: 10.1007/s00181-012-0562-8.

Balcilar, M., Ozdemir, Z. A., & Arslanturk, Y. (2010). Economic Growth and Energy Consumption Causal Nexus Viewed through a Bootstrap Rolling Window. *Energy Economics, 32*(6), 1398–1410, doi: 10.1016/j.eneco.2010.05.015.

Baum, C. F., Hurn, S., & Otero, J. (2021). The Dynamics of U.S. Industrial Production: A Time-varying Granger Causality Perspective. Econometrics and Statistics, doi: 10.1016/J.ECOSTA.2021.10.012.

Chauhan, S., Pande, R., & Sharma, S. (2020). The Causal Relationship between Indian Energy Consumption and the GDP: A Shift from Conservation to Feedback Hypothesis Post Economic Liberalisation. *Theoretical and Applied Economics, 3*(624), 203–212.

Destek, M. A. (2016). Natural Gas Consumption and Economic Growth: Panel Evidence from OECD Countries. *Energy, 114*, 1007–1015, doi: 10.1016/J.ENERGY.2016.08.076.

Dickey, D. A., & Fuller, W. A. (1981). Likelihood Ratio Statistics for Autoregressive Time Series with a Unit Root. *Econometrica, 49*(4), 1057–1072, doi: 10.2307/1912517.

Dolado, J. J., & Lütkepohl, H. (1996). Making Wald Tests Work for Cointegrated VAR Systems. *Econometric Reviews, 15*, 369–386, doi: 10.1080/07474939608800362.

Emirmahmutoglu, F., Zulal, D., Omay, T., & Tiwari, A. K. (2021). Regime Dependent Causality Relationship between Energy Consumption and GDP Growth: Evidence from OECD Countries. *Applied Economics*, *53*(19), 2230–2241, doi: 10.1080/00036846.2020.1857330.

Ghysels, E., Hill, J. B., & Motegi, K. (2016). Testing for Granger Causality with Mixed Frequency Data. *Journal of Econometrics, 192*(1), 207–230, doi: 10.1016/J.JECONOM.2015.07.007.

Granger, C. W. J. (1996). Can We Improve the Perceived Quality of Economic Forecasts? *Journal of Applied Econometrics, 11*(5), 455–473, doi: 10.1002/(SICI)1099-1255(199609)11:5%3C455::AID-JAE408%3E3.3.CO;2-5.

Granger, C. W., & Ding, Z. (1996). Varieties of Long Memory Models. *Journal of Econometrics, 73*, 61–77, doi: 10.1016/0304-4076(95)01733-X.

Hacker, R. S., & Hatemi-J., A. (2006). Tests for Causality Between Integrated Variables Using Asymptotic and Bootstrap Distributions: Theory and Application. *Applied Economics, 38*, 1489–1500. doi: 10.1080/00036840500405763.

Hansen, B. E. (1992). Tests for Parameter Instability in Regressions with I(1) Processes. *Journal of Business and Economic Statistics, 10*(3), 321–336, doi: 10.1080/07350015.1992.10509908.

Johansen, S. (1991). Estimation and Hypothesis Testing of Cointegration Vectors in Gaussian Vector Autoregressive Models. *Econometrica, 59*(6), 1551–1580.

Johansen, S. (1995). *Likelihood-Based Inference in Cointegrated Vector Autoregressive Models*. Oxford University Press.

Li, Z.-G., Cheng, H., & Gu, T.-Y. (2019). Research on Dynamic Relationship between Natural Gas Consumption and Economic Growth in China. *Structural Change and Economic Dynamics*, *49*(C), 334–339, doi: 10.1016/J.STRUECO.2018.11.006.

Mantalos, P. (2000). A Graphical Investigation of the Size and Power of the Granger-Causality Tests in Integrated-Cointegrated VAR Systems. *Studies in Non-Linear Dynamics & Econometrics, 4*(1), 17–33, doi: 10.2202/1558-3708.1053.

Mantalos, P., & Shukur, G. (1998). Size and Power of the Error Correction Model Cointegration Test: A Bootstrap Approach. *Oxford Bulletin of Economics and Statistics, 60*(2), 249–255, doi: 10.1111/1468-0084.00097.

Nyblom, J. (1989). Testing for the Constancy of Parameters over Time. *Journal of the American Statistical Association, 84*(405), 223–230, doi: 10.1080/01621459.1989.10478759.

Pandelara, D., Kristjanpoller, W., Michell, K., & Minutolo, M. C. (2021). A Fuzzy Regression Causality Approach to Analyze Relationship between Electrical Consumption and GDP. *Energy, 239*, doi: 10.1016/J.ENERGY.2021.122459.

Pesaran, M. H., & Timmermann, A. (2005). Small Sample Properties of Forecasts from Autoregressive Models under Structural Breaks. *Journal of Econometrics, 129*(1–2), 183–217, doi: 10.1016/j.jeconom.2004.09.007.

Phillips, P. C. B., & Perron, P. (1988). Testing for a Unit Root in Time Series Regression. *Biometrika, 75*(2), 335–346, doi: 10.1093/biomet/75.2.335.

Qin, M., Su, C. W., Pirtea, M. G., & Peculea, A. D. (2023). The Essential Role of Russian Geopolitics: A Fresh Perception into the Gold Market. *Resour. Policy, 81*, 103310.

Qin, M., Wu, T., Tao, R., Su, C. W., & Petru, S. (2022). The Inevitable Role of Bilateral Relation: A Fresh Insight into the Bitcoin Market. *Ekon. Istraz. – Econ. Res, 35*(1), 4260–4279.

Richard, P. O. (2019). Residual Bootstrap Tests in Linear Models with Many Regressors. *Journal of Econometrics, 208*(2), 367–394, doi: 10.1016/J.JECONOM.2018.10.002.

Shahzad, S. J. H., Nor, S. M., Hammoudeh, S., & Shahbaz, M. (2017). Directional and Bidirectional Causality between U.S. Industry Credit and Stock Markets and Their Determinants. *Int. Rev. Econom. Financ., 47*, 46–61.

Shukur, G., & Mantalos, P. (2000). A Simple Investigation of the Granger-Causality Test in Integrated-Cointegrated VAR Systems. *Journal of Applied Statistics, 27*(8), 1021–1031, doi: 10.1080/02664760050173346.

Sims, C. A. (1980). Macroeconomics and Reality. *Econometrica, 48*(1), 1–48.

Sims, C. A. (2003). Implications of Rational Inattention. *Journal of Monetary Economics, 50*, 665–690. doi: 10.1016/S0304-3932(03)00029-1.

Sims, C. A., Stock, J. H., & Watson, M. W. (1990). Inference in Linear Time Series with Some Unit Roots. *Econometrica, 58*(1), 113–144, doi: 10.2307/2938337.

Su, C. W., Pang, L. D., Umar, M., & Lobont, O. R. (2022). Will Gold Always Shine Amid World Uncertainty? *Emerg. Mark. Finance Trade, 58*(12), 3425–3438.

Su, C. W., Qin, M., Tao, R., & Zhang, X. Y. (2020). Is the Status of Gold Threatened by Bitcoin. *Ekon. Istraz.-Econ. Res., 33*(1), 420–437.

Sysoev, I. V., & Sysoeva, M. V. (2015). Detecting Changes in Coupling with Granger Causality Method from Time Series with Fast Transient Processes. *Physica D: Nonlinear Phenomena, 309*, 9–19, doi: 10.1016/J.PHYSD.2015.07.005.

Toda, H. Y., & Yamamoto, T. (1995). Statistical Inference in Vector Autoregressions with Possibly Integrated Processes. *Journal of Econometrics, 66*(1–2), 225–250, doi: 10.1016/0304-4076(94)01616-8.

Zeileis, A., Leisch, F., Hornik, K., & Kleiber, C. (2005). Monitoring Structural Change in Dynamic Econometric Models. *Journal of Applied Econometrics, 20*, 99–121, doi: 10.1002/jae.776.

Renate Bratu, Bogdan Mârza, and Răzvan Şerbu

Chapter 5 Exploring a metamorphosed world economy by the impact of artificial intelligence on the contemporary economic trends

Abstract: The world is undergoing a profound transformation driven by diverse perspectives and augmented by innovations especially nowadays artificial intelligence (AI). This expedition toward the future is distinct by adaptability, resilience, and collaboration, where sustainability, technology, and societal shifts meet and melt together unprecedentedly. As quantum computing, blockchain, and AI attract our attention more and more, businesses play a vital role in shaping sustainable growth through innovation, scalability, and collaboration. However, the challenge lies in cultivating agility and ethical practices to succeed on our way to solve more problems with less resource successfully. The evolution of AI, from science fiction to its current capabilities, underscores the need for these perspectives in understanding its impact on society and creativity. Human-machine interactions call for flexibility and a well-adjusted approach, given the complex nature of AI's influence. The history of AI, traversing theoretical foundations to modern applications, reflects humanity's determination to innovate and this chapter emphasize the importance of this collaborative efforts among AI researchers, legal experts, and policymakers and their responsibility in establishing an ethical framework that respects individual rights while cultivating creativity. As the uncertainty continues evolving, in economy and society, it's our cooperative duty to shape a future where AI enhances human potential, upholds ethics, and preserves our human essence.

Keywords: world economy, artificial intelligence, sustainable development, environment, ethics

1. Introduction

The transformation that the world has encountered is truly remarkable, not solely due to COVID but also because of our different perspectives towards the future within the new revolutions. In many ways, we could argue that the future is already unfolding before our eyes, yet we might not have fully comprehended it. We are now increasingly realizing this shift, particularly with the emergence of artificial intelligence, which we are going to spend a part of our life with.

The subject of sustainable development was in the attention of many researchers, it should and will be until these problems will be solved. The rise of stakeholder interest globally in sustainable business practices has resulted in a rise in demands from stakeholders that companies report on the environmental and social impacts of their business activities. (Moodaley & Arnesh, 2023).

With this chapter we intend to offer some insights that will push some of the contemporary problem close to solution. We are very optimistic, especially now when we have these new tools, quantum computers, blockchain and especially Artificial Intelligence.

2. The imperative of sustainable development

Climate change became a climate urge, and despite any other shock that the planet encounters nowadays, like COVID, the Ukraine-Russia war, or others, sustainability remains in the debate at all levels social, economic, and political. The first problems that we mentioned were impacting recently, the population of the world, direct or indirect, but hopefully are now winding down. The director-general of the United Nations World Health Organization (WHO) has officially declared with hope, the end of COVID-19 as a public health emergency, expressing optimism. Unfortunately, we cannot say the same about the war, even if it seems that things cooled down a little bit, Ukraine will need reconstructions and from that point of view the process of sustainability should be taken in consideration. The good news is that we have more and new tools to solve sustainability through technology. The times we pass seem to be quite different than what we were used to, so the new dynamic is requesting more flexibility, adaptation, agility, and resilience.

Business-led innovation is a vital driver for sustainable and for economic growth due to their capacity for advance, market-driven solutions, financial resources, scalability, job creation, collaboration, supply chain influence, responsiveness to consumer preferences, and adherence to new regulatory requirements. For any successful endeavor to achieve sustainable development, the active involvement of companies is indispensable.

The challenge lies in each company's ability to develop a unique form of agility that is robust and can be maintained over the long term to withstand market pressures. We can imagine that a company which is producing significant CO2 will not intend to reduce it, if this cost will lead to competitive disadvantage compared to competition there will not motivate the company to pursue the sustainable development's goal. In other words, sustainability is the degree to which human well- being is shaped by the circumstances in which people live and the way they take care of the environment. (Tanasescu & Oprean, 2013).

The environment should inspire companies to sort their action into the framework of sustainable development goals, to highlight the societal returns, and their timeline, the effort needed to cooperate in creating a right puzzle for a sustainable and growing economy and world. This pressure is higher and higher so we hope that this paper will support companies, especially people that are forming those companies in setting agendas, and prioritizing tasks effectively bridging the gap between aspirational goals and tangible one impactful actions. At the core of their responsibilities is the crucial work of identifying key priorities and facilitating the formation of appropriate partnerships. Through collaboration and strategic alliances, they can expedite the process of implementing sustainable and inclusive initiatives, ensuring that real-world progress is achieved swiftly and efficiently. This requires a proactive approach, strong leadership, and a deep understanding of the interconnected challenges and opportunities related to sustainable, inclusive growth. Additionally, they must continuously evaluate and adapt their strategies to stay aligned with evolving market dynamics and societal needs, all while remaining committed to the long-term vision of a sustainable and inclusive future.

According to Rohit et al. (2020), AI cannot be a panacea for all our complex environmental sustainability problems. Historically, new technologies have promised to solve immediate problems, but in time proved unsustainable (Rohit et al., 2020) Furthermore, the convergence of AI with other emerging technologies, such as blockchain, is expected to generate industry-wide benefits (Hughes et al., 2019)

3. The evolving transformations

Both the private and the public companies and institutions need to adapt and to think a little bit differently about this new environment shaped by the new revolutions that becomes natural with every moment that is passing.

In our opinion an important step before speaking about the future to know about the past, so we should see how we got here, what is the evolution of Artificial Intelligence, and how was the journey of challenges and triumphs

Artificial Intelligence (AI) has captivated the human imagination since its early depictions in science fiction, especially during the golden age of science fiction (1938–1946), from the heartless Tin man in "The Wizard of Oz" to the humanoid robot Maria in "Metropolis." Over the years, AI has evolved from mere fantasy into a field of scientific exploration and innovation, transforming industries and shaping the way we live and work. We must mention here also Isaac Asimov's and the "Three Laws of Robotics" that can be adjust to artificial intelligence also. In the world of science fiction, Asimov's story has captivated our imaginations, presenting a framework to keep humans in control of intelligent machines. These laws emphasize the obedience of robots to humans and their obligation never to harm us.

Asimov's stories serve as a brilliant exploration of the challenges in devising problem-free laws to govern complex intelligences. They highlight the inherent difficulty, if not impossibility, of creating a concise set of rules to regulate the interactions between machines, artificial intelligence, and humans. A recent paper in Science Robotics further underlines this complexity, warning against the belief that a small set of simple rules can effectively design or regulate intricate machines and human interactions. Any attempt to control AI with rigid laws might lead to loopholes or exceptions that could compromise the very protection they seek to provide. One of Asimov's stories, "That Thou Art Mindful of Him," offers a prescient twist. In a world where robots define "human" as possessing "apex intelligence," it raises profound questions about our understanding of humanity. If AI surpasses humans in creativity and high intelligence, do they gain a greater claim to being considered "human" in sense of consciences? This challenge extends beyond a mere threat to our way of life; it fundamentally challenges our understanding of human identity.

As AI continues to advance, it becomes essential to distinguish what is created by humans from what is produced by machines. Many of us will still seek assurance that the novels, poems, songs, or artworks we engage with are crafted by human hands and minds. This desire for human involvement maintains the unique connection between creators and their creations.

In this dynamic landscape, it is crucial to approach AI with a nuanced perspective. Most of the experts, encourage thoughtful consideration of the complexities surrounding AI and the potential implications of regulating it through rigid laws. Embracing the intricacies of human-machine-A.I. interactions and cultivating flexibility in our approach will be key to navigating this transformative era responsibly. Only through a balanced and well-informed strategy can we harness the full potential of AI while safeguarding our understanding of humanity and creativity.

With these early pioneers the times brought the theoretical foundations for the real artificial intelligence. In the 1950s, AI gained momentum as a theoretical concept, thanks to pioneers like Alan Turing, a young British polymath. Turing explored the mathematical possibilities of AI, suggesting that machines, like humans, could use available information and reason to solve problems and make decisions. His groundbreaking 1950 paper, "Computing Machinery and Intelligence," laid the logical framework for building intelligent machines and testing their abilities.

Despite the theoretical promise of AI, challenges of early implementation and practical obstacles hindered its progress. Computers lacked the capability to store commands, limiting their potential for intelligence. Moreover, the exorbitant cost of computing in the 1950s made AI exploration accessible only to prestigious universities and major technology companies. Convincing funding sources of the value of machine intelligence required a proof of concept and advocacy from influential individuals.

We can consider "The Dartmouth Conference" a milestone in artificial intelligence history. Five years after Turing's seminal paper, the Dartmouth Summer Research Project on Artificial Intelligence (DSRPAI) marked a pivotal moment in AI history. This conference, led by John McCarthy and Marvin Minsky, brought together top researchers to discuss the potential of AI. While the conference fell short of some expectations, it united experts in the belief that AI was achievable. The event catalyzed the next two decades of AI research and funding.

The Flourishing Era of AI was about to start. From 1957 to 1974, AI flourished with the advancement of computer technology. Faster, cheaper, and more accessible computers enabled the storage of vast amounts of information, enhancing AI capabilities. Machine learning algorithms improved, enabling researchers to apply the right tools to their problems. Demonstrations like the General Problem Solver and ELIZA showed promise in problem-solving and natural language interpretation.

The advocacy of leading researchers, including attendees of the DSRPAI, convinced government agencies like the Defense Advanced Research Projects Agency (DARPA) to fund AI research. Government interest centered around machines capable of transcribing and translating spoken language, as well as high throughput data processing. Optimism was high, with some envisioning machines possessing the general intelligence of an average human being within a few years. While progress demonstrated the basic principles, AI was still far from achieving complex tasks like natural language processing and abstract thinking.

The lack of computational power presented a significant barrier to substantial AI achievements. Communicating and understanding words required massive amounts of data storage and processing, far beyond the capabilities of computers at the time. Funding dwindled, and research stagnated for a decade.

AI experienced a revival in the 1980s, driven by an expanded algorithmic toolkit and increased funding. "Deep learning" techniques by John Hopfield and David Rumelhart enabled computers to learn through experience. Expert systems, introduced by Edward Feigenbaum, mimicked human decision-making processes. Though ambitious goals set by projects like Japan's Fifth

Generation Computer Project (FGCP) were not fully met, the project inspired a new generation of talented engineers and scientists.

Remarkably, the field of AI demonstrated resilience and significant progress despite the lack of substantial government funding and limited public attention. The landmark achievement in 1997, where IBM's Deep Blue triumphed over the world chess champion Gary Kasparov, exemplified AI's prowess in decision-making tasks. Furthermore, the integration of speech recognition software into the Windows platform marked a noteworthy milestone in advancing AI's capabilities in interpreting spoken language. The once seemingly elusive dominion of emotions was also conquered by AI, as evidenced by the development of robots like Kismet, capable of recognizing and expressing emotions. These remarkable achievements underscore the continuous evolution of AI technology, driven by a relentless pursuit of enhancing its cognitive capabilities and widening its scope of application.

4. Artificial intelligence in the age of big data

Today, AI's potential is boundless in the age of "big data." Colossal amounts of information, too cumbersome for human processing, are now manageable through AI's brute force learning. Technology, banking, marketing, and entertainment industries have already reaped the benefits of AI implementation. Although Moore's Law may be slowing, the influx of data ensures AI's momentum continues to surge forward.

Understanding the history of AI is vital to grasp the challenges and triumphs that shaped this remarkable field. Over the past few years, organizations are increasingly turning to AI to gain business value following a deluge of data and a strong increase in computational capacity. Nevertheless, organizations are still struggling to adopt and leverage AI in their operations (Enholm et al., 2022).

From its theoretical beginnings to the breakthroughs in big data and mass computing, AI's journey can be described like a testament to human ingenuity and innovation. To maintain the good road to the future of mankind it is important to establish some limits and ethics that the right way for humanity depends on. The idea of Kelly (2016) it is close to a good vision of the phenomena. In the paper The Inevitable: Understanding the 12 Technological Forces That Will Shape Our Future he wrote: "This is not a race against the machines. If we race against them, we lose. This is a race with the machines. You'll be paid in the future based on how well you work with robots. Ninety percent of your coworkers will be unseen machines… We've been redefining what it means to be human. As we invent more species of AI, we will be forced to surrender more of what is supposedly unique about humans. Each step of surrender—we are not the only mind that can play chess, fly a plane, make music, or invent a mathematical law – will be painful and sad. We'll spend the next three decades – indeed, perhaps the next century – in a permanent identity crisis, continually asking ourselves what humans are good for. In the grandest irony of all, the greatest benefit of an everyday, utilitarian AI will not be increased productivity or an economics of abundance or a new way of doing science – although all those will happen. The greatest benefit of the arrival of artificial intelligence is that AIs will help define humanity. We need AIs to tell us who we are" (Kelly, 2016, p. 29).

5. A new vision for technological progress – embracing 'Protopia'

Kelly (2016) is also the first author that introduce the term "protopia" in 2009 to describe a society that makes incremental progress over time thanks to technological advancements. This concept offers a more realistic and inclusive pathway to a better future, as opposed to the existing binary of dystopia or utopia. "Protopia" has gained traction in recent years as a more desirable option. In the land of progress and transformation, "protopia" stands as a dynamic contrast to both utopias, where an ideal state is believed to have already been attained, and dystopia, where the envisioned "ideal" turns out to be far from desirable. "Protopia" embraces the concept of continuous improvement and evolution, emphasizing the journey of becoming rather than a fixed destination. The prefix "pro" in "protopian" originates from the essence of process and progress, acknowledging that the state of "protopia" is an ongoing and ever-evolving state of advancement. The notion of "protopia" proves to be deeply intriguing, as it underscores the fluidity and adaptability of human aspirations and endeavors. In the pursuit of progress, "protopia" serves as a guiding principle that inspires us to embrace change and growth, thru innovation, and the potential for a brighter and more prosperous future.

The biggest problem that the past, present and most probably future is struggling with, is the ethical consideration that will govern the AI world.

In the domain of AI research, the capacity for AI algorithms to adopt social roles has emerged as a significant aspect, necessitating the establishment of innovative design principles, notably transparency and predictability. As AI algorithms advance in generality, their actions may deviate from predictability, compelling the implementation of fresh safety assurance measures and artificial ethical frameworks. Notably, certain highly sophisticated AI systems could potentially attain moral standing, akin to persons, albeit with unique characteristics and potentially subject to distinct rules.

6. The ethics of AI: Challenges, triumphs and boundaries

The arrival of AI boasting superhuman intelligence and capabilities presents a daunting challenge: devising algorithms capable of consistently generating super ethical conduct. While these challenges might seem far-reaching, it is reasonable to expect their eventual confrontation, and they offer invaluable insights to steer contemporary research. As we continue to propel AI technology forward, addressing these concerns remains paramount to ensure the responsible and ethical integration of AI into society. The principles of transparency, safety assurance, and ethical considerations must be front and center in AI development, fostering a future where AI harmoniously and ethically complements human endeavors. By embracing these principles, we can navigate the uncharted territory of AI evolution responsibly and with a profound understanding of its impact on humanity. To do this, AI systems need to be human-centric, resting on a commitment to their use in the service of humanity and the common good, with the goal of improving human welfare and freedom (European Commission, 2019).

At this right moment, the most popular AI that is used on the market, "Chat GPT" offers a line at the end of a response message that is considered implying consciences or ethics, letting the user now that: "However, it is essential to ensure that AI applications are carefully validated, and ethical considerations are considered to guarantee their responsible and beneficial use." It is a starting point, but our hope is that will not be an ending point, for the good of the "proptopia" we were mentioned before.

Recently the actors' union, American Federation of Television and Radio Artists "SAG-AFTREA" representing over 150,000 actors entered on strike and merge the Writers Guild of America "WGA" marching protection and regulation for the use of AI. It's the first time since 1960 when both unions have been on strike simultaneously asking studios for higher pay and to rethink a more constrict regulation on the use of artificial intelligence in creative projects.

In the rapidly evolving landscape of AI, another pressing concern revolves around the implementation of "diffusion models" and the fusion of human creativity with these models. Diffusion models, such as text-to-video and other text to image diffusion models, are advancing at an astounding pace, leading to profound resolutions in images and unleashing unprecedented creativity. Even in the absence of traditional artistic tools like pen and paper or pixel manipulation on a screen, graphic artists are now harnessing their creativity textually, setting scenes and creating intricate artworks with the help of AI. The creative process endures, albeit through novel means, as AI becomes a collaborative partner in the artistic journey.

Consider the scenario where an AI, engages language to instruct another AI, specialized in image creation, to produce a profound new form of art. This collaboration unlocks the potential for creating awe-inspiring pictures, and as we venture into the empire of movies, the possibilities for crafting entire cinematic experiences with virtual characters and interactions become conceivable. The current level of creativity with AI might not yet match a full-length movie, but the trajectory points to it becoming a reality within months.

However, within this technological phenomenon, an essential question reveals huge – the issue of ownership. As AI-generated outputs can replicate our faces, voices, and digital identities, the matter of who owns this extended digital identity becomes increasingly controversial. Already, we witness instances where AI simulates living or deceased individuals, leading to critical debates about patentability, copyright, and the foundation of capitalism itself.

For the moment the answer from the most popular AI, "Chat GPT", about the ownership is simple: "As an AI language model, I don't have ownership over any specific text [...]" so "we the people" must put our mind and effort again together trying to build the order again. The phrase "we the people" is more actual than any time before. an important and iconic phrase that is stated in the beginning of the United States Constitution. "We the People [...], in Order to form a more perfect Union, establish Justice, insure domestic Tranquility, provide for the common defense, promote the general Welfare, and secure the Blessings of Liberty to ourselves and our Posterity, do ordain and establish this Constitution [...]" (Preamble to the United States Constitution).

The urgency for a comprehensive digital law for AI like a constitution of digital rights is incontestable. We need a robust framework that addresses ownership rights for AI-generated outputs, data inputs (including behavioral patterns of individuals), and their results. Without such legislation, the ownership vacuum will persist, leaving individuals vulnerable to exploitation and raising complex legal dilemmas. Courts will grapple with determining rights and remedies in cases where AI-generated content infringes upon someone's likeness or identity.

The notion of a digital law for AI might seem daunting, given the rapid pace at which AI technology evolves. However, if we fail to act promptly, we risk undermining the very essence of individual identity and creative ownership in a technologically driven society. Thus, a proactive approach to establish regulations is paramount, safeguarding the rights of creators and individuals alike.

7. Conclusions

To address these multifaceted challenges, interdisciplinary collaboration among AI researchers, legal experts, ethicists, and policymakers becomes imperative. By coming together to craft a comprehensive and adaptive legal framework, we can ensure that the transformative power of AI aligns with ethical values and human rights. Deliberations surrounding the ownership of AI-generated content must be driven by principles of fairness, accountability, and transparency.

The convergence of human creativity and AI-powered diffusion models promises to reshape the artistic landscape profoundly. However, the rise of this technological proficiency necessitates the formulation of robust legal and ethical foundations to govern ownership rights in the digital kingdom. By proactively establishing a digital law for AI and embracing a constitution of digital rights, we can create a solid ground for an inclusive and responsible AI-driven society that empowers individuals, upholds creativity, and protects digital identities.

The interest in sustainable development is evident in the contributions made by countries and institutions of various origins, apart from the geographical and intellectual variety. According to a growing number of articles and citations, sustainable development appears to be an increasing trend. Finally, from all the results and discussion, we conclude that AI has a positive impact on sustainable entrepreneurship (Gupta et al., 2023).

The time for action is now, and our collective efforts will determine how we navigate the vast expanse of AI's transformative potential while preserving the essence of humanity.

The future of AI holds immense promise, and it is up to researchers and players of this industry to continue pushing the boundaries of this transformative technology, paving the way for a more intelligent and automated future where AI and human collaboration will shape new frontiers in technology and beyond hopefully good for the humanity.

Acknowledgment: This work was supported by Hasso Plattner Foundation through the grant LBUS-UA-RO-2023, financed by the Knowledge Transfer Center of the Lucian Blaga University of Sibiu.

Bibliography

Constitution of the United States: A Transcription. National Archives, U.S. National Archives and Records Administration, 4 May (2020), https://www.archives.gov/founding-docs/constitution-transcript [Accessed July 1st 2023].

Enholm, I.M., Papagiannidis, E., & Mikalef, P. (2022). Artificial Intelligence and Business Value: A Literature Review. *Inf Syst Front*, 24, https://doi.org/10.1007/s10796-021-10186-w.

European Commission. (2019). *Ethics Guidelines for Trustworthy AI* https://ec.europa.eu/newsroom/dae/document.cfm?doc_id=60419. [Accessed 4 July 2023].

Gupta, B.B., Gaurav, A., Panigrahi, P.K., & Arya, V. (2023). Analysis of Artificial Intelligence-Based Technologies and Approaches on Sustainable Entrepreneurship. *Technol. Forecast. Soc. Change*, 186, Part B, https://doi.org/10.1016/j.techfore.2022.122152.

Hughes, L., Dwivedi, Y.K., Misra, S.K., Rana, N.P., Raghavan, V., & Akella, V. (2019). Blockchain Research, Practice and Policy: Applications, Benefits, Limitations, Emerging Research Themes and Research Agenda. *International Journal of Information Management*, 49, 114–129, https://doi.org/10.1016/j.ijinfomgt.2019.02.005.

Kelly, K. (2016). *The Inevitable: Understanding the 12 Technological Forces That Will Shape Our Future.* Publishing by Viking.

Moodaley, W., & Arnesh, T. (2023). Greenwashing, Sustainability Reporting, and Artificial Intelligence: A Systematic Literature Review. *Sustainability*, 15(2), 1481. https://doi.org/10.3390/su15021481.

Rohit, N., Kennedy, M., & Corbett, J. (2020). Artificial Intelligence for Sustainability: Challenges, Opportunities, and a Research Agenda. *International Journal of Information Management*, 53, https://doi.org/10.1016/j.ijinfomgt.2020.102104.

Tanasescu, C.R., & Oprean, C. (2013). Towards a Sustainable Well-being. *Review of Applied Socio-Economic Research*, 5(1), 170–178.

Nadia Sghaier

Chapter 6 Recent global crises and sectoral stock market returns

Abstract: This chapter compares the effect of the Covid-19 pandemic and the invasion of Ukraine on the dynamic of the stock market return of the world and 11 individual sectors under heterogenous behaviors of investors from 31 December 2019 to 30 March 2023. The econometric approach is based on Markov Regime Switching model that allows the presence of two different regimes. The empirical results show evidence of significant impacts of the crises that varies across sectors. These findings indicate how the investors could diversify their portfolios during each type of crises.

Keywords: stock market return, heterogenous behaviors of investors, Covid-19 pandemic, invasion of Ukraine, Markov Regime Switching model

1. Introduction

During the last three decades, both developed and developing countries have been submitted to serious crises with distinct features (financial, health and geopolitical) that did not only cause numerous disruptions in the global economy but also in the financial markets.

On 11 March 2020, the World Health Organization had declared that the Covid-19 pandemic, initially discovered on 31 December 2019 in China, as a global pandemic. Two years later, on 24 February 2022, Russia had officially invaded Ukraine. The intensity and duration of each of these crises as well as its effect on the stock markets have been extensively researched in the finance literature.

For the Covid-19 crisis, empirical evidence suggests a negative impact on stock market returns (Al-Awadhi et al., 2020; Ashraf, 2020; Topcu, & Gulal, 2020; Khan et al., 2020) and a positive effect on their volatilities (Zaremba et al., 2022; Chaudhary et al., 2020; Bai et al., 2021; Aslam et al., 2021). In particular, some studies argued that the effect of the Covid-19 pandemic varied across countries and among sectors (Harjoto et al., 2021; Singh & Shaik, 2021). Compared to previous infectious pandemics, the Covid-19 pandemic presents the most forceful effect on stock markets (Baker et al., 2020; Zhang et al., 2020).

In addition, the repercussions of the Covid-19 crisis are greater to that of the global financial crisis (Shehzad et al., 2020; Gunay, 2021; Yarovaya et al., 2022).

As for the invasion of Ukraine, several studies investigated its implications on stock market returns and volatilities and reported heterogeneous effects (Boungou, & Yatié, 2022; Yousaf et al., 2022; Boubaker et al., 2022; Ahmed et al., 2022).

Although previous studies pointed to the significant effect of these crises on stock markets, they did not shed light on investor behavior during these particular events. However, it is well known that investors show numerous changing psychological drives that can lead to variation in stock prices and consequently on market dynamics. Consequently, the standard finance models which assume that investors are homogenous and show rational expectations about future variables need to reconsidered. Accordingly, an alternative theory which takes into account the heterogenous behavior of investors has emerged yielding a growing body of research on behavioral finance.

In this chapter, we compare the effects of the Covid-19 pandemic and the invasion of Ukraine on the dynamic of stock market returns of the world and 11 individual sectors in the presence of heterogenous investor behavior during a period stretching from 31 December 2019 to 30 March 2023. We extend the behavior finance literature in various ways. First, we compare the effect of the two most severe crises on stock market returns under heterogenous investor behavior. Second, we consider both world and sectoral indices that represent developed and emerging markets. Third, we apply the Markov Regime Switching model that takes into account different regimes.

2. Literature review

Behavioral finance examines the effect of psychological dimensions of investors. It specifically examines the effect of aspirations, emotions, expectations and beliefs on stock market. Numerous models known as "Heterogenous Agent models" have been developed to model different types of investors (Day, & Huang, 1990; Chiarella, 1992; Brock, & Hommes, 1998).

We retain two types of investors which are the fundamentalists and the chartists. The first one assumes that the stock price will mean revert towards a certain fundamental price and that investors buy assets when they are undervalued and sell them when they are overvalued. In contrast, the second type does not take market conditions into account but base their trading strategies on past prices.

Empirical evidence on heterogenous investor behavior has been found by several authors. Earlier authors applied the Markov Regime-Switching model and found significant behavioral heterogeneity in stock markets (De Grauwe & Grimaldi, 2005; Boswijik et al., 2007; Li, & Miu, 2020). Other authors rely on nonlinear models (Frijns et al., 2010; Hommes & Veld, 2017; Jawadi et al., 2017). Later studies focused on the effect of the financial crisis on investor behavior (Lam et al., 2011).

Recent empirical studies have focused on the heterogenous behavior of investors during the Covid-19 crisis. Gao (2022) examined the behavior of different investors in the American stock market and found strong evidence on behavioral heterogeneity among different groups of traders. Solihat and Nugraha (2020) studied also the effect of the Covid-19 pandemic on investor behavior and revealed significant change in their behavior during the Covid-19 pandemic.

In addition to the Covid-19 crisis, financial markets have suffered from the effect of the invasion of Ukraine. Using linear regression panel data models, Boungou and Yatié (2022) highlighted the negative effect of the invasion of Ukraine on 94 stock market returns and found that the effects are most pronounced in neighboring countries to Russia and Ukraine. Similarly, Yousaf et al. (2022) examined the effect of the Russian invasion on 26 stock markets. They found that the stock markets of Hungary, Russia, Poland and Slovakia are negatively affected while those of the other European and Asian Regions are adversely affected. Applying an event study methodology, Boubaker et al. (2022) documented that the invasion of Ukraine had heterogenous effects on 47 emerging stock market returns and that the effects varied across countries. In the same vein, Ahmed et al. (2022) found significant effects of the invasion of Ukraine on European stock markets.

3. Empirical methodology

3.1 Heterogeneous agent models

To compare the empirical effect of the Covid-19 pandemic and the invasion of Ukraine on stock market returns in the presence of heterogenous investor behavior, we apply an heterogeneous agent model (Chiarella et al., 2012) with two types of investors (fundamentalists and chartists). The fundamentalists are supposed to have information about the long-term fundamental stock price, u_t, given by:

$$E_{t-1}^{f}\left(p_t\right)=u_t \tag{1}$$

They buy (resp. sell) the stock when market price (p_{t-1}) is below (resp. above) the fundamental price of the stock (u_{t-1}). Their demand function is:

$$D_t^f = \alpha^f \left(E_{t-1}^f(p_t) - p_{t-1}\right) = \alpha^f \left(u_t - p_{t-1}\right) \tag{2}$$

Where $\alpha^f > 0$ measures the speed of mean-reversion of market price to the fundamental value.

The chartists do not have information about the fundamental price. They trade based on market conditions and historical prices. They extrapolate market price on market price deviation from the short-term value:

$$E_{t-1}^c(p_t) = p_{t-1} + \beta(p_{t-1} - v_{t-1}) \tag{3}$$

Where $\beta \neq 0$ is the extrapolation rate of the chartists.

Their demand function is determined by:

$$D_t^c = \beta^c \left(E_{t-1}^c(p_t) - p_{t-1}\right) = \beta^c \left(p_{t-1} - v_{t-1}\right) \tag{4}$$

All chartists hold the same beliefs about the short-term market value which is updated in every period to reproduce market conditions. However, they engage in two different trading strategies according to which they are classified into two types (momentum traders and contrarian traders). Momentum traders believe that $\beta > 0$, thus, the stock price will deviate further away from the current price. Contrarian traders believe that $\beta < 0$, i.e., the stock price will reverse in the next period.

As suggested by Chiarella et al. (2012), we consider that stock price variation is calculated using:

$$\Delta p_t = p_t - p_{t-1} = \alpha(u_t - p_{t-1}) + \beta(p_{t-1} - v_{t-1}) + \varepsilon_t \tag{5}$$

To determine the long-term fundamental stock price, we apply the Hodrick and Prescott (1997) filter technique which consists in decomposing an observed variable into its long-term trend and transitory fluctuations.

3.2 Markov Regime Switching model

The Markov regime switching model is introduced by Hamilton (1989) and contains several equations that can reproduce investor behavior in different regimes. The main feature of this model is that the switching mechanism from one regime to another is determined by an unobservable state variable, s_t, which takes 0 (Regime 1) or 1 (Regime 2). Formally, we reproduce the dynamic of the stock market return using the two-state Markov regime switching model:

$$r_{i,t} = \alpha_{i,t} detrend_{i,t-1} + \beta_{i,t} r_{i,t-1} + \varepsilon_{i,t} \tag{6}$$

Where $detrend_{i,t-1}$ is the past detrended stock market index, $r_{i,t-1}$ is the past stock market return, $\alpha_{i,t}$ is the coefficient of the fundamentalist and $\beta_{i,t}$ is the coefficient of the chartist. $\varepsilon_{i,t}$ are independent and identically distributed normal error with mean 0 and variance σ_i^2. i denotes the world or the sector and t is time.

The matrix of transition probabilities is given by:

$$P = \begin{pmatrix} P(s_t = 0|s_{t-1} = 0) & P(s_t = 1|s_{t-1} = 0) \\ P(s_t = 0|s_{t-1} = 1) & P(s_t = 1|s_{t-1} = 1) \end{pmatrix} = \begin{pmatrix} p_{11} & p_{12} \\ p_{21} & p_{22} \end{pmatrix} \tag{7}$$

Where $p_{ij}(i, j = 0,1)$ means the transition probability of $s_t = j$ given that $s_{t-1} = i$. The transition probabilities satisfy $p_{11} + p_{12} = 1$ and $p_{21} + p_{22} = 1$.

Given the estimated transition probabilities, we can compute the expected duration by:

$$E(D_s) = \frac{1}{1 - p_{ij}} \tag{8}$$

The parameters of the Markov Regime-Switching model are estimated using the maximum likelihood method (Hamilton, 1994).

4. Data and descriptive statistics

4.1 Data

For the empirical study, we consider the daily closing indices of the stock market of the world (Morgan Stanley Capital International World Index) and 11 individual sectors (Global Industry Classification Standard) from 31 December 2019 to 30 Mach 2023. All indices are expressed in US dollars and obtained from Datastream. Table 6.1 presents name and notation of the indices.

Tab. 6.1: Stock market indices

Index	Notations
World Stock Market	PWS
Communication Service	PCS
Consumer Discretionary	PCD
Consumer Staples	PCST
Energy	PENG
Financial	PFIN
Health	PHC
Industrials	PIND
Information Technology	PIT
Materials	PMAT
Real estate	PRE
Utilities	PUTI

We omitted observations for which the indices were not available because the market was closed. The final dataset consists of 848 observations. The stock market return is calculated using the first difference of stock index transformed in logarithm form:

$$r_{i,t} = \log(p_{i,t}) - \log(p_{i,t-1}) \tag{9}$$

Where $p_{i,t}$ is the stock index.

To reproduce the effect of the Covid-19 pandemic and the invasion of Ukraine, we consider two separate subperiods: Covid-19 period (from 31 December 2019 to 23 February 2020, 562 observations) and Invasion of Ukraine period (from 24 February 2022 to 31 December 2022, 286 observations). Following previous studies, we consider 31 December 2019 as the day of the first Covid-19 case while 24 February 2022 is the starting date of the invasion of Ukraine.

We examined stationarity of all series using unit root tests. The obtained results (not reported here for space purposes) indicate that all series follow a stationary process.

Figures 6.1 and 6.2 present the evolution of the stock market indices and returns respectively.

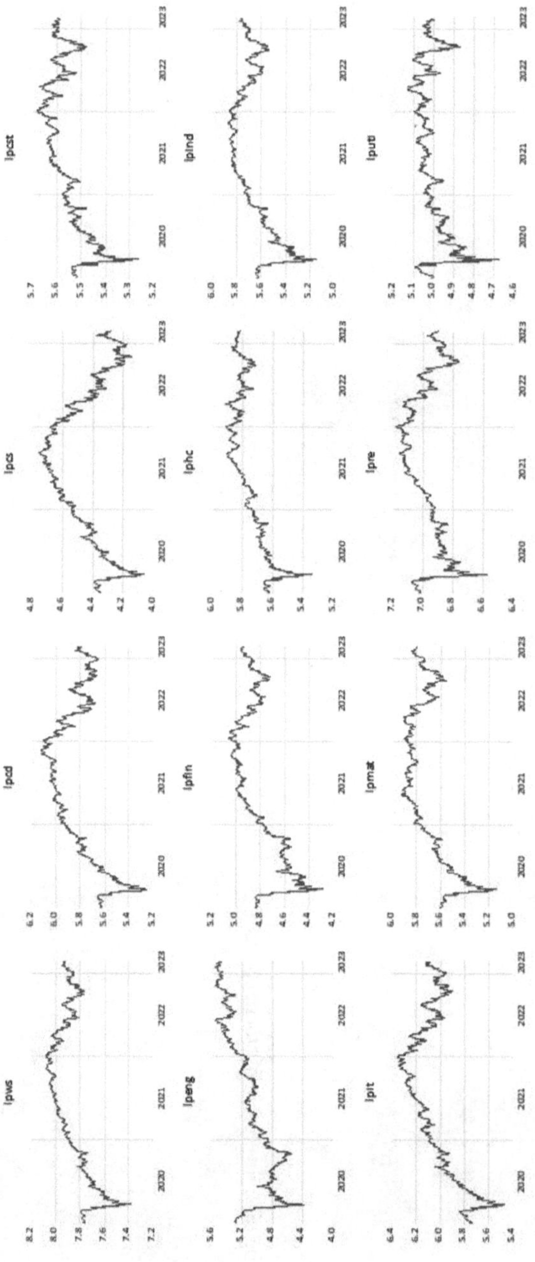

Fig. 6.1: Evolution of stock indices

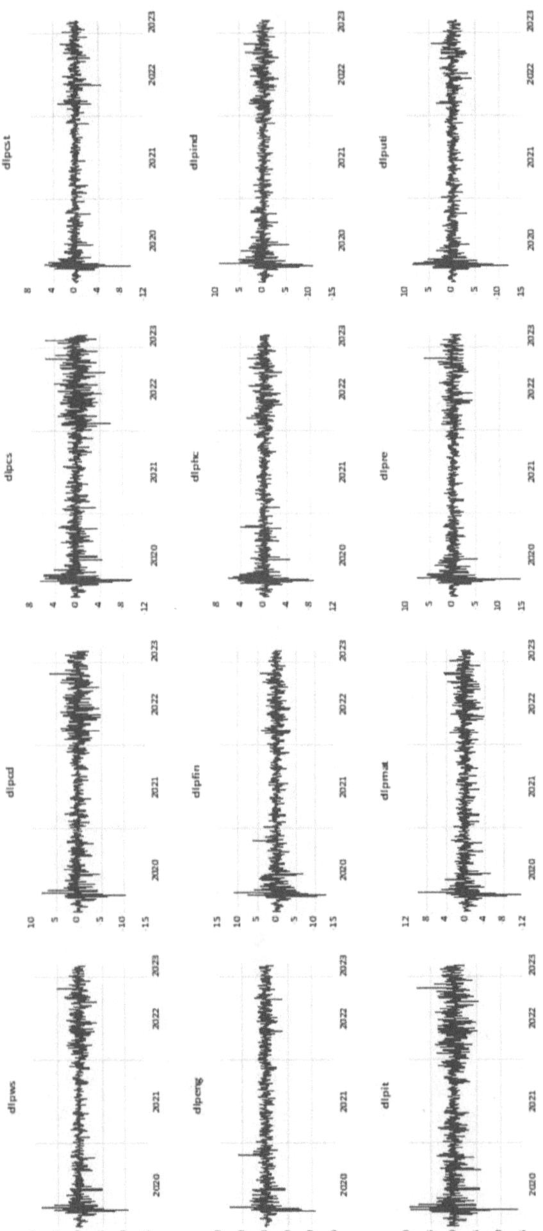

Fig. 6.2: Evolution of stock returns

4.2 Descriptive statistics

Table 6.2 reports the descriptive statistics of return series for each subperiod. During Covid-19 all period, the means of all returns are positive with the highest 7.6 % for information technology while the lowest 0.1 % for utilities. Stock market risk is measured by the standard deviation and the highest 2.517 is for energy sector.

We examine the stability of the means using Bai and Perron (2003) test which assumes that the date of the break is unknown. We found evidence of structural breaks on 4 May 2020. Therefore, we reexamine the descriptive statistics over two separate subperiods: From 31 December 2019 to 4 May 2020 and from 5 May 2020 to 23 February 2022. In the first subperiod, we found that all returns are negative, reflecting the severe effect of the Covid-19 pandemic. In the second subperiod, all returns become positive. This could relate to the announcement of the vaccination program. During the invasion of Ukraine period, all returns except that of energy, health care, industrial and utilities sectors are negative. This can be attributed to the dramatic effect of the invasion of Ukraine.

5. Empirical results

Table 6.3 reports the empirical results of the two-state Markov Regime Switching model, given by Equation (6), for each subperiod.

5.1 Covid-19 subperiod 1

We see clearly that the coefficients of the fundamentalists, in Regime 1, as well as that, in Regime 2, are negative and statistically significant for all series. This indicates a mean reversion trading strategy towards the fundamental in the two regimes. In particular, we notice that the coefficients of the fundamentalists in Regime 1 are higher than those in Regime 2 in the communication service, consumer discretionary, financial service and real estate sectors. This reflects that the presence of fundamentalists is more important.

However, for other sectors and the world, the coefficients of the fundamentalists in Regime 2 are higher than those in Regime 1.

In addition, we notice that the coefficients of the chartists in Regime 1 are significant in some sectors. This indicates that the chartists are active simultaneously with the fundamentalists. The sign of this coefficient is positive, suggesting that the trading activities of momentum traders dominated those of contrarians.

5.2 Covid-19 subperiod 2

We see that in Regime 1, the coefficients of the fundamentalists are significant and negative in all sectors, except the real estate sector whereas in Regime 2 all coefficients of the fundamentalists are also significant and negative in all sectors, except financial and real estate sectors where the coefficient of the fundamentalists is not significant. In particular, we found that some coefficients increase while others decrease. This could be attributed to the dramatic impact of the Covid-19 pandemic on the fundamentalists, which seems to vary across sectors.

For the chartists, we notice that all their coefficients are significant and positive in Regime 1 in all countries while in Regime 2 all coefficients are significant and positive in all sectors, except the consumer discretionary and real estate sectors where the coefficients of chartists are not significant. Then, the trading activities of momentum traders dominated those of contrarians.

These results are similar to those obtained by previous studies which found significant varying effects of the Covid-19 on stock market returns across sectors (He et al., 2020; Singh & Shaik, 2021).

Tab. 6.2: Descriptive statistics of returns

	RWS	RCD	RCS	RCST	RENG	RFIN	RHC	RIND	RIT	RMAT	RRE	RUTI
Covid-19 All Period												
Mean	0.037	0.029	0.053	0.021	0.007	0.029	0.031	0.022	0.076	0.043	0.005	0.001
Standard Deviation	1.359	1.423	1.455	1.012	2.517	1.751	1.188	1.426	1.829	1.438	1.491	1.426
Covid-19 Subperiod 1												
Mean	-0.173	-0.099	-0.141	-0.123	-0.527	-0.402	-0.020	-0.294	-0.021	-0.226	-0.243	-0.151
Standard Deviation	2.761	2.558	2.651	2.061	4.662	3.414	2.373	2.767	3.421	2.722	3.053	3.003
Covid-19 Subperiod 2												
Mean	0.078	0.054	0.090	0.049	0.109	0.112	0.041	0.082	0.094	0.094	0.052	0.030
Standard Deviation	0.864	1.082	1.088	0.641	1.836	1.185	0.784	0.974	1.330	1.022	0.932	0.842
Invasion of Ukraine Period												
Mean	-0.018	-0.059	-0.042	-0.008	0.048	-0.054	0.003	0.004	-0.005	-0.024	-0.072	0.001
Standard Deviation	1.256	1.673	1.735	0.905	1.893	1.327	1.001	1.170	1.906	1.387	1.297	1.132

Tab. 6.3: Estimation results of the Markov Regime Switching model

	RWS	RCD	RCS	RCST	RENG	RFIN	RHC	RIND	RIT	RMAT	RRE	RUTI
Covid-19 Subperiod 1												
c_1												
α_1	-2.437***	-0.382	-0.587*	-3.651***	-3.117***	-1.593***	-3.837***	-2.081***	-2.869***	-3.073***	-1.330***	-3.312***
	[-5.379]	[-1.159]	[-1.811]	[-4.591]	[-8.528]	[-3.396]	[-10.214]	[-7.194]	[-2.494]	[-6.535]	[-3.521]	[-7.088]
β_1	2.667***	0.065	0.036	4.053***	3.345***	0.767**	4.030***	3.129	2.868	3.179***	1.673	3.641***
	[5.934]	[0.226]	[0.120]	[4.965]	[9.694]	[2.064]	[10.209]	[7.870]	[2.916]	[7.478]	[4.677]	[6.962]
c_2												
α_2	-1.713***	-3.552***	-4.279***	-1.301	-0.816***	-2.359***	-0.575*	-0.896**	-1.452***	-0.644*	-2.442***	-1.354*
	[-3.422]	[-7.740]	[-9.230]	[-1.663]	[-2.634]	[-5.318]	[-1.644]	[-2.065]	[-2.689]	[-1.650]	[-6.444]	[-1.692]
β_2	0.881**	3.446***	3.907***	0.630	0.411*	2.713***	0.023	0.378	0.727	0.227	1.451***	0.618
	[2.201]	[8.469]	[8.381]	[0.986]	[1.627]	[6.575]	[0.066]	[1.160]	[1.491]	[0.649]	[4.375]	[0.990]
Covid-19 Subperiod 2												
c_1		-0.222*	0.034									0.030
		[-1.799]	[0.744]									[0.408]
α_1	-8.847***	-1.856***	-1.447***	-2.011***	-0.883***	-1.687***	-1.953***	-1.257***	-5.161***	-1.594***	-0.026	-1.377***
	[-3.349]	[-6.105]	[-8.505]	[-4.932]	[-4.423]	[-10.909]	[-4.886]	[-7.155]	[-3.350]	[-5.300]	[-0.169]	[-9.686]
β_1	7.215***	1.600***	1.337***	1.489***	0.890***	1.469***	1.344***	1.214***	3.402***	1.774***	-0.117	1.164***
	[2.659]	[7.011]	[8.421]	[4.340]	[5.002]	[10.732]	[3.964]	[7.686]	[2.813]	[6.117]	[-0.480]	[8.850]
c_2		0.466*	-2.725***									-1.719***
		[1.738]	[-5.796]									[-3.747]

	RWS	RCD	RCS	RCST	RENG	RFIN	RHC	RIND	RIT	RMAT	RRE	RUTI
α_2	-1.430***	-0.154	-2.316	-1.248***	-4.834***	0.550	-1.365***	-8.918***	-1.404***	-1.206***	0.003	-5.472***
	[-9.791]	[-0.236]	[-1.252]	[-3.955]	[-7.587]	[1.177]	[-5.191]	[-10.234]	[-8.256]	[-4.057]	[0.008]	[-2.836]
β_2	1.304***	0.387	1.073	1.313***	3.803***	1.268*	1.467***	11.210***	1.279***	1.031***	0.603***	5.299***
	[9.676]	[0.709]	[0.593]	[4.328]	[6.986]	[2.399]	[5.760]	[21.180]	[8.301]	[4.109]	[2.440]	[2.858]
Invasion of Ukraine Period												
c_2			-0.360**									
			[-2.220]									
α_2	-0.483	-2.309***	-1.611	-1.033***	-1.995***	-1.684***	-0.066	-1.966***	-2.491***	-0.584**	0.394	-0.698**
	[-1.557]	[-8.964]	[-7.136]	[-5.211]	[-5.279]	[-6.289]	[-0.895]	[-8.063]	[-4.671]	[-2.176]	[0.610]	[-2.143]
β_1	0.681***	1.942***	1.506***	1.108***	1.519***	1.225***	-0.022	1.584***	1.982***	0.882***	-0.252	0.905***
	[2.478]	[7.023]	[7.144]	[6.212]	[4.532]	[5.046]	[-0.129]	[7.666]	[4.103]	[3.736]	[-0.402]	[3.787]
c_2			1.902***									
			[3.623]									
α_2	-2.127***	-0.022	-0.977	-4.781***	-1.219***	-1.056***	-0.067	-0.673***	-0.428	-2.201***	-2.333***	-1.875***
	[-8.103]	[-0.037]	[-1.193]	[-3.802]	[-3.285]	[-3.733]	[-0.406]	[-2.510]	[-1.141]	[-5.958]	[-6.366]	[-8.484]
β_1	1.758***	0.262	0.843	3.250***	1.436***	1.281***	0.663**	0.887***	0.591*	1.642***	2.148***	1.422***
	[7.058]	[0.537]	[1.189]	[3.027]	[3.854]	[4.894]	[2.224]	[3.854]	[1.747]	[5.155]	[6.812]	[7.017]

Notes: ***, ** and *denote statistical significance at the 1 %, 5 % and 10 % levels respectively

5.3 Invasion of Ukraine period

We notice the presence of fundamentalists in both Regime 1 and 2 for all sectors. Furthermore, the coefficient of the fundamentalists increased in some sectors like financial and information technology, whereas it decreased in other sectors like energy.

In Regime 1 and Regime 2, we observe that the coefficients of the chartists are significant and positive in some sectors. Similar to the two previous subperiods, the trading activities of momentum investors still dominate those of contrarian investors.

These results are consistent with those of previous studies which found significant varying effects of the invasion of Ukraine on stock market returns across sectors.

The switching beliefs of fundamentalists and chartists during the two distinct states as reproduced by the transition probabilities expressed by Equation (7) and durations, defined by Equation (8), in each subperiod are summarized in Table 5. We see a significant change in both probabilities and durations.

Tab. 6.4: Transition probabilities and durations

	RWS	RCD	RCS	RCST	RENG	RFIN	RHC	RIND	RIT	RMAT	RRE	RUTI
Covid-19 Subperiod 1												
P_{11}	0.291	0.613	0.666	0.199	0.000	0.339	0.218	0.193	0.121	0.199	0.623	0.286
P_{22}	0.350	0.315	0.252	0.255	0.563	0.374	0.351	0.313	0.576	0.479	0.377	0.173
D_1	1.410	2.585	2.991	1.249	1.000	1.513	1.279	1.238	1.138	1.248	2.650	1.401
D_2	1.538	1.459	1.337	1.342	2.291	1.597	1.541	1.456	2.357	1.918	1.509	1.210
Covid-19 Subperiod 2												
P_{11}	0.300	0.769	0.982	0.289	0.896	0.915	0.008	0.984	0.134	0.242	0.666	0.880
P_{22}	0.890	0.364	0.229	0.338	0.032	0.050	0.417	0.124	0.961	0.101	0.250	0.289
D_1	1.000	4.328	55.861	1.000	9.626	11.830	1.000	6.159	1.155	1.000	3.000	5.190
D_2	18.050	1.572	1.296	1.511	1.000	1.053	1.714	1.000	2.596	1.112	1.333	1.000
Invasion of Ukraine Period												
P_{11}	0.001	0.116	0.813	0.912	0.001	0.001	0.833	0.020	0.001	0.425	0.399	0.001
P_{22}	0.044	0.001	0.057	0.001	0.158	0.116	0.542	0.043	0.305	0.001	0.592	0.117
D_1	1.000	1.130	5.356	11.376	1.000	1.000	5.977	1.021	1.000	1.738	1.664	1.000
D_2	1.046	1.000	1.061	1.000	1.188	1.132	2.185	1.044	1.438	1.000	2.448	1.133

Notes: P_{11} (resp. P_{22}) is estimated probability of remaining in state 1 (resp 2) in next period given that the process is in state 1 (resp. 2) in current period. D_1 (resp D_2) is the duration of Regime 1 (resp. 2).

6. Conclusions

This chapter compared the effect of the Covid-19 pandemic and the Invasion of Ukraine on the dynamics of stock market returns of the world and 11 individual sectors, in the presence of heterogeneous investors (reproduced by the fundamentalists and the chartists). The econometric approach used the Markov Regime Switching model that allows for considering two regimes. The empirical results have shown that both fundamentalists and chartists are present in stock markets but with some difference across sectors. In addition, we found that the Covid-19 pandemic has affected the behavior of all investors in all sectors. However, the Invasion of Ukraine presented adverse effects that varied across sectors. These findings have important implications for investors to make appropriate hedging decisions against boom-and-bust markets, for risk managers to better manage their risk and for investors to diversify their portfolios by choosing stocks of sectors that are positively related to the crises.

Bibliography

Ahmed, S., Hasan, M.M., & Kamal, M.R. (2022). Russia-Ukraine Crisis: The Effects on the European Stock Market. *European Financial Management*, 1–41, doi: 10.1111/eufm.12386.

Al-Awadhi, A.M, Alsaifi, K., Al-Awadhi, A., & Alhammadi, S. (2020). Death and Contagious Infectious Diseases: Impact of the COVID-19 Virus on Stock Market Returns. *Journal of Behavioral and Experimental Finance*, 1–5, doi: 10.1016/j.jbef.2020.100326.

Ashraf, B.N. (2020). Stock Markets' Reaction to COVID-19: Cases or Fatalities? *Research in International Business and Finance*, 54, 101249, https://doi.org/10.1016/j.ribaf.2020.101249.

Aslam, M.-F., Silveira Ferreira, P.J., Mughal, K.S., & Bashir, B. (2021). Intraday Volatility Spillovers among European Financial Markets during COVID-19. *International Journal of Financial Studies*, 9(1), 5, https://doi.org/10.3390/ijfs9010005.

Bai, L., Wei, Y., Wei, G.W., Li, X., & Zhang, S. (2021). Infectious Disease Pandemic and Permanent Volatility of International Stock Markets: a Long-term Perspective. *Finance Research Letters*, 40(101709), 1–10, https://doi.org/10.1016/j.frl.2020.101709.

Bai, J. & Perron, P. (2003). Computation and Analysis of Multiple Structural Change Models, *Journal of Applied Econometrics*, 18(1), 1–22, https://doi.org/10.1002/jae.659.

Baker, S.R., Bloom, N., Davis, S.J., Kost, K., Sammon, M., & Viratyosin, T. (2020). The Unprecedented Stock Market Reaction to COVID-19. *The Review of Asset Pricing Studies*, 10(4), 742–758, https://doi.org/10.1093/rapstu/raaa008.

Boswijk, H.P., Hommes, C.H., & Manzan, S. (2007). Behavioral Heterogeneity in Stock Prices, *Journal of Economic Dynamics and Control*, 31(6), 1938–1970, https://doi.org/10.1016/j.jedc.2007.01.001.

Boubaker, S., Goodell, J.W., Pandey, D.K., & Kumari, V. (2022). Heterogeneous Impacts of Wars on Global Equity Markets: Evidence from the Invasion of Ukraine. *Finance Research Letters*, 48, 102934, https://doi.org/10.1016/j.frl.2022.102934.

Boungou, W., & Yatié A. (2022). The Impact of the Ukraine-Russia War on World Stock Market Returns. *Economics Letters*, 215, 110516, https://doi.org/10.1016/j.econlet.2022.110516.

Brock, W.A., & Hommes, C.H. (1998). Heterogeneous Beliefs and Routes to Chaos in a Simple Asset Pricing Model. *Journal of Economic Dynamics and Control*, 22, 1235–1274, https://doi.org/10.1016/S0165-1889(98)00011-6.

Chaudhary, M., Sodani, P.R., & Das, S. (2020). Effect of COVID-19 on Economy in India: Some Reflections for Policy and Programme. *Journal of Health Management*, 22(2), 169–180, https://doi.org/10.1177/0972063420935541.

Chiarella, C. (1992). The Dynamics of Speculative Behaviour. *Annals of Operations Research* 37, 101–123, https://doi.org/10.1007/BF02071051.

Chiarella, C., He, X.-Z., Huang, W., & Zheng, H. (2012). Estimating Behavioural Heterogeneity under Regime Switching. *Journal of Economic Behavior and Organization*, 83(3), 446–460.

Day, R.H., & Huang, W. (1990). Bulls, Bears and Market Sheep. *Journal of Economic Behavior and Organization*, 14, 299–329.

De Grauwe, P., & Grimaldi, M. (2005). Heterogeneity of Agents, Transaction Costs and the Exchange Rate. *Journal of Economic Dynamics and Control*, 29(4), 691–719, https://doi.org/10.1016/j.jedc.2004.01.004.

Frijns, B., Lehnert, T., & Zwinkels, R.C.J. (2010). Behavioral Heterogeneity in the Option Market. *Journal of Economic Dynamics and Control*, 34(11), 2273–2287, https://doi.org/10.1016/j.jedc.2010.05.009.

Gao, S. (2022). Modelling and Forecasting Methods in Financial Economics, PhD Thesis, CUNY Academic Works. https://academicworks.cuny.edu/gc_etds/4779.

Gunay, S. (2021). Comparing COVID-19 with the GFC: A Shockwave Analysis of Currency Markets. *Research in International Business and Finance*, 56(101377), 1–13, https://doi.org/10.1016/j.ribaf.2020.101377.

Hamilton, J.D. (1989). A New Approach to the Economic Analysis of Nonstationary Time Series and the Business Cycle. *Econometrica*, 57(2), 357–384, https://doi.org/10.2307/1912559.

Hamilton, J.D. (1994). *Times Series Analysis*. Princeton University Press.

Harjoto, M.A., Rossi, F., Lee, R., & Sergi, B.S. (2021). How Do Equity Markets React to COVID-19? Evidence from Emerging and Developed Countries. *Journal of Economics and Business*, 115, 105966, https://pubmed.ncbi.nlm.nih.gov/33518845/

He, P., Sun, Y., Zhang, Y., & Li, T. (2020). COVID–19's Impact on Stock Prices Across Different Sectors—An Event Study Based on the Chinese Stock Market. *Emerging Markets Finance and Trade*, 56(10), 2198–2212, https://doi.org/10.1080/1540496X.2020.1785865.

Hodrick, R.J., & Prescott, E.C. (1997). Postwar US Business Cycles: an Empirical Investigation. *Journal Money Credit Bank*, 29(1), 1–16.

Hommes, C., & in't Veld, D. (2017). Booms, Busts and Behavioural Heterogeneity in Stock Prices. *Journal of Economic Dynamics and Control*, 80, 101–124, https://doi.org/10.1016/j.jedc.2017.05.006.

Jawadi, F., Namouri, H., & Ftiti, Z. (2017). An Analysis of the Effect of Investor Sentiment in a Heterogeneous Switching Transition Model for G7 Stock Markets. *Journal of Economic Dynamics and Control*, 1–16, https://doi.org/10.1016/j.jedc.2017.10.004.

Khan, K., Zhao, H., Zhang, H., Yang, H., Shah, M. H., & Jahanger, A. (2020). The Impact of COVID-19 Pandemic on Stock Markets: An Empirical Analysis of World Major Stock Indices, *Journal of Asian Finance, Economics and Business*, 7 (7), 463–474, https://doi.org/10.13106/jafeb.2020.vol7.no7.463.

Lam, C.F., DeRue, D.S, Karam, E.P., & Hollenbeck, J.R. (2011). The Impact of Feedback Frequency on Learning and Task Performance': Challenging the "More is Better" Assumption. *Organizational Behavior and Human Decision Processes*, 116(2), 217–228, doi: 10.1016/j.obhdp.2011.05.002.

Li, L., & Miu, P. (2020). Behavioral Heterogeneity in the Stock Market Revisited: What Factors Drive Investors as Fundamentalists or Chartists? *Journal of Behavioral Finance*, 23(1), 1–19, doi: 10.1080/15427560.2020.1841767.

Shehzad, K., Xiaoxing, L., & Kazouz, H. (2020). COVID-19's Disasters are Perilous than Global Financial Crisis: a Rumor or Fact?. *Finance Research Letters*, 36(101669), 1–8, https://doi.org/10.1016/j.frl.2020.101669.

Singh, G., & Shaik, M. (2021). The Short-Term Impact of COVID-19 on Global Stock Market Indices. *Contemporary Economics*, 15(1), 1–18, https://ssrn.com/abstract=3848616.

Solihat, A., & Nugraha, N. (2020). How Behavioral Finance during Pandemic COVID-19? *Business Innovation & Entrepreneurship Journal*, 2(2), 131–137, https://doi.org/10.35899/biej.v2i2.126.

Topcu, M., & Gulal, O.S. (2020). The Impact of COVID-19 on Emerging Stock Markets. *Finance Research Letters, 36,* https://doi.org/10.1016/j.frl.2020.101691.

Yarovaya, L., Brzeszczyński, J., Goodell, J.W., Lucey, B., & Lau, C.K.M. (2022). Rethinking Financial Contagion: Information Transmission Mechanism during the COVID-19 Pandemic. *Journal of International Financial Markets, Institutions and Money*, 79, 101589, https://doi.org/10.1016/j.intfin.2022.101589.

Yousaf, I., Patel, R., & Yarovaya, L. (2022). The Reaction of G20+ Stock Markets to the Russia–Ukraine Conflict "black-swan" Event: Evidence from Event Study Approach. Journal of Behavioral and Experimental Finance, 35. https://doi.org/10.1016/j.jbef.2022.100723.

Zaremba, A., Cakici, N., Demir, E., & Long, H. (2022). When Bad News Is Good News: Geopolitical Risk and the Cross-Section of Emerging Market Stock Returns. *Journal of Financial Stability*, 58, 100964. https://doi.org/10.1016/j.jfs.2021.100964

Zhang, D., Hu, M., & Ji, Q. (2020). Financial Markets under the Global Pandemic of COVID-19. *Finance Research Letters,* 36, 101528, https://doi.org/10.1016/j.frl.2020.101528.

Marian Pompiliu Cristescu, Dumitru Alexandru Mara, Raluca Andreea Nerişanu, and Lia Cornelia Culda

Chapter 7 Leveraging free tools in financial sentiment analysis

Abstract: In a world where financial news are easily accessible, stock prices are influenced by the sentiments of their investors and the news related to them. In order to make informed decisions, it is viable to assess all relevant factors that may influence stock prices. As a result, investors may take in consideration the sentiment of the news regarding a specific stock. In order to do this, sentiment analysis provides a way to categorize the positive, negative, or neutral attitude that news convey. Also, integrating sentiment analysis into investment strategies enhances understanding of market sentiment and may lead to better timed trading decisions. This paper aims to provide a guide on how to use free tools for conducting sentiment analysis on financial news. Firstly, we mined textual data using a free API provided by polygon.io, a comprehensive platform offering the latest financial markets data through query capabilities. Afterwards, we used the TextBlob and BERT library to process textual data and evaluate the sentiment polarity of financial news titles. Furthermore, we provided an example of analysis the obtained results using Pandas (Python Data Analysis Library) and export the results. We expect to develop a useful script and procedure for sentiment analysis of financial news, especially for analyzing large quantities of data that has the potential to be automated.

Keywords: sentiment analysis, financial news, free tools, TextBlob library, BERT, Pandas (Python Data Analysis Library)

1. Introduction

Financial news sentiment analysis incorporates technology, psychology, market dynamics, and worldwide connections. It enriches investing strategies, democratizes complex analytical tools, and improves our understanding of how emotions and attitudes affect the financial landscape (Claessens, 2017). Sentiment trends influence stock market movements and investor behavior, requiring nuanced understanding and technological innovation for real-world decision-making (Bollen et al., 2011).

The world of financial markets is characterized by its volatility intertwined with the ever-shifting sentiment of financial news. This sentiment is, at times, swayed by a complex web of political currents. According to Vancea et al. (2017), political events do wield an impact on financial markets. However, it's noteworthy that this influence doesn't have a uniform effect across all sectors.

Sentiment analysis holds a significant advantage in the realm of financial decision-making due to its capacity to offer a more holistic and nuanced comprehension of market sentiment, surpassing the insights provided by conventional financial metrics in isolation. (Cristescu et al., 2022).

1.1. Sentiment analysis

Data mining is the act of uncovering patterns, relationships, and insights from massive datasets and can help companies (Bâra & Lungu, 2012). Sentiment analysis requires data mining knowledge. Stancu et al. (2020) suggests focusing on data extraction for decision assistance to make a decision support system work well. Sentiment analysis and data mining enable firms to use textual data for sophisticated decision support, gaining a competitive edge.

Sentiment analysis also known as opinion mining, opinion extraction, sentiment mining, subjectivity analysis, affect analysis, emotion analysis, and review mining. This interdisciplinary field is concerned with analyzing and understanding people's attitudes, emotions, opinions, and sentiments (Liu, 2012). By leveraging natural language processing, machine learning, and data mining techniques, sentiment analysis aims to extract valuable insights from textual data, offering valuable applications in market research (Pang & Lee, 2008; Cambria et al., 2013).

Sentiment analysis requires massive internet data collecting and processing (Nassirtoussi et al., 2014). Web content mining – extraction of information from web documents – is central to this process (Atanasova et al., 2010). Web mining is necessary to comprehend and extract feelings from financial news stories, which are mostly posted online. Web mining gives the foundation to identify and analyze the intricacies of thoughts, feelings, and sentiments in the huge financial web material.

Investor sentiment affects asset prices and stock market behavior, according to extensive finance and behavioral economics research. There is strong evidence that investor sentiment drives the market's tendency to overreact to new information, causing excessive volatility and asset mispricing (Hong & Stein, 1999). This shows that market players' emotions and prejudices may dominate logical decision-making during moments of high sentiment, resulting in exaggerated price movements that vary from fundamentals (Zhou, 2018).

Investor sentiment and media impact asset values. Tetlock (2007) discovered that media coverage profoundly affects investors' perceptions and sentiments.

News, social media, and financial pundits can spread sentiments and affect market players. These channels' constant flow of information and narratives can affect investors' decisions and cause herding, where market participants follow prevailing sentiment rather than undertaking independent analysis.

Moreover, Investor emotions and media coverage feed each other, intensifying market dynamics. Investor sentiment drives asset price swings, which draw media attention and reinforce investor sentiment. This amplification effect can cause speculative bubbles or panics, causing market exuberance or pessimism (Da et al., 2015).

1.2. Free tools for sentiment analysis

In data science, open-source tools help organizations understand and use their data (Provost & Fawcett, 2013). Python modules like Pandas, NumPy, and scikit-learn and R and its packages offer flexible data processing, visualization, and statistical analysis. Open-source technologies let firms use cutting-edge methods, algorithms, and models without expensive proprietary software. The open-source community encourages continuous development, so these tools are updated and improved regularly, giving firms access to the latest data science advances (Peng & Matsui, 2016). Organizations can efficiently use open-source technologies to make data-driven decisions, streamline processes, and gain vital insights that drive corporate success and competitiveness in the data-centric market.

Free tools such as R, Python, and Weka have become increasingly popular in data analytics for their accessibility and versatility (Wickham & Grolemund, 2017).

There are different approaches to sentiment analysis. One involves the use of TextBlob, renowned for its straightforward usability, which is a lexicon-based sentiment. Another approach would be the use of the BERT model, a cutting-edge and context-aware approach that demonstrates a high level of proficiency in understanding intricate textual relationships (Devlin et al., 2018; Loria, n.d.; Sun et al., 2019). The BERT model is widely used as the initial layer to generate vector representations for words in a sentence. Due to its attention mechanism, the same word can have different representations depending on its context, making it well-suited for capturing nuanced relationships in text. BERT's output has been applied in predicting aspects, emotional polarity, and domain perspectives (Devlin et al., 2018; Colasanto et al., 2022; Phan & Ogunbona, 2020; Karimi et al., 2021; Xu et al., 2020). Additionally, novel models like DomBERT have been introduced to leverage BERT's capabilities for aspect detection, in combination with linguistic ideas (Xu et al., 2020; Wu et al., 2019; Li et al., 2019).

The integration of BERT's contextual information with linguistic methodologies aims to enhance the efficiency and accuracy of aspect identification in sentiment analysis tasks.

This research relies on free tools like Pandas and Matplotlib. The study's focus on moving from lexical analysis to context-aware sentiment analysis is supported by platforms like polygon.io. These free tools provide a more complete picture of human emotions and help researchers comprehend financial news sentiment. Free tools enable the democratization and automation of these strategies, which lowers barriers to entry and makes the field more accessible to individual and institutional investors.

2. Methodology

Our methodology involved data extraction from a financial news API, sentiment analysis of news titles and descriptions, storage and organization of results, and graphical representation of the sentiment trend.

The study began with the goal of analyzing the sentiment of financial news titles and their short descriptions and chose news related to Tesla Inc. as it is a highly discussed stock. We implemented a three-phase methodology. Initially, we used TextBlob, a simple lexical-based sentiment analysis tool, and subsequently, we upgraded to the BERT model, a more sophisticated, context-aware approach.

The first step in our methodology was data collection. We used the Polygon.io's news API (Polygon, n.d.) to retrieve news data. The API endpoint provided data in JSON format which included key details like the article title, the time of publishing (in UTC), and a short description of the news. Our script focused on retrieving articles that specifically related to TSLA.

Secondly, we have applied sentiment analysis to the news titles and descriptions. We used TextBlob initially, a straightforward yet effective tool that classifies text as positive, neutral, or negative based on the polarity of the words used (Loria, n.d.).

However, understanding that TextBlob's lexical approach could be limited in interpreting nuanced sentiments, we decided to utilize BERT (Devlin et al., 2018), a transformer-based model known for its ability to comprehend intricate context dependencies. The BERT model used was made available through the Hugging Face's Transformers library (Wolf et al., 2019).

Thirdly, the results of the sentiment analysis (sentiment labels and sentiment scores) were then stored in an excel file along with the corresponding news data (title, published UTC, description) in a Pandas DataFrame (McKinney, 2010). Finally, we visualized the temporal change in sentiment scores using matplotlib

(Hunter, 2007). This allowed us to gain insights into the overall sentiment trend over time regarding TSLA in the news.

The utilization of both TextBlob and BERT in our approach allows for a comprehensive comparison between a simpler lexical-based tool and a more advanced, context-aware model.

3. Results

3.1. TextBlob

The obtained Python script leverages free and open-source tools to conduct sentiment analysis on financial news. Specifically, this script retrieves Tesla (TSLA) news articles from Polygon.io's news API (Polygon, n.d.) and performs sentiment analysis on the article titles and descriptions using the TextBlob library (Loria, n.d.).

The script begins by importing the necessary libraries and modules:

```
import requests
import json
import pandas as pd
from textblob import TextBlob
import matplotlib.pyplot as plt
```

Fig. 7.1: Importing the libraries used to retrieve and parse the data

The requests and JSON libraries are used to retrieve and parse the data from Polygon.io's news API. Pandas (pd) is a powerful data manipulation library that allows us to work with structured data efficiently. TextBlob is a library for processing textual data, providing a simple API for diving into common natural language processing (NLP) tasks such as part-of-speech tagging, noun phrase extraction, sentiment analysis, and more. Matplotlib is a library for creating static, animated, and interactive visualizations in Python.

```
def get_data(api_url):
    response = requests.get(api_url)
    data = json.loads(response.text)
    articles_data = []
    for result in data['results']:
        if result.get('tickers', []) == ["TSLA"]:
            title = result.get('title', '')
            published_utc = result.get('published_utc', '')
            description = result.get('description', '')
            articles_data.append((title, published_utc, description))
    return articles_data
```

Fig. 7.2: Function for extracting news titles related to TSLA from the Polygon API

Next, the code fetches JSON data from the Polygon.io's news API:

```
def main():
    api_url = "https://api.polygon.io/v2/reference/news?ticker=TSLA&
    order=desc&limit=1000&sort=published_utc&
    apiKey=dklAHm9iNtPIfMZ20h9xtb7PXqBKI6d3"
    articles_data = get_data(api_url)
    write_to_excel(articles_data)
```

Fig. 7.3: Defining the Polygon API url

This get_data function sends a GET request to the API, and the json.loads function is used to parse the JSON response. The function is passed the ticker symbol (e.g., 'AAPL' for Apple, 'TSLA' for Tesla) and the API key as arguments.

Next, the code proceeds to define the analyze_sentiment function:

```
def analyze_sentiment(text: str):
    analysis = TextBlob(text)
    polarity = analysis.sentiment.polarity
    if polarity > 0:
        return 'Positive', polarity
    elif polarity == 0:
        return 'Neutral', polarity
    else:
        return 'Negative', polarity
```

Fig. 7.4: Sentiment analysis function using TextBlob

The analyze_sentiment function uses TextBlob to perform sentiment analysis on a given piece of text (either a title or a description). TextBlob provides a simple API for diving into common natural language processing (NLP) tasks such as part-of-speech tagging, noun phrase extraction, and sentiment analysis (Loria, n.d.). It is built on the foundations of NLTK and another package called Pattern. TextBlob returns polarity in the range of −1 to 1, where a value closer to 1 indicates a more positive sentiment, and a value closer to −1 indicates a more negative sentiment. This function categorizes the sentiment as 'Positive', 'Neutral', or 'Negative', based on the polarity, and returns both the categorized sentiment and the polarity.

The write_to_excel function creates a Pandas DataFrame from the article data, applies the analyze_sentiment function to the titles and descriptions to create new DataFrame columns for sentiment and polarity, and writes the DataFrame to an Excel file. It then plots the title and description polarities over time, giving a visual representation of sentiment trends.

```
def write_to_excel(articles_data):
    title_sentiments = []
    title_polarities = []
    description_sentiments = []
    description_polarities = []
    for article in articles_data:
        title_sentiment, title_polarity = analyze_sentiment(article[0])
        description_sentiment, description_polarity = analyze_sentiment
        (article[2])
        title_sentiments.append(title_sentiment)
        title_polarities.append(title_polarity)
        description_sentiments.append(description_sentiment)
        description_polarities.append(description_polarity)

    df = pd.DataFrame(articles_data, columns=['Title', 'Published UTC',
    'Description'])
    df['Title Sentiment'] = title_sentiments
    df['Title Polarity'] = title_polarities
    df['Description Sentiment'] = description_sentiments
    df['Description Polarity'] = description_polarities

    # DataFrame columns
    df = df[['Published UTC', 'Title', 'Title Sentiment', 'Title
    Polarity', 'Description', 'Description Sentiment', 'Description
    Polarity']]

    df.to_excel('article_data_with_sentiment.xlsx', index=False)

    # Plotting Title Polarity
    df['Title Polarity'].plot(kind='line')
    plt.title('Title Sentiment Polarity Over Time')
    plt.show()

    # Plotting Description Polarity
    df['Description Polarity'].plot(kind='line')
    plt.title('Description Sentiment Polarity Over Time')
    plt.show()
```

Fig. 7.5: Function to write to excel and plot the results of the sentiment analysis

The resulted excel file of TextBlob processer is presented in the Fig. 7.6.

A	B	C	D	E	F	G
Published UTC	Title	Title Sentiment	Title Polarity	Description	Description Sentiment	Description Polarity
2023-07-17T12:32:00Z	Why Tesla (TSLA) Might Surprise This Earning	Neutral	0	Tesla (TSLA) is seeing favor	Positive	0.227272727
2023-07-17T11:56:00Z	After years of delays, Tesla builds its first Cyt	Positive	0.25	After years of delays, Tesla	Positive	0.25
2023-07-17T09:27:02Z	Elon Musk Poses 'Top Risk' To Tesla, Says EV E	Positive	0.111111111	As the electric vehicle mark	Positive	0.082979798
2023-07-17T06:31:25Z	Why Tesla Will Likely Stay Quiet About Mode	Neutral	0	Tesla, Inc. (NASDAQ:TSLA) i	Positive	0.039166667
2023-07-16T13:52:22Z	Ahead Of Tesla's Q2 Results, Analyst Says To I	Positive	0.05	Tesla, Inc. (NASDAQ:TSLA) i	Negative	-0.066021324
2023-07-16T11:30:00Z	Tesla: Buy, Sell, or Hold?	Neutral	0	Tesla just made a strategic i	Neutral	0
2023-07-16T10:00:00Z	1 Unstoppable Stock That Could Join Apple, M	Neutral	0	The $1 trillion market capit	Negative	-0.2
2023-07-16T08:46:00Z	Tesla Has Skyrocketed by $532 Billion in Valu	Neutral	0	Up more than double so far	Positive	0.25
2023-07-16T08:45:00Z	Tesla Issues Stark Warning	Negative	-0.2	The company posted a warn	Neutral	0
2023-07-15T14:15:00Z	Tesla Is Crushing It, and We're Just Getting St	Positive	0.4	Here's everything you need	Neutral	0
2023-07-14T21:41:00Z	Is Tesla Stock a Buy?	Neutral	0	The leading EV maker has s	Neutral	0
2023-07-14T08:36:41Z	After Tesla, Warren Buffett-Backed BYD Sets	Neutral	0	This story was first publishe	Positive	0.086666667
2023-07-14T06:07:35Z	Tesla Analyst Predicts 6% Beat On Q2 EPS — (	Positive	0.45	With less than a week rema	Positive	0.015123457

Fig. 7.6: The results of the sentiment analysis using TextBlob

Thus, by utilizing these libraries and API, researchers and analysts can automate the process of collecting and analyzing the sentiment of financial news. This can assist in understanding market sentiment trends, which are increasingly recognized as influencing financial markets (Bollen et al., 2011).

3.2. BERT

We also adapted the script to use the BERT model. As it can be seen in the Fig. 7.7, we imported 'transformers' for state-of-the-art Natural Language Processing. Afterwards, the script initializes the sentiment-analysis pipeline from Hugging Face's Transformers library (Hugging Face, n.d.).

```
_bert.py
import requests
import json
import pandas as pd
import matplotlib.pyplot as plt
from transformers import pipeline

# Initialize the sentiment-analysis pipeline
nlp = pipeline("sentiment-analysis")
```

Fig. 7.7: Importing libraries that will be used for the sentiment analysis using BERT

The analyze_sentiment function is where the sentiment analysis of the text happens. In this case, it's leveraging the capabilities of a BERT model via the Hugging Face's Transformers library.

```
def analyze_sentiment(text: str) -> (str, float):
    result = nlp(text)[0]
    return result['label'], result['score']
```

Fig. 7.8: Sentiment analysis function that uses BERT

The function accepts a string of text, processes it through the BERT-based sentiment-analysis pipeline (initialized as nlp), and returns a sentiment label (Positive or Negative) and a sentiment score.

BERT (Bidirectional Encoder Representations from Transformers) is an advanced NLP model (Devlin et al., 2018). BERT is built on Transformers (Vaswani et al., 2017) and pre-trained on a large corpus of text to predict missing words in sentences and consider context from both left and right (hence the term "bidirectional"). TextBlob uses simpler methods based on lexical approaches like counting positive and negative words (Loria, n.d.).

BERT captures complex context relationships in text data during pre-training, which is essential for sentiment analysis. BERT can capture the sentiment of a word depending on its preceding and following words, while simpler approaches may not.

BERT then leverages this pre-trained information and fine-tunes it to categorize text sentiment as positive or negative, offering a more accurate and nuanced analysis than TextBlob (Sun et al., 2019).

The resulted excel file, of the BERT analyzer, is presented in the Fig. 7.9.

1	Published UTC	Title	Description	Title Sentiment	Title Score	Description Sentiment	Description Score
2	2023-07-17T06:31:25Z	Why Tesla Will Likely Stay Quiet About Model 3 Highland Launch Timeline On Q2 Call: Analyst	Tesla, Inc. (NASDAQ:TS	NEGATIVE	0.990719557	NEGATIVE	0.999361813
3	2023-07-17T01:10:00Z	After years of delays, Tesla builds its first Cybertruck	After years of delays, T	POSITIVE	0.991744697	NEGATIVE	0.989731967
4	2023-07-16T13:52:22Z	Ahead Of Tesla's Q2 Results, Analyst Says To Brace For Short-Term Margin Disappointment Bu	Tesla, Inc. (NASDAQ:TS	POSITIVE	0.999371231	POSITIVE	0.794618309
5	2023-07-16T11:30:00Z	Tesla: Buy, Sell, or Hold?	Tesla just made a strat	NEGATIVE	0.989073813	POSITIVE	0.997637272
6	2023-07-16T10:00:00Z	1 Unstoppable Stock That Could Join Apple, Microsoft, Nvidia, Amazon, and Alphabet in the $	The $1 trillion market c	NEGATIVE	0.895038545	NEGATIVE	0.998861194
7	2023-07-16T08:46:00Z	Tesla Has Skyrocketed by $532 Billion in Value This Year: Here's What Investors Need to Know	Up more than double s	NEGATIVE	0.997020304	POSITIVE	0.999094486
8	2023-07-16T08:45:00Z	Tesla Issues Stark Warning	The company posted a	NEGATIVE	0.99521178	NEGATIVE	0.9973737
9	2023-07-15T14:15:00Z	Tesla Is Crushing It, and We're Just Getting Started	Here's everything you	NEGATIVE	0.939287961	NEGATIVE	0.965362012
10	2023-07-14T21:41:00Z	Is Tesla Stock a Buy?	The leading EV maker I	NEGATIVE	0.993395627	POSITIVE	0.999344289
11	2023-07-14T08:36:41Z	After Tesla, Warren Buffett-Backed BYD Sets Sights On India's EV Market With $1B Proposal	This story was first pub	POSITIVE	0.592169166	NEGATIVE	0.987629831
12	2023-07-14T06:07:35Z	Tesla Analyst Predicts 6% Beat On Q2 EPS — But Tells Investors To Focus On 4 'More Importan	With less than a week	NEGATIVE	0.880994081	NEGATIVE	0.994796455

Fig. 7.9: The results of the sentiment analysis using BERT

4. Discussion

This paper provides an academic and practical introduction to using free sentiment analysis tools for financial news. We used a three-stage process and suggested various free tools (Pandas, NumPy, scikit-learn, Matplotlib) in the first section of the paper. We mined textual data using polygon.io's free API. Second, we used TextBlob and BERT library to analyze financial news titles' sentiment polarity. Thirdly, we showed how to analyze and export Pandas results. The analysis is three-stage and two-dimensional process, using TextBlob and BERT libraries for textual data processing.

The news was extracted from Polygon.io's, which provided a free API key, that allowed us to evaluate the polarity of the sentiment associated with each news.

In Figs. 7.6 and 7.9 it can be observed many differences between results obtained with TextBlob and BERT libraries. For example, in case of the first news, entitled "Why Tesla Will Likely Stay Quiet About Model 3 Highland Launch Timeline On Q2 Call: Analyst Weighs In", results from the TextBlob processing generated a neutral, 0, score, while the results processed with BERT generated a −0.99 negative sentiment for the title (for a scale from −1 to 1). For the description: "Tesla, Inc." (NASDAQ:TSLA) is scheduled to host its second-quarter earnings [...]. What Happened: Tesla management may not discuss the launch timing of the Model 3 [...] the sentiment score processed using TextBlob library was positive, at 0.035 (for a scale from −1 to 1), while the score processed using BERT library was negative, as −0.999 (for a scale from −1 to 1). The main difference in contrary results of the description analysis from TextBlob and BERT, outlines the limitation of simpler lexically-based tools, such as TextBlob, in comparison with context-aware models, such as BERT. TextBlob uses a NLTK (Natural Language ToolKit), being a lexicon-sentiment processor, it uses its predefined rules, based on a words dictionary and associated weights, which generate the final score, also being called rule-based sentiment analyzers. It is based on a naive Bayesian classifier and an implementation from the Pattern library (Kotelnikova et al., 2022). In contrast, BERT, a transformer-based model known for its ability to learn latent representations of words and sentences in context, being pre-trained on two tasks: language modeling and next sentence prediction. For the analyzed news, the analysis that used TextBlob identified the words from the description as being generally positive, while the BERT processing has scored a negative sentiment for the context of the description presented.

The Pearson correlation between the two results is 0.32, positive, and significant at a 10 % significance level. Results using both text processors are presented in Fig. 7.10. It can be observed not any linear correlation between the two types of processing, while there are news that are evaluated as positive by TextBlob and negative by BERT, and vice versa.

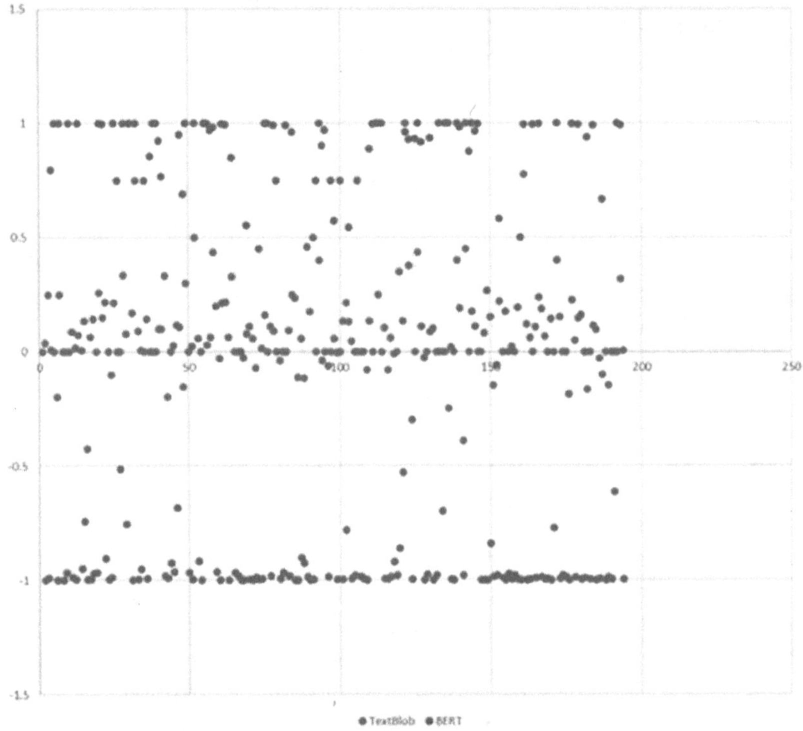

Fig. 7.10: Scatter plot of the daily prices and sentiment scores

From a deeper analysis it can be observed that TextBlob has a high rate of bias results, as seen in (Aljedaani et al., 2022) , where the probability of wrong labels cannot be overlooked where the subjectivity of human experts, the influence of the mental state, human error, and bias can lead to wrong labels. Also, in the same article, TextBlob provides a better precision than other lexicon-based processors, like VADER and Afinn (Aljedaani et al., 2022).

Recent technological progress, especially in machine learning and big data, has notably enhanced predictive analysis capabilities (Stoica & Stoica 2021) and big data analytics combined with the use of sentiment analysis may prove useful in stock market redictions.

Future research may focus on a deeper comparison between Textblob and BERT, including the confusion matrix and accuracy analysis.

5. Conclusions

The role of media in shaping general opinion and investors sentiments on future behavior of stock and other financial assets has increased since the reach of the news is made in real-time, thus the interpretation of its significance over the financial performance of the asset it is a short-time decision. Many free Lexicon-based and context-based sentiment analyzers were proposed in the present paper, of which two were used and compared, TextBlob and BERT. The analysis proposes a three-stage structure, starting with mining textual data using a free API provided by polygon.io. Secondly, by using Text Blob and BERT library we have processed textual data and evaluate the sentiment polarity of financial news titles, gained from polygon.io news repository. Thirdly, we provided an example of analysis the obtained results using Pandas (Python Data Analysis Library) and exported the results. Results show that the Pearson correlation between the two results series is 0.32, positive, and significant at a 10 % significance level.

Bibliography

Aljedaani, W., Rustam, F., Mkaouer, M.W., Ghallab, A., Rupapara, V., Washington, P.B., Lee, E., & Ashraf, I. (2022). Sentiment Analysis on Twitter Data Integrating TextBlob and Deep Learning Models: The Case of US Airline Industry. Knowledge-Based Systems. https://doi.org/10.1016/j.knosys.2022.109780.

Atanasova, T., Kasheva, M., Sulova, S., & Vasilev, J. (2010). Analysis of the Possible Application of Data Mining, Text Mining and Web Mining in Business Intelligent Systems. The 33rd International Convention MIPRO, 1294–1297. https://doi.org/10.13140/2.1.1027.5840.

Bâra, A., & Lungu, I. (2012). Improving Decision Support Systems with Data Mining Techniques. In A. Karahoca (ed.), Advances in Data Mining Knowledge Discovery and Applications. InTech. https://doi.org/10.5772/47788.

Bollen, J., Mao, H., & Zeng, X. (2011). Twitter Mood Predicts the Stock Market. *Journal of Computational Science*, 2(1), 1–8. https://doi.org/10.1016/j.jocs.2010.12.007.

Cambria, E., Schuller, B., Xia, Y., & Havasi, C. (2013). New Avenues in Opinion Mining and Sentiment Analysis. *IEEE Intelligent Systems*, 28(2), 15–21. https://doi.org/10.1109/MIS.2013.30.

Claessens, S. (2017). Global Banking: Recent Developments and Insights from Research. *Review of Finance*, 21(4), 1513–1555. https://doi.org/10.1093/rof/rfw045.

Colasanto, F., Grilli, L., Santoro, D., & Villani, G. (2022). BERT's Sentiment Score for Portfolio Optimization: A Fine-tuned View in Black and Litterman Model. *Neural Computing & Applications*, 34, 17507–17521. https://doi.org/10.1007/s00521-022-07403-1.

Cristescu, M. P., Nerişanu, R. A., Mara, D. A., & Oprea, S.-V. (2022). Using Market News Sentiment Analysis for Stock Market Prediction. Mathematics, 10(22). https://doi.org/10.3390/math10224255.

Da, Z., Engelberg, J., & Gao, P. (2015). The Sum of All FEARS Investor Sentiment and Asset Prices. *The Review of Financial Studies*, 28(1), 1–32. https://doi.org/10.1093/rfs/hhu072.

Devlin, J., Chang, M. W., Lee, K., & Toutanova, K. (2018). Bert: Pre-training of Deep Bidirectional Transformers for Language Understanding. *arXiv preprint* arXiv:1810.04805. https://doi.org/10.48550/arXiv.1810.04805.

Hong, H., & Stein, J. C. (1999). A Unified Theory of Underreaction, Momentum Trading, and Overreaction in Asset Markets. *The Journal of Finance*, 54, 2143–2184. https://doi.org/10.1111/0022-1082.00184 .

Hugging Face. (n.d.). *Transformers*. Retrieved from https://huggingface.co/transformers/.

Hunter, J. D. (2007). Matplotlib: A 2D Graphics Environment. *Computing in Science & Engineering*, 9(3), 90–95. https://doi.org/10.1109/MCSE.2007.55.

Karimi, A., Rossi, L., & Prati, A. (2021). *AEDA: An Easier Data Augmentation Technique for Text Classification*. Findings of the Association for Computational Linguistics, Findings of ACL: EMNLP 2021, 2748–2754. https://doi.org/10.18653/v1/2021.findings-emnlp.234.

Kotelnikova, A. et al. (2022). Lexicon-Based Methods vs. BERT for Text Sentiment Analysis. Lecture Notes in Computer Science (including subseries Lecture Notes in Artificial Intelligence and Lecture Notes in Bioinformatics), 13217 LNCS, pp. 71–83. https://doi.org/10.1007/978-3-031-16500-9_7.

Li, X. Bing, L., Zhang, W., & Lam, W. (2019). Exploiting BERT for End-to-End Aspect-based Sentiment Analysis. In *Proceedings of the 5th Workshop on Noisy User-generated Text (W-NUT 2019)*, pp. 34–41, Hong Kong, China. Association for Computational Linguistics. https://doi.org/10.18653/v1/d19-5505.

Liu, B. (2012). Sentiment Analysis and Opinion Mining (Synthesis Lectures on Human Language Technologies). Morgan & Claypool Publishers. ISBN-10: 1608458849.

Loria, S. (n.d.). *TextBlob: Simplified Text Processing*. Retrieved from https://textblob.readthedocs.io/en/dev/ .

McKinney, W. (2010). Data Structures for Statistical Computing in Python. In S. van der Walt & J. Millman (Eds.), Proceedings of the 9th Python in Science Conference (pp. 56–61). https://doi.org/10.25080/Majora-92bf1922-00a.

Nassirtoussi, A. K., Aghabozorgi, S., Wah, T. Y., & Ngo, D. C. L. (2014). Text Mining for Market Prediction: A Systematic Review. *Expert Systems with Applications*, 41(16), 7653–7670. https://doi.org/10.1016/j.eswa.2014.06.009.

Pang, B., & Lee, L. (2008). Opinion Mining and Sentiment Analysis. *Foundations and Trends® in Information Retrieval*, 2(1–2), 1–135. http://dx.doi.org/10.1561/1500000011.

Peng, R. D., & Matsui, E. (2016). *The Art of Data Science. A Guide for Anyone Who Works with Data*. Skybrude Consulting, LLC. ISBN 10: 1365061469.

Phan, M. H., & Ogunbona, P. O. (2020). Modelling Context and Syntactical Features for Aspect-based Sentiment Analysis. In Proceedings of the 58th Annual Meeting of the Association for Computational Linguistics, pp. 3211–3220. https://doi.org/10.18653/v1/2020.acl-main.293.

Polygon.io. (n.d.). *Stock Market Data*. Retrieved from https://polygon.io/stocks.

Provost, F., & Fawcett, T. (2013). *Data Science for Business*. O'Reilly. ISBN: 978-1-449-36132-7.

Stancu, A.R., Pompiliu, C.M., & Stoyanova, M. (2020). Data Mining Algorithms for Knowledge Extraction. In Springer Proceedings in Business and Economics. Springer International Publishing. doi: 10.1007/978-3-030-43449-6_20.

Stoica, F., & Stoica, L. F. (2021). Integrated Tool for Assisted Predictive Analytics. In D. Simian & L. F. Stoica (Eds.), Modelling and Development of Intelligent Systems (pp. 149–166). Springer International Publishing. http://dx.doi.org/10.1007/978-3-030-43449-6_20.

Sun, C., Qiu, X., Xu, Y., & Huang, X. (2019). How to Fine-tune BERT for Text Classification? In China National Conference on Chinese Computational Linguistics, pp. 194–206. Cham: Springer. https://doi.org/10.48550/arXiv.1905.05583.

Tetlock, P. C. (2007). Giving Content to Investor Sentiment: The Role of Media in the Stock Market. *The Journal of Finance*, 62, 1139–1168. https://doi.org/10.1111/j.1540-6261.2007.01232.x.

Vancea, C., Kamer-Ainur, A., & Duhnea, C. (2017). Political Uncertainty and Volatility on the Financial Markets-the Case of Romania. *Transformations in Business and Economics*, 16, 457.

Vaswani, A., Shazeer, N., Parmar, N., Uszkoreit, J., Jones, L., Gomez, A. N., Kaiser, L., & Polosukhin, I. (2017). Attention Is All You Need. *arXiv:1706.03762* [cs. CL]. https://doi.org/10.48550/arXiv.1706.03762 .

Wickham, H., & Grolemund, G. (2017). *R for Data Science: Import, Tidy, Transform, Visualize, and Model Data*. O'Reilly Media, Inc. ISBN 10: 1491910399.

Wolf, T., Debut, L., Sanh, V., Chaumond, J., Delangue, C., Moi, A., et al. (2019). HuggingFace's Transformers: State-of-the-art Natural Language Processing. *ArXiv*, abs/1910.03771.

Wu, X., Lv, S., Zang, L., Han, J., & Hu, S. (2019). Conditional BERT Contextual Augmentation. Lecture Notes in Computer Science (including subseries Lecture Notes in Artificial Intelligence and Lecture Notes in Bioinformatics), 11539 LNCS, 84–95. https://doi.org/10.1007/978-3-030-22747-0_7.

Xu, C., Baevski, A., Edunov, S., Fan, A., & Auli, M. (2020). BERT-of-Theseus: Compressing BERT by Progressive Module Replacing. In Proceedings of the 2020 Conference on Empirical Methods in Natural Language Processing (EMNLP). Stroudsburg, PA, USA: Association for Computational Linguistics, pp. 7859–7869. doi: https://doi.org/10.18653/v1/2020.emnlp-main.633.

Xu, H., Shu, L., Yu, P. S., & Liu, B. (2020). Understanding Pre-trained BERT for Aspect-based Sentiment Analysis. In Proceedings of the 28th International Conference on Computational Linguistics (COLING 2020). Retrieved from arXiv:2011.00169. https://doi.org/10.48550/arXiv.2011.00169.

Zhou, G. (2018). Measuring Investor Sentiment. *Annual Review of Financial Economics*, 10, 239–259. https://doi.org/10.1146/annurev-financial-110217-022725.

Emil Dinga

Chapter 8 On cyclicality and intrinsic rhythm in time series

Abstract: The paper aims to discuss the theoretical and methodological possibility to consider a time series (no matter the nature of its registrations) as a causally isolated one related to other time series, so to calculate an intrinsic rhythm (time) in which the continuous registrations that occur inside the economic phenomenology tend to their mean. This discussion implies the concept of (fundamental) cycle of a generic time series, which is introduced and formalized in the paper. A necessary consequence of this discussion is the concept of economic number, which is presented in Annex. The entire analysis leads to the crucial concept of the natural value (price, return and so on), that, in my opinion, must be exactly the mean of the time series, towards which it naturally goes according to its intrinsic rhythm and cycle.

Keywords: time series, cycle, intrinsic rhythm, regression towards mean, propensity

1. Introduction

Cyclicality is an intrinsic property of any social process (in this case, economic, financial, etc.) and is derived, from a logical point of view, on the one hand from the psychological traits of the individual seen as an economic agent (e.g., alternative successive 'waves' of optimism and pessimism respectively), and, on the other hand, from the normative framework of the society in question (Dinga, 2016). In particular, "responsible" for cyclicality in general are the stabilizers (either discretionary or automatic) which exist and operate both at the level of the individual and at the level of the societal normative framework. Although talking about the cycle of a time series seems a bit strange, I recall that the records/observations of a time series are only quasi-automatic reflections of the decisions and actions (that is, the behaviors) of economic agents, where those decisions and actions are always carried out within the framework of psychological, respectively normative constraints (including ethical ones). So, the cycle or cyclicality of a time series is only what we can measure, more or less adequately, from the actual cyclicality of the behavior of economic agents themselves.

Economic activities are those activities resulting from the action (acts or abstentions, as the case may be) of countless individuals pursuing their own economic goal/interest (e.g., we can accept that each of them pursues the maximization of a specific utility function, as orthodox/neoclassic economic theory proceeds). Inherently, through the simple game of chance, there is a reversion/coming back or, at least, a tendency/regression towards the mean in economic processes/phenomena. The tendency to return toward the mean is an empirical discovery of behaviorism applied in economics (Kahneman, 2012) (regression toward the mean, was only re-discovered by behavioral economics, since it was suggested by Francis Galton). The tendency towards the mean of economic phenomena is, of course, an effect of economic behavior but, in the hypothesis considered in the present study, it will be considered as a property intrinsic of the involved time series. At the same time, the tendency towards the mean (as an intrinsic property of the time series) must be considered as a propensity (in the literature (especially philosophical) dedicated to this problem, the term disposition (or, sometimes, finkish disposition) is also used, having a quasi-identical meaning – see, especially, the works of David Lewis (1997) on this subject) of this time series, i.e. as an inalienable characteristic of the series in the case.

2. About the propensity of the time series

The (modern) concept of propensity (even if not the term as such, which is, of course, subsequent and relative to the concept) is already known since Aristotle, who built his Physics (wrong, as Galileo proved) based on the necessary tendency of entities (objects) to go to their natural places. Without explicitly establishing a link between tendency and environment (or rather, the set of conditions under which a phenomenon occurs), Aristotle nevertheless captured the relationship between the type of entities in question and the type of tendency of motion, that is, he intuited a very interesting concept which today is called (relative) propensity of entities (either objects or events). Later, Thomas Aquinas held that human inclinations represent the substrate/ground of human actions (the reference to the modern concept of preference is more than obvious here) (Simboli, 2017).

From historical point of view, in modern times, the concept of propensity is due to the fact that, in Quantum Theory, where we have what is called pure/genuine indeterminism (Johansson, 2009), an objective probability of the singular case/event (the singular case is also specific to the economy (the social domain, in general), therefore the concept of propensity is very useful in the modeling (either logical or quantitative) of the economic phenomenon, although for now it is only addressed by philosophy and the theory of probabilities) is needed. As is known, in the standard ("orthodox") conception there is only one type of objective probability, namely frequential probability. This is, however, a probability of the repeatable case (namely over as long a repeating sequence as possible – ideally, an infinite sequence). The first systematic proposal of a propensity theory (of probability) belongs to Karl Popper (1959) and can be described as follows:

- an entity (object, event, process) has an internal inclination, a disposition, a tendency to pass from one state to another;
- this tendency is a property of that entity, a property called propensity;
- propensity is not an absolute property; it manifests itself, objectively, in the singular case, only in accordance with the conditions in which the event takes place;
- the propensity thus considered is the (objective) probability of the singular case (event);
- the absolute propensity (which cannot be known as such, but only through its manifestation as the disposition of the targeted entity) is invariant precisely as a result of its "declaration" as absolute. The problem here is that, being invariant, even if one accepts the derivation of the objective probability of the singular case from the relative propensity, we cannot go back from probability to propensity.

3. The cycle of time series

3.1. General considerations

By cycle of a time series I propose to understand the following properties that can be identified, by appropriate instrumental means, in the generic time series:

- what *should not* be understood by the cycle/cyclicity of a time series
  - o it is not about a resumption of the numerical values of the time series observations, with a certain periodicity. Of course, this is not a cyclical repetition of these numerical values at exactly the same level, say: $\left\{x_1^{(0)}, x_2^{(0)}, \ldots, x_n^{(0)}\right\}$, after a period k, that is: $\left\{x_{1+k}^{(1)}, x_{2+k}^{(1)}, \ldots, x_{n+k}^{(1)}\right\}$ but a more general (and more realistic) situation can also be accepted, e.g., $\left\{\alpha \cdot x_{1+k}^{(1)}, \alpha \cdot x_{2+k}^{(1)}, \ldots, \alpha \cdot x_{n+k}^{(1)}\right\}$, with α either subunit or superunitary;
  - o it is not about the so-called seasonal cyclicity, which is removed from the time series when its trend is determined;
- what *should* be understood by the cycle/cyclicity of a time series
  - o the cycle of a time series must be estimated at some levels of depth of the records/observations contained in the time series. These levels of depth

could be those indicated/suggested by my proposal in Annex, regarding the concept of economic numbers;
- o the cycle period of the time series should be established based on the determination of a certain "oscillation" of own (internal, intrinsic) rhythm/ time of the type series
- o an important issue here is the stability of this cyclicality – in other words, clear conditions/criteria must be established on the basis of which to "decide" on the cyclicality of the time series.

3.2. The own/eigen rhythm of a time series

We will equate the average value of a variable measuring an economic phenomenon (which, in turn, is "synthesized" in the time series in question) with the natural value (Dinga et al., 2020) of that phenomenon. There are several reasons for this option:

- a causally isolated time series, as we consider in this study, has already taken over all the causal/correlational/conditional impacts from the other time series (describing the other economic phenomena/processes), in addition, integrating also the reaction function of economic agents "responsible" for that time series;
- as a result, the respective time series (more precisely, the records/observations it contains) is somewhat in the equilibrium state as possible following all these interactions;
- the state of equilibrium, as we have shown above, is likely to generate natural values;
- if the individual values of the time series are likely to express natural values (or values close to natural ones), then, *a fortiori*, the average of these individual values will express, so to speak, the "most natural" value of the time series .

Based on the above, we will now determine the proper rhythm/time of a generic/ abstract time series.

Let the time series be $\mathcal{S}^{(k)} = \left\{x_1^{(k)}, x_2^{(k)}, \ldots, x_{n_{(k)}}^{(k)}\right\}$. The (time) series of coefficients of variation is formed: $\mathcal{v}_j^{(k)}$, where: for $j = 1$, the coefficient of variation refers to the individual values $x_1^{(k)}$ and $x_2^{(k)}$, for $j = 2$, the coefficient of variation refers to the individual values $x_1^{(k)}$, $x_2^{(k)}$ and $x_3^{(k)}$, in general, for $j = t$, the coefficient of variation refers to the individual values $x_1^{(k)}$, $x_2^{(k)}$,..., $x_{t+1}^{(k)}$. The (time) series of the average of the coefficients of variation is formed: $\mathcal{m}_q^{(k)}$, where: for $q = 1$, the average refers to the individual values $\mathcal{v}_1^{(k)}$ and $\mathcal{v}_2^{(k)}$, for $q = 2$, the average refers to the individual values $v_1^{(k)}$, $v_2^{(k)}$ and $v_2^{(k)}$, in general, for $q = p$, the average refers to the individual values $v_1^{(k)}$, $v_2^{(k)}$, ... $v_{p+1}^{(k)}$. So, for a given time series: $S^{(k)} = \left\{x_1^{(k)}, x_2^{(k)}, \ldots, x_{n_{(k)}}^{(k)}\right\}$, which we can call the *primary* time series, we have the following derived time series:

- *secondary* time series (series of coefficients of variation): $\mathcal{V}^{(k)} = \left\{v_1^{(k)}, v_2^{(k)}, \ldots, v_{n(k)-1}^{(k)}\right\}$;
- *tertiary* time series (of averages of coefficients of variation): $\left\{m_1^{(k)}, m_2^{(k)}, \ldots, m_{n(k)-2}^{(k)}\right\}$

Nota bene: the series of averages of the coefficients of variation must be stationary, either at the level of absolute values or at the level of differences (of different orders, as the empirical case presents itself).

I introduce, at this point, the concept of *force of regression toward the mean* – FRTM. Formally, FRTM can be described as follows:

$$\mathfrak{f}_1 \equiv v_4^{(k)} = v_3^{(k)} + (-1)^{sign} \cdot \varepsilon \cdot \left(v_3^{(k)} - m_1^{(k)}\right)$$

$$\mathfrak{f}_2 \equiv v_5^{(k)} = v_4^{(k)} + (-1)^{sign} \cdot \varepsilon \cdot \left(v_4^{(k)} - m_2^{(k)}\right)$$

$$\mathfrak{f}_{n-4} \equiv v_{n-1}^{(k)} = v_{n-2}^{(k)} + (-1)^{sign} \cdot \varepsilon \cdot \left(v_{n-2}^{(k)} - m_{n-4}^{(k)}\right)$$

$$\mathfrak{f}_{n-3} \equiv v_n^{(k)} = v_{n-1}^{(k)} + \varepsilon \cdot (-1)^{sign} \cdot \left(v_{n-1}^{(k)} - m_{n-3}^{(k)}\right)$$

where: $\mathfrak{f}_i$ is the FRTM related to the mean i of the time series of the averages of the coefficients of variation (according to the denominations above, related to the mean i of the tertiary time series); ε is a proportionality or adaptation (the possibility that the parameter ε can alternatively be considered an adaptation parameter is derived from the formal similarity of the FRTM equation to Milton Friedman's permanent income equation – and indeed, more generally, to equations containing adaptive expectations. Nota bene: not rational anticipations/expectations!) coefficient applicable to the difference between the individual value in the secondary time series and the average of the values prior to that individual value, in the tertiary time series, and the *sign* variable is defined as follows (the variable sign is similar to the well-known Kronecker symbol):

$$sign = \begin{cases} 0, & for\ v_j^{(k)} \leq m_{j-2}^{(k)} \\ 1, & for\ v_j^{(k)} > m_{j-2}^{(k)} \end{cases}$$

Of course, the f values constitute their own records of a *quaternary* time series, which we will name time series of the mean-reverting force. We always keep in mind that when we refer to the average, we have in mind the averages of the tertiary time series, that is, we have in mind the averages of the coefficients of variation (moving averages, as it follows from the proposed calculation formulas). This concept is characterized by the following:

- the function f is directly proportional to the gap between the individual value of the secondary time series and the average (found in the tertiary time series) of the individual values prior to that individual value; the degree of proportionality obviously depends on the value of the parameter ε; indeed, if $\left(v_j^{(k)} - m_{j-2}^{(k)}\right) > 0$, then $v_j^{(k)} > m_{j-2}^{(k)}$, so $sign = -1$, so individual value (of the coefficient of variation) $v_{j+1}^{(k)}$ will be "pulled" down, towards the mean;
$j+1$
conversely for the case $\left(v_j^{(k)} - m_{j-2}^{(k)}\right) < 0$: $v_j^{(k)} < m_{j-2}^{(k)}$, so $sign = 1$, so individual value (of the coefficient of variation) $v_{j+1}^{(k)}$ will be "pulled" upwards, towards the mean;
- therefore, the function f can be considered an automatic stabilizer, inside the causally isolated time series (it always acts anti-cyclically, as a result of the variable values denoted *sign*) the intensity depending, as we have already demonstrated, on the characteristics of the time series in question – namely of empirical value ε.

We formulate the following conjecture: the function f is, from a quantitative point of view, symmetrical, that is, it acts with the same intensity both when the individual value in the secondary series rises above the average, and when this value falls below the average. Obviously, we are talking about an equal intensity but of the opposite (algebraic) sign: when the individual value rises above the average, it is lowered towards the average (or, at the limit, it is lowered to the average), and when the individual value falls below the average, the individual value is raised towards average (or, at the limit, it is raised to average). On the basis of this symmetry, the analysis can be carried further, namely until the construction of a prime integral that generates a conservation law (i.e., an invariance – see, here, Noether's theorem on conservation laws). However, such a conjecture is not unproblematic, so I raise here some questions that remain to be examined elsewhere (or by other researchers interested in the matter):

- *first of all*, there is the issue of lag (respectively, symmetrically, of lead): is a deviation of an individual value $v_j^{(k)}$ from the "corresponding" mean $m_{j-2}^{(k)}$ will generate an impact, from the function f, "exactly" at the individual $v_{j+1}^{(k)}$? Why not for the individual $v_{j+\tau'}^{(k)}$, where τ is the lag? Or, symmetrically, why not, already, at $v_{j-\mu}^{(k)}$, where μ denotes the lead (or anticipation – this time, we are dealing with rational expectations, not adaptive expectations (such as those in the analytic formula of the function f_i))? Both questions are difficult and require extensive further analysis and more analytical finesse;

- *secondly*, there is the question of the relationship (including causality or, at least, conditionality) between the propensity and the function f: is it possible to formulate the conjecture that the function f expresses precisely a quantitative value of the propensity of the time series in the case? As is known, in the specialized literature, a numerical value (or some quantitative relation – such as the function f proposed here) for the propensity of a phenomenon/ process has not yet been proposed. In this sense, the function f could be a candidate for propensity "quantification" (at least for the particular case of causally isolated time series), but obviously, as in the case of the previous problem, such a line of research needs to be carried out separately and distinct.

Figure 8.1 shows a synoptic of the relationship between the four kind of time series introduced above.

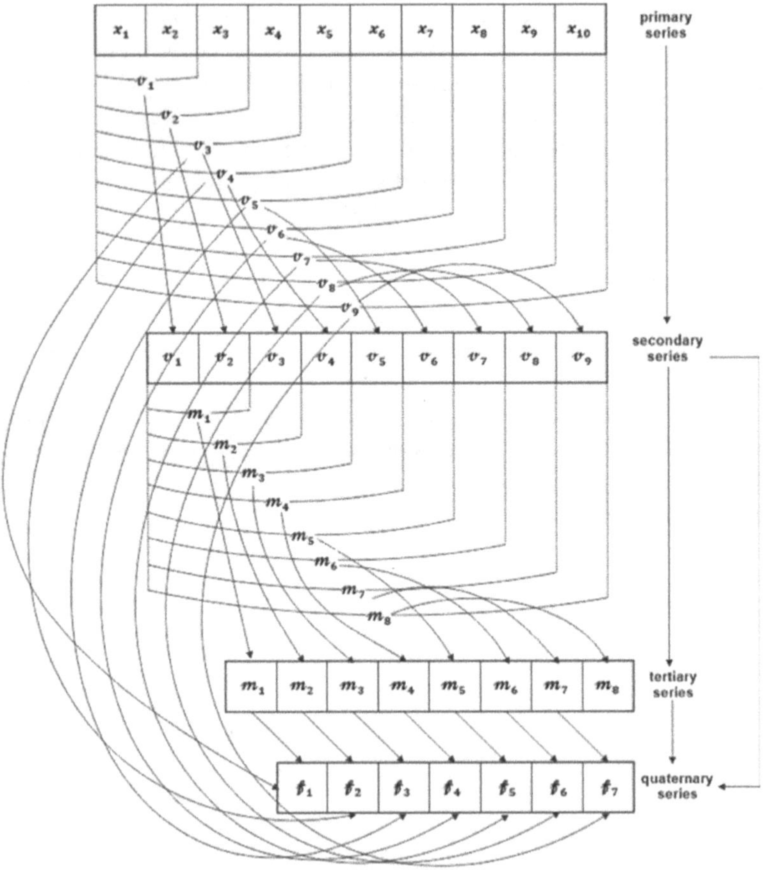

Fig. 8.1: The four kind of time series for the analysis of the eigen rhythm of the time series

Source: Created by the author

3.3. Additional comments

The proper time/pace of a time series should be understood, as previously shown, as a tendency (propensity) of that series to stabilize itself at or near its average level; although oscillations may persist around this value (which should be considered the natural value of the time series), the important thing is that these oscillations occur according to the "logic" of the function f. Suppose we have found, within a time series data, that the function f acts as an automatic stabilizer – for example, it reduces the individual value of the coefficient of variation when it rises above the mean; is this enough to establish the own (intrinsic) rhythm/time of the time series? Obviously not, since it is possible, for example, that the function no longer behaves as expected (i.e., symmetrically) if the individual value of the coefficient of variation subsequently falls below the mean, and when, therefore, the function $\mathscr{f}$ should "pull" up this individual value. We therefore argue that the natural rhythm/time of a time series can only be established after the function $\mathscr{f}$ behaves anti-cyclically (i.e., as designed) at least after producing two symmetric switches of the individual coefficients of variation . For example, if we have some number of "upward" stabilizations of individual values, no matter how large this number is, it is still not conclusive to establish the proper rhythm/time of the time series – we have to wait until at least a "down" stabilization occurs. The question arises: should the occurrence of an equal number of stabilizations in one direction be expected if, until that moment, a number of consecutive stabilizations have been recorded in the opposite direction? My view is that a negative answer must be given here (I will return to this point below, when I discuss the intrinsic cycle of the time series).

Based on the above, I will now discuss in a more analytical (and relatively more concrete) way about establishing the proper rhythm/time of the causally isolated time series.

Suppose we have a number λ^+ of consecutive cases in which the function $\mathscr{f}$ increased the individual value of the coefficient of variation in the secondary time series, after which the first case occurs in which the function $\mathscr{f}$ decreases the individual value of the coefficient of variation (we agree to write with λ^0 if the individual value of the coefficient of variation is invariant). Let us assume that there are λ^- consecutive cases of reduction of the value in question (including the first case), after which the first case of individual value increase occurs, i.e. of the λ^+ type. My view is that regardless of whether further λ^+ or λ^- type processes occur, the analysis should be stopped as sufficiently significant after the first λ^+ case (in this hypothetical description). Based on the above, the proper (intrinsic) rhythm/time of the time series is the (clock) interval between two consecutive cases of type λ^+ (of course, one can start, symmetrically with cases of λ^-, so, in this case, the proper rhythm/time is the (clock) interval between two consecutive cases of type λ^-). For example, if the recording/observation frequency in the time series is *t*: quarter, then the natural rhythm/time of that series is: $\varphi = \lambda^+ + \lambda^- + \lambda^0 + 1$. It should be noted that the calculation mode is not influenced by the fact that the action of the function $\mathscr{f}$ starts with adjustments of the type λ^+or with adjustments of the type λ^- (the reason, expressed pedantical, is that the addition, in the set of natural numbers, is commutative, i.e. $\lambda^{+} + \lambda^{-} = \lambda^{-} + \lambda^{+}$). (*Nota bene*: obviously,$\lambda^{+} \in \mathbb{N}$, and $\lambda^{-} \in \mathbb{N}$). Thus, if the recording frequency in the time series is the quarter, $\lambda^{+} = 3$, $\lambda^{-} = 2$, $\lambda^{0} = 0$, then $\varphi = 6$ quarters.

3.4. The cycle of the time series causally isolated

To examine the concept of the cycle of causally isolated time series, I will introduce the concept (well-known in economic theory) of the natural (numerical) value of an economic variable. In general, by natural value is meant a value towards which an economic phenomenon/process to which that variable is associated, fundamentally tends, through the game of oscillations generated by the actions carried out on the whole market or in the respective field. The expression *to tend fundamentally* means, of course, to make a connection between this tendency and the concept of propensity – in other words, the natural value of a variable is that (numerical) value likely to act as an attractor (e.g., the tendency towards the mean, identified by Kahneman, can be considered as such a propensity towards the natural value). Most approaches to natural values are based on considerations of economic equilibrium (generally macroeconomic), using the equilibrium model, from the simplest (Walras) to the most sophisticated (DSGE) (Boland, 2014). Within the natural value concept, the time series cycle concept can be characterized as follows:

- any cycle of the time series begins with reaching the natural value of the phenomenon described (recorded) by that time series;
- the cycle period ends when the natural value is reached again. Of course, here comes the important issue of the invariance of the natural value – I will present some considerations here:
  - o given that natural value is given by one or another configuration of causal/conditional "forces" acting (e.g., in the market, the ratio of demand and supply), it is obvious that the ratio of these forces changes over time, so the absolute invariance of the natural value cannot be conjectured;
  - o it follows that the natural value is an intrinsic property of the time series, although non-invariant;
  - o one of the most stable and idiosyncratic properties of a time series is, of course, its mean;
  - o in what follows, we will consider as the natural value of a time series the very average of that series;
- the following problem arises at this point in the discussion: the mean of a time series is the result/effect of the numerical values of the records in that time

series. In other words, we do not know what the mean of a time series is unless and after we know the numerical values of all the records in question. How exactly will we know, then, that the time series (its records) are "reverting" to the mean? The problem is fundamental, so I will develop this topic in a somewhat more analytical way:

- o indeed, here we have a principled asymmetry (more precisely, a definitional or methodological asymmetry, because it is based on the definition of the average): having the individual values, the average is unique but having the average, the individual values are not unique;
- o however, there is no need to return from the average to individual values, because the stability of the proper rhythm/time of the time series, which is of particular interest here, does not require such a return;
- o it is true, however, that for prediction needs, the own rhythm/time, based on the average of the coefficients of variation, can be used with full confidence;

- we can formulate the assumption that the natural value of the time series expresses, in a sui generis way, the proper/intrinsic time of the time series in question: more precisely, we could say that the cycle of a time series (measured from the period perspective). A cycle (in our case, an economic cycle) can have several measures/measurements (Dinga, 2016): a) amplitude; b) period; c) the trend; d) the evolutionary angle) expresses precisely the size of this proper time (or proper beat) of the time series;
  - o so, in order to establish the natural value of the time series, it is necessary to return from the mean to the individual values – in fact, in this case, one returns from the average of the coefficients of variation to the average of the individual values (so not to the individual values themselves (x_i) in the primary time series), or, in other words, from tertiary time series to primary time series;
  - o the problem of identifying the natural value (that is, the return from the mean or, equivalently, from the coefficient of variation, to the individual values) of a time series is a matter that will be addressed in another context, not being one of the objectives of the present study;
- based on the above, the definition of the cycle concept of the time series can be synthesized: a set of records/observations of that series, in which a unit of own time is produced (passes). On this basis, the cycle period of a time series is the very value of φ established above.

Nota bene: an (interesting) development of the idea of the cycle of the time series, associated with the proper rhythm or time of the series, could be in the direction of quantifying the series, that is, in the direction of establishing the amount of action or the amount of change of the series, namely, a quantum of action/change of the time series is that variation of individual values that corresponds to a cycle of the time series. Of course, this direction will not be followed in the present study, but it can be an impetus for other researchers interested in this matter.

3.5. On the fundamental cycle of a causally isolated time series

The fundamental cycle concept is a somewhat more esoteric concept that refers to the case where $\lambda^+ = \lambda^- = \lambda^0 = 1$, in other words, the case where the increase or decrease or maintenance of the individual values of coefficients of variation (secondary time series), by means of the function $\mathfrak{f}$ are alternating one after the other, without any inertia (or moment, according to the terminology adopted by financial market theory, for example). A somewhat more precise terminological variant would be the fundamental cycle period of a causally isolated generic time series.

Figure 8.2 provides a synoptic view of the own/intrinsic time, of the cycle (specifically cyclic period), of the quantum action, and of the fundamental cycle of the generic time series.

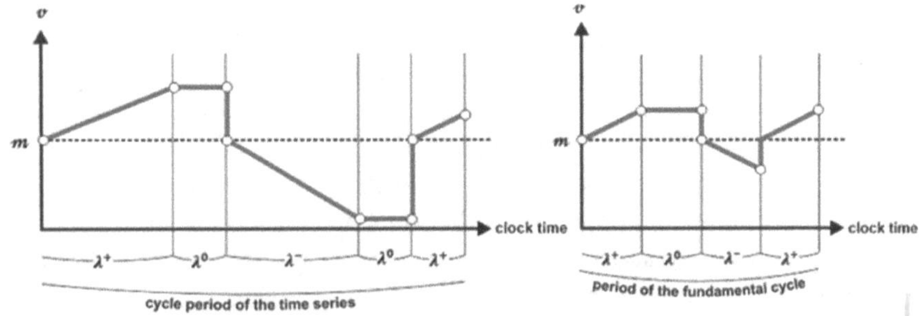

Fig. 8.2: The cyclic period of a generic time series and its fundamental cycle
Source: Created by the author

3.6. On the autonomy of the cyclicality of causally isolated time series

The question can be asked: how autonomous is the cyclicity (e.g., its own rhythm/time, so also the quantum of change/modification) of a time series. In my opinion, the important aspects in this matter are the following:

- the function $\mathscr{f}$ is dependent on the coefficients of variation ($\mathscr{v}$) and the mean ($\mathscr{m}$) of the time series; as the coefficients of variation are dependent on the individual values of the series (x), it seems, *prima facie*, that the cyclicity is dependent on the individual values of the series, i.e. we cannot speak of an autonomy (at the limit, of an invariance) of the cyclicity (i.e. of the own rhythm/time) of the time series;
- and yet, we should also consider the following aspects:
  - o the stability of a real number is the greater the greater the degree of constraint that that number has; thus, a nominal number (so to speak) has no constraint, it presents itself as such, nominally, e.g., the number 5;
  - o a sum of nominal numbers (e.g., 2+5+14), or, symmetrically, a difference, has one degree of constraint – the sum depends on the contained terms; likewise a product of several terms, or a ratio between two nominal numbers, or an index (it should be noted that it is not the number of terms that gives the degree of constraint, but the number of calculation operations that are involved: addition is involved in the sum, addition and a ratio (division) are involved in the arithmetic mean, etc);
  - o an average (of whatever type) has two degrees of constraint, because it is determined by calculating a sum, which has one degree of constraint and a ratio – the ratio of that sum to the number of terms that enter the sum (if we consider the arithmetic average. For example, the geometric mean is also of degree 2 of constraint: it involves a multiplication and a root extraction of order equal to the number of terms involved); likewise an ordinary rhythm or an average rhythm;
  - o a marginal quantity has degree of constraint three: we have two subtraction operations and one reporting operation. I mention that the degree of constraint is an additive quantity, like, for example, entropy. Moreover, it is not without interest to make a connection between entropy and the number of degrees of constraint of a (real) number: thus, for example, one could conjecture that entropy is inversely proportional to the number of degrees of constraint. In this way, a new meaning of entropy could be established, namely that of the degree of stability of a number, in addition to the now majority one, namely of the degree of order/organization of a process/ system;
  - o an elasticity has degree of constraint five: we have two rhythms, each with degree of constraint two, and a reporting;
- let's apply these reasonings to the case of the function $\mathscr{f}$:
  - o from the formal relation of the function $\mathscr{f}$:

$\mathscr{f}_i \equiv \mathscr{v}_{i+3}^{(k)} = \mathscr{v}_{i+2}^{(k)} + (-1)^{sign} \cdot \varepsilon \cdot \left(\mathscr{v}_{i+2}^{(k)} - \mathscr{m}_i^{(k)}\right)$, with $i = \overline{1,(n-3)}$

- it follows that we have the following degrees of constraint (algebraically additive):
  - o for the variable $\mathscr{v}$: calculation of the dispersion of individual values from the primary time series (x_i): (1) calculation of the average: 2 cd (by cd we denote the constraint degree); (2) calculation of the difference between the individual values and the mean: 1 cd; (3) squaring the above difference: 1 cd; (4) sum of squared differences: 1 cd; (5) reporting to $n-1$, where n is the number of terms of the primary time series: 1 cd; (6) calculation of the standard deviation: 1 cd. So the cd number of the variable $\mathscr{v}$ is: 6
- for variable $\mathscr{m}$: (1) summation of values of variable $\mathscr{v}$: 1 cd; (2) reporting the amount to the number of values taken into account: 1 cd. So the cd number of variable $\mathscr{m}$: 2
- for the difference $\left(\mathscr{v}_{i+2}^{(k)} - \mathscr{m}_i^{(k)}\right)$: cd number is 1
- for the product $\varepsilon \cdot \left(\mathscr{v}_{i+2}^{(k)} - \mathscr{m}_i^{(k)}\right)$: cd number is 1
- for the sum $\mathscr{v}_{i+2}^{(k)} + (-1)^{sign} \cdot \varepsilon \cdot \left(\mathscr{v}_{i+2}^{(k)} - \mathscr{m}_i^{(k)}\right)$: cd number is 1

Summing up all the constraint degrees we arrive at a number of 11. Obviously, with such a number of constraints, the function $\mathscr{f}$ seems particularly stable, so somehow it "qualifies" to identify/calculate a quasi-invariance for a generic time series, causally isolated, like the proper rhythm/time of such a series.

Bibliography

Boland, L.A. (2014). *Model Building in Economics: Its Purposes and Limitations.* Cambridge University Press.

Dinga, E. (2016). *Economic Cyclicality* (in Romanian: *Ciclicitatea Economică*). Bucharest: Ed. Academiei Române.

Dinga, E., Tănăsescu, C.-R., & Ionescu, G.-M. (2020). Social Entropy and Normative Network. *Entropy* (Basel), 22(9), 1051. doi: 10.3390/e22091051.

Johansson, L.-G. (2009). Propensities. *Uppsala Philosophical Studies*, 57, 161–175.

Kahneman, D. (2012). *Thinking, Fast and Slow.* Penguin.

Lewis, D. (1997). Finkish Dispositions. *The Philosophical Quarterly*, 47(187), 143–158.

Popper, K. (1959). The Propensity Interpretation of Probability. *The British Journal for the Philosophy of Science*, 10(37).

Simboli, B. (2017). *An Aristotelian-Thomistic Propensity Theory of Probability: Towards a 'Naturalized' Social Science and Econometrics*, http://dx.doi.org/10.2139/ssrn.2711887

Annex: The economic number

1. *Measure/measurement stability*

From the perspective of the problem discussed above – the stability of a measure (or measurements) as a function of the number of degrees of constraint to which the measure is subjected (to which it endures) (the real number, in the last instance) I will now discuss a proposal, which I make here, and which can help economic analysis, both for the special case of the subject of the present study, and for more general (and, of course, more frequent) cases. The question therefore arises: how stable is a measure (more precisely, a measurement) of a record/observation in the time series? This is an old problem, of course, but satisfactory solutions have not been found, at least for the social (in this case, economic) field. According to my information, a theory that comes very close to providing a solution in the matter is the so-called complexity theory (Nota bene: I have insisted many times and in many places on this erroneous name, so we give up and here), or chaos theory (deterministic) or, still, the theory of non-linear dynamic systems – namely through the concepts of attractor and source respectively. In my opinion, a topological approach is much more appropriate in this sense (what I propose here is a topological approach). When I say that no satisfactory solutions have been given to the problem of the stability of the measure/measurement, I am not referring to the field of mathematics, where, obviously, such solutions were given a long time ago, but to the economic field (the application of mathematical solutions to processes/phenomena economics cannot be considered a solution to the problem – I recall here the *homo œconomicus mathematical model* which is undoubtedly a resounding failure rewarded, unfortunately, with too many Nobel prizes).

Next, I propose a method very simple (and subjective enough, like the Bayesian Probability – but, probably, in the economic phenomenon the subjectivity should be dominant) to ensure the stability of the measure/measurement, based on the concept of economic number.

2. *Degrees of calculation of numerical values – the concept of economic number*

Any economic phenomenon, to the extent that a numerical value can be associated with it, can be considered to take place in a four-dimensional space:

- a nominal dimension: n
- a temporal dimension: t

- an intensive dimension: c
- an extensive dimension: e

Future economic phenomena (not yet produced, but possibly produced) are characterized by uncertainty. By uncertainty we mean the current impossibility of deciding on the exact (punctual) numerical values that must be associated with future phenomena. In this sense, from our point of view, uncertainty is also the source of what we call risks: by risk we mean an eventuality that the economic phenomenon of interest has, in the considered time horizon, an associated numerical value that exceeds (in algebraic module) the acceptable margin (of for example, from the perspective of expected profit). I will give some definitions:

- the nominal dimension (n) is given by the very numerical value associated with that phenomenon;
- the temporal dimension (t) is given by the time horizon to which the nominal value in question refers (as a result, the nominal value of a future phenomenon must be adjusted to include a measure of this uncertainty; this measure must also be numerical, to be able to add up to the nominal value);
- the intensive dimension (c) is given by the degree of calculation of the nominal value of interest; the degree of calculation is important because, depending on it, the nominal value presents a lower or higher uncertainty; the uncertainty generated by the degree of calculation depends, inversely proportionally, on the stability of the nominal quantity in question, and this stability depends, directly proportionally, on the degree of calculation;
- the extensive dimension (e) is given by the degree of aggregation of the economic size signified by the nominal value in question.

For the *nominal* dimension (numerical values for n) we have the values as given (standard real numbers)

For the *temporal* dimension (numerical values for t), I propose:

- for the current period: $t = 1$
- for a double period: $t = 2$
- for a triple period: $t = 3$
- for a period 4 times longer: $t = 4$
- for a period five times greater: $t = 5$
- for a period 6 times greater or greater than $t = 6$

Nota bene: beyond a sixfold multiplication of the time interval one can admit an uncertainty so relevant to the observer that its further increase is no longer meaningful.

For the *intensive* dimension (the numerical values for c), I propose:

- for absolute nominal values (minimum degree of calculation, therefore maximum instability): $c = 6$
- for nominal absolute values applied to themselves (averages, differences of order 1): $c = 5$
- for relative nominal values (indices, rhythms): $c = 4$
- for marginal nominal values or for differences of order 2: $c = 3$
- for nominal values of elasticities: $c = 2$
- for normative type nominal values (maximum degree of calculation): $c = 1$

For the *extensive* dimension (numerical values for e), I propose:

- for nominal values related to the generic individual (average): $e = 6$
- for nominal values related to microeconomic systems (economic actors): $e = 5$
- for nominal values related to mesoeconomic (regional) systems: $e = 4$
- for nominal values related to macroeconomic systems: $e = 3$
- for nominal values related to sub-global integrated economic systems: $e = 2$
- for nominal values related to global economic systems: $e = 1$

Based on the above, any economic quantity related to an economic phenomenon can be written in the form of a quaternion (I remind that the concept of quaternion was proposed by the Irish mathematician William Rowan Hamilton in 1843, being intended for application in three-dimensional space, especially for rotation operations, which constitute a group of transformations). A quaternion is written: $a + bi + cj + dk$, under the condition $i^2 = j^2 = k^2 = ijk = -1$):

$n_f = n + it + jc + ke$, where n_f is the value of the economic number

Nota bene: here the quantities i, j, k are the established quantities from the analytical form of the quaternion (e.g., for the case of a 'relative' with only two dimensions of the quaternion, i.e. in the case of a complex number, we will have $n_f = n + it$).

Since the theory of quaternions is well developed by mathematicians, economists can simply borrow that technology to work with their own quaternions.

The transformation of the quaternion into a nominal economic number can be done based on the following algorithm:

- *Step 1*: calculation of the adjustment operator (ξ): $\xi(n_f) = \log_2(t \cdot c \cdot e)$
- *Step 2*: calculation of the generic nominal calibration adjustment (δ): $\delta = n \cdot \xi / 100$
- *Step 3*: calculation of the adjusted nominal value $(\tilde{n}_f)$:$\tilde{n}_f = n \mp \delta$
- *Step 4*: forming the numerical range (one-dimensional real space): $\tilde{n}_f \in [n - \delta, n + \delta]$

Nota bene: it is easy to see that, here, things happen in a similar way to what happens in the case of fuzzy sets (the adjustment operator only sets the limits – left-right – of the membership set of an object to a considered set, which, in fuzzy logic, makes the membership function).

So the adjustment operator transforms a zero-dimensional quantity (a real number) into a one-dimensional quantity (a real interval).

Nota bene: of course, one can investigate how, in turn, a one-dimensional quantity can be transformed, by a suitable operator, into a two-dimensional quantity (i.e., a surface), etc.

Based on the above, I will make a proposal to simplify the formalism of the quaternion, which can be written, in a simplified form, as follows:

$$n_f = n + it + jc + ke \equiv n_{tce}$$

Nota bene: it is noted that the writing proposal is analogous to Einstein's proposal to simplify the writing of a mathematical tensor.

An (didactic) illustration of the above is as follows (this way of writing and operating with the real numbers associated with economic phenomena could be useful in making non-point predictions, but without using fuzzy theory (which is excessively subjective in the area of setting the values of set membership functions). Needless to say, probabilities are no longer needed either, since we no longer have statistical probability distributions at large numbers. In the case of this proposal, a certain (initial) subjectivity is contained in the establishment of the classes of values for t, c, and e, but even here the objective character can be greatly increased by putting into public debate the number of these classes and the content of each. In this way, uncertainty would be treated according to its nature, without all the distortions that confuse uncertainty with risk (despite Knight's long-advised cautions). Moreover, by using these numbers, which I call *economic numbers*, the risk is no longer just a complete *ex ante* calculation problem, namely a *complete* calculation problem):

Be a nominal current value equal to 3 (i.e., $n = 3$); let us presuppose it is desired to calculate this value for:

- a time horizon equal to 4 (so, $t = 4$)
- a quantity of marginal type (so, $c = 2$)
- for a macroeconomic phenomenon (so, $e = 2$)

Then the quaternion will have the expression:: $n_f = 3 + i4 + j2 + k2 \equiv 3_{422}$

The way to calculate the 'correction' to be applied to dimension 3 is as follows:

- we calculate the nominal adjustor: $\xi(3_{422}) = \delta = \log_2(4 \cdot 2 \cdot 2) = \log_2 4 + \log_2 2 + \log_2 2 = 4$
- then we calculate the calibrated nominal adjustor is: $\tilde{\delta} = n \cdot \frac{\delta}{100} = 3 \cdot \frac{4}{100} = 0.12$
- then the adjusted nominal value is: $\tilde{n}_f = n \mp \tilde{\delta} = 3 \mp 0.12$, i.e., the real range is reached: $\tilde{n}_f \in [2.88; 3.12]$, which replaces the point value 3.

Vasile Brătian and Camelia Oprean-Stan

Chapter 9 Option pricing using the Black-Scholes methodology vs. using the Feynman-Kac theorem: Comparative approach

Abstract: Two methods of pricing option derivatives are discussed in this chapter with the main goal of capturing potential variations between call and put prices. The application of the Black-Scholes methodology for the selection of explicit solutions for Call and Put is one approach we will first take into consideration in this regard. Similar to the heat equation in physics, where we find words like diffusion in a homogeneous medium, reaction, and convection, the Black-Scholes equation, which underlies the explicit solutions for Call and Put, is a differential equation with second-order random variables. We'll also take into account using the Feynman-Kac Theorem in conjunction with Monte Carlo simulations to estimate the value of the underlying asset at maturity. These types of simulations enable the generation of potential outcomes in relation to the stochastic evolution of the underlying asset at various future maturities. The empirical findings obtained by using the two methods mentioned above do not show any significant variations in European-style option prices. The DAX stock index is used as the underlying asset when calculating the results for European call and put options.

Keywords: the Black-Scholes equation, explicit solutions for Call and Put, Feynman-Kac theorem, Monte Carlo simulations

1. Introduction

The Black-Scholes equation, the explicit solutions for the European Call and Put, and the application of this methodology to the underlying asset of the DAX (GDAXI) stock index are presented in the following sections. The numerical findings obtained are then compared to those produced using Monte Carlo simulations of the underlying asset at various maturities of the option derivative using the Feynman-Kac theorem for determining Call and Put prices.

The Black-Scholes equation was developed in 1969 by Fisher Black and Myron Scholes, creating a million-billion-dollar industry (Stewart, 2013), and was published in 1973, when the first regulated market for standardized, tradable options was born in Chicago. Contributions to the mathematical model, developed by Fisher Black and Myron Scholes for option pricing, were later made by Robert Merton, producing extensions of it, a mathematical model accepted by academia and the industry as a robust model (Karoui et al.,1998).

Explicit solutions for European-type calls and puts provide academics and investors with a rational way to price options and are a very important contribution to the field of finance (Copeland & Weston, 1988). Did it contribute to the 2007 financial crisis or not? Opinions are divided (Smith, January 21/2008, *Daily News*; Pollak, April 30/2012, *Financial Times*; Stewart, February 12/2012, *The Guardian*; Weatherall, February14/2013, *Financial Times*). Here we recall another critique of the Black-Scholes model found in Haug and Taleb (2011).

However, an alternative to the Black-Scholes methodology is based on Monte Carlo simulation of the underlying asset's future price. In this way, the price for Call and Put can be determined using Monte Carlo simulation in the form of various scenarios on the evolution of the price of the underlying asset and the Feynman-Kac theorem. The Feynman-Kac theorem relates stochastic processes to parabolic partial differential equations (PDEs), and the Black-Scholes equation is an equation that obeys these characteristics.

Therefore, as can be seen from the above, solving the Black-Scholes equation can be done mainly by two methods (Negrea & Damian, 2015):

- by using the classical theory of solving equations with parabolic partial derivatives;
- by Monte Carlo simulations of the price of the underlying asset at option maturity and using the Feynman-Kac theorem, thus providing a probabilistic solution to this equation.

2. Methodology

We will provide the methodology in the following order: we will define the concept of option derivatives and categories; we will present the Black-Scholes equation and the explicit solutions for European-type Call and Put; and we will present the Feynman-Kac theorem utilized for option pricing.

2.1. On the concept of option and categories

The concept of option means a derivative or derivative product characterized by the following sufficient predicates:

- it is a forward contract;
- it is based on an underlying asset (share, bond, stock index, etc.);
- it is conditional on the buyer (it gives the buyer the right, but not the obligation, to buy or sell the underlying asset at maturity at the strike price; the seller has the right, but also the obligation, to sell or buy the underlying asset at maturity at the strike price).

The categories of options are:

1. Call option, with the following sufficient predicates: (a) the buyer has the right, but not the obligation, to buy in the future a quantity of the underlying asset at the strike price, hoping that the price of the underlying asset will rise; (b) the seller has the obligation, at the buyer's request, to sell in the future a quantity of the underlying asset at the strike price, hoping that the price will fall;
2. Put option, with the following sufficient predicates: (a) the buyer has the right, but not the obligation, to sell in the future a quantity of the underlying asset at the strike price, hoping that the price of the underlying asset will fall; (b) the seller has the obligation, at the buyer's request, to buy in the future a quantity of the underlying asset at the strike price, hoping that the price will rise.

2.2. On the Black-Scholes equation and explicit solutions for Call and Put

The mathematical model developed by Black and Scholes is based on a number of assumptions (Black & Scholes, 1973), namely: "the short-term interest rate is known and is constant through time; the stock price follows a random walk in continuous time with a variance rate proportional to the square of the stock price. Thus, the distribution of possible stock prices at the end of any finite interval is lognormal. The variance rate of the return on the stock is constant; the stock pays no dividends or other distributions; the option is "European", that is, it can only be exercised at maturity; there are no transaction costs in buying or selling the stock or the option; it is possible to borrow any fraction of the price of a security to buy it or to hold it, at the short-term interest rate; there are no penalties to short selling. A seller who does not own a security will simply accept the price of the security from a buyer, and will agree to settle with the buyer on some future date by paying him an amount equal to the price of the security on that date".

2.2.1. The Black-Scholes equation

To obtain the Black-Scholes equation we consider the following (Brătian et al., 2016; Brătian, 2018) assumptions of the above mathematical model: we note with $V = V(S,t)$ the option value, given by two factors (S = price of the underlying asset and t = time moment); we denote by Π the value of a portfolio consisting of a long position on one unit of the derivative and a short position on a quantity of the underlying asset (ΔS).

On the basis of these notations above, we can write successively the following (Wilmott, 2007; Brătian, 2019):

$$\Pi = V - \Delta S \tag{1}$$

We know that the dynamics of the underlying asset price is in the form of a geometric Brownian motion (GBM):

$$dS = \mu S dt + \sigma S dB \tag{2}$$

The infinitesimal dynamics (from t to $t+dt$) of the portfolio value is given by the following formal expression:

$$d\Pi = dV - \Delta dS \tag{3}$$

We know that $V = V(S,t)$ and using Taylor series development for dV, we obtain:

$$\begin{aligned} dV &= \sum_{k=1}^{\infty} \frac{1}{k!}\left(\frac{\partial V}{\partial S} dS + \frac{\partial V}{\partial t} dt\right)^k = \\ &= \frac{\partial V}{\partial S} dS + \frac{\partial V}{\partial t} dt + \frac{1}{2}\left(\frac{\partial V}{\partial S} dS + \frac{\partial V}{\partial t} dt\right)^2 + R = \\ &= \frac{\partial V}{\partial S} dS + \frac{\partial V}{\partial t} dt + \frac{1}{2}\left(\frac{\partial^2 V}{\partial S^2} dS^2 + \frac{\partial^2 V}{\partial t^2} dt^2 + 2\frac{\partial^2 V}{\partial S \partial t} dS dt\right) \end{aligned} \tag{4}$$

where: $R \approx 0$

In stochastic calculus we know that:

$$dt \cdot dt = 0; dt \cdot dB = 0; dB \cdot dB = dt \tag{5}$$

From (4) and (5) we have:

$$dV = \frac{\partial V}{\partial t} dt + \frac{\partial V}{\partial S} dS + \frac{1}{2}\sigma^2 S^2 \frac{\partial^2 V}{\partial S^2} dt \tag{6}$$

From (3) and (6) we have:

$$d\Pi = \frac{\partial V}{\partial t} dt + \frac{\partial V}{\partial S} dS + \frac{1}{2}\sigma^2 S^2 \frac{\partial^2 V}{\partial S^2} dt - \Delta dS \tag{7}$$

Terms containing dS in equation (7) are portfolio risk terms. Thus, if we want to eliminate risk, we will have $\left(\frac{\partial V}{\partial S}dS - \Delta dS\right) = 0$ which implies: $\left(\frac{\partial V}{\partial S} - \Delta\right)dS = 0$.

As a result, if the portfolio is completely risk-free, the portfolio dynamics are:

$$d\Pi = \frac{\partial V}{\partial t}dt + \frac{1}{2}\sigma^2 S^2 \frac{\partial^2 V}{\partial S^2}dt \Rightarrow d\Pi = \left(\frac{\partial V}{\partial t} + \frac{1}{2}\sigma^2 S^2 \frac{\partial^2 V}{\partial S^2}\right)dt \tag{8}$$

If the portfolio dynamics are completely risk-free, then this can be considered equivalent to remunerating an amount of money, the size of the portfolio, at a risk-free interest rate (r).

In the above sense, we will have:

$$\begin{aligned} &d\Pi = r\Pi dt = \\ &= \int_0^t \frac{1}{\Pi} d\Pi = r\int_0^t dt = \\ &= \ln \Pi(t) = \ln \Pi(0) + \ln e^{rt} = \\ &= \Pi(t) = \Pi(0)\cdot e^{rt} \end{aligned} \tag{9}$$

As a result, from equations (8) and (9) we have:

$$\left(\frac{\partial V}{\partial t} + \frac{1}{2}\sigma^2 S^2 \frac{\partial^2 V}{\partial S^2}\right)dt = r\Pi dt$$

$$\frac{\partial V}{\partial t} + \frac{1}{2}\sigma^2 S^2 \frac{\partial^2 V}{\partial S^2} = r\Pi \tag{10}$$

From equation (1) and knowing that $\Delta = \frac{\partial V}{\partial S}$, we have:

$$\Pi = V - \frac{\partial V}{\partial S}S \tag{11}$$

As a result, from (11) and (10) we have:

$$\frac{\partial V}{\partial t} + \frac{1}{2}\sigma^2 S^2 \frac{\partial^2 V}{\partial S^2} = r\left(V - \frac{\partial V}{\partial S}S\right)$$

$$\frac{\partial V}{\partial t}+\frac{1}{2}\sigma^2 S^2\frac{\partial^2 V}{\partial S^2}+rS\frac{\partial V}{\partial S}-rV=0 \tag{12}$$

Equation (12) represents the Black-Scholes equation, being a second order parabolic differential equation, similar to the heat equation in physics.

2.2.2. On explicit solutions for Call and Put

The Black-Scholes equation (12) does not specify which type of option, Call or Put, is being valued. But what we do know is that its price is a function of the value of the underlying asset at maturity (*T*). As a result, we must write a function $V(S_T,T)$ representing the profit or loss at maturity for each type of option. So we have (Wilmott, 2002):

1. For Call: $C=V(S_T,T)=max(S_T-E,0)=Payoff(S)$ (13)
2. For Put: $P=V(S_T,T)=max(E-S_T,0)=Payoff(S)$ (14)

where: S_T = the price of the underlying asset at maturity; E = the strike price.

The explicit solution for the Call option can be determined as follows (Negrea, 2006; Brătian et al., 2016):

(a) If we take into account the time remaining until the deadline $(T-t=\tau)$ of the Call option, under a risk-neutral probability, the option price is given by the following expression:

$$C=V(S,t)=e^{-r(T-t)}E^{Q}\left[max(S_T-E,0)|F_t)\right] \tag{15}$$

where: E^Q = expectation under a risk-neutral probability.

(b) The expectation of a continuous random variable is given by the following expression:

$$E[X]=\int_{-\infty}^{+\infty} xf_X(x)dx \tag{16}$$

(c) Applying expression (16) to expression (15), we have:

$$C=e^{-r(T-t)}\int_{-\infty}^{+\infty}\max(S_T-E,0)f(S_T)dS_T \tag{17}$$

or, otherwise written:

$$C = \frac{\int_{-\infty}^{+\infty} \max(S_T - E, 0) f(S_T) dS_T}{e^{r\tau}} \tag{18}$$

(d) Price of the underlying asset at maturity (S_T) can be written as follows: $S_T = Se^R$, where $R = ln\frac{S_T}{S}$ is the return on the underlying asset at maturity.

In this sense, the option price C can be written as follows:

$$C = \frac{\int_{-\infty}^{+\infty} \max(Se^R - E, 0) f(R) dR}{e^{r\tau}} \tag{19}$$

(e) Since R obeys the normal law, the distribution density of R, $f(R)$ is given by the following expression:

$$f(R) = \frac{1}{\sigma\sqrt{2\pi\tau}} e^{-\frac{\left[R - \left(r - \frac{1}{2}\sigma^2\right)\tau\right]^2}{2\sigma^2\tau}}, \tag{20}$$

and the distribution function (distribution) of R is given by the following expression:

$$F(R) = \frac{1}{\sigma\sqrt{2\pi\tau}} \int_{-\infty}^{+\infty} e^{-\frac{\left[R - \left(r - \frac{1}{2}\sigma^2\right)\tau\right]^2}{2\sigma^2\tau}} dR \tag{21}$$

(f) Substituting into expression (19) expression (20), we obtain:

$$C = \frac{\int_{-\infty}^{+\infty} \max(Se^R - E) \frac{1}{\sigma\sqrt{2\pi\tau}} e^{-\frac{\left[R - \left(r - \frac{1}{2}\sigma^2\right)\tau\right]^2}{2\sigma^2\tau}} dR}{e^{r\tau}}, \tag{22}$$

expression that can be written like this:

$$C = e^{-r\tau} \int_{-\infty}^{+\infty} \max\left(Se^{R} - E\right) \frac{1}{\sigma\sqrt{2\pi\tau}} e^{-\frac{\left[R-\left(r-\frac{1}{2}\sigma^2\right)\tau\right]^2}{2\sigma^2\tau}} dR \tag{23}$$

(g) Next, to remove the *max* function from expression (23) use the fact that $Se^{R} \geq E \leftrightarrow R \geq ln\frac{E}{S}$ and as such we have:

$$C = e^{-r\tau} \int_{ln\frac{E}{S}}^{+\infty} \left(Se^{R} - E\right) \frac{1}{\sigma\sqrt{2\pi\tau}} e^{-\frac{\left[R-\left(r-\frac{1}{2}\sigma^2\right)\tau\right]^2}{2\sigma^2\tau}} dR \tag{24}$$

$$\Rightarrow$$

$$C = e^{-r\tau} Se^{R} \int_{ln\frac{E}{S}}^{+\infty} \frac{1}{\sigma\sqrt{2\pi\tau}} e^{-\frac{\left[R-\left(r-\frac{1}{2}\sigma^2\right)\tau\right]^2}{2\sigma^2\tau}} dR - e^{-r\tau} E \int_{ln\frac{E}{S}}^{+\infty} \frac{1}{\sigma\sqrt{2\pi\tau}} e^{-\frac{\left[R-\left(r-\frac{1}{2}\sigma^2\right)\tau\right]^2}{2\sigma^2\tau}} dR$$

$$\Rightarrow$$

$$C = S \int_{ln\frac{E}{S}}^{+\infty} e^{R-r\tau} \frac{1}{\sigma\sqrt{2\pi\tau}} e^{-\frac{\left[R-\left(r-\frac{1}{2}\sigma^2\right)\tau\right]^2}{2\sigma^2\tau}} dR - e^{-r\tau} E \int_{ln\frac{E}{S}}^{+\infty} \frac{1}{\sigma\sqrt{2\pi\tau}} e^{-\frac{\left[R-\left(r-\frac{1}{2}\sigma^2\right)\tau\right]^2}{2\sigma^2\tau}} dR \tag{25}$$

(h) If a change of variable is made $v = \sqrt{\frac{\left[R-\left(r-\frac{1}{2}\sigma^2\right)\tau\right]^2}{\sigma^2\tau}} =$

$= \frac{R-\left(r-\frac{1}{2}\sigma^2\right)\tau}{\sigma\sqrt{\tau}}$, term $\int_{ln\frac{E}{S}}^{+\infty} \frac{1}{\sigma\sqrt{2\pi\tau}} e^{-\frac{\left[R-\left(r-\frac{1}{2}\sigma^2\right)\tau\right]^2}{2\sigma^2\tau}} dR$ can be written as follows:

$$\int_{ln\frac{E}{S}}^{+\infty} \frac{1}{\sigma\sqrt{2\pi\tau}} e^{-\frac{\left[R-\left(r-\frac{1}{2}\sigma^2\right)\tau\right]^2}{2\sigma^2\tau}} dR = \int_{-z_2}^{+\infty} \frac{1}{\sqrt{2\pi}} e^{-\frac{v^2}{2}} dv$$

where: $z_2 = \dfrac{ln\frac{S}{E} + \left(r - \frac{1}{2}\sigma^2\right)\tau}{\sigma\sqrt{\tau}}$

(i) Further, knowing that: $\int_{-z_2}^{+\infty} \frac{1}{\sqrt{2\pi}} e^{-\frac{v^2}{2}} dv = \int_{-\infty}^{z_2} \frac{1}{\sqrt{2\pi}} e^{-\frac{v^2}{2}} dv$, the term

$$\int_{ln\frac{E}{S}}^{+\infty} \frac{1}{\sigma\sqrt{2\pi\tau}} e^{-\frac{\left[R-\left(r-\frac{1}{2}\sigma^2\right)\tau\right]^2}{2\sigma^2\tau}} dR = \int_{-z_2}^{+\infty} \frac{1}{\sqrt{2\pi}} e^{-\frac{v^2}{2}} dv = \int_{-\infty}^{z_2} \frac{1}{\sqrt{2\pi}} e^{-\frac{v^2}{2}} dv = \tag{26}$$
$$= \Phi(z_2)$$

(j) Also making the same variable change, $v = \dfrac{R - \left(r - \frac{1}{2}\sigma^2\right)\tau}{\sigma\sqrt{\tau}}$ for the term:

$\int_{ln\frac{E}{S}}^{+\infty} e^{R-r\tau} \frac{1}{\sigma\sqrt{2\pi\tau}} e^{-\frac{\left[R-\left(r-\frac{1}{2}\sigma^2\right)\tau\right]^2}{2\sigma^2\tau}} dR$ wewillhave: $\int_{ln\frac{E}{S}}^{+\infty} e^{R-r\tau} \frac{1}{\sigma\sqrt{2\pi\tau}} e^{-\frac{\left[R-\left(r-\frac{1}{2}\sigma^2\right)\tau\right]^2}{2\sigma^2\tau}} dR =$

$$= \int_{-z_2}^{+\infty} e^{\left(r\tau - \frac{1}{2}\sigma^2\tau + v\sigma\sqrt{\tau} - r\tau\right)} \frac{1}{\sqrt{2\pi}} e^{-\frac{v^2}{2}} dv$$

$$\Rightarrow$$

$$\int_{-z_2}^{+\infty} e^{\left(r\tau - \frac{1}{2}\sigma^2\tau + v\sigma\sqrt{\tau} - r\tau\right)} \frac{1}{\sqrt{2\pi}} e^{-\frac{v^2}{2}} dv = \int_{-z_2}^{+\infty} \frac{1}{\sqrt{2\pi}} e^{-\frac{\left(v-\sigma\sqrt{\tau}\right)^2}{2}} dv$$

(k) Next, if the variable change is made $u = v - \sigma\sqrt{\tau}$ then:

$$\int_{-z_2}^{+\infty} \frac{1}{\sqrt{2\pi}} e^{-\frac{(v-\sigma\sqrt{\tau})^2}{2}} dv = \int_{-z_2-\sigma\sqrt{\tau}}^{+\infty} \frac{1}{\sqrt{2\pi}} e^{-\frac{u^2}{2}} du \tag{27}$$

(l) Knowing the symmetry property of the normal law, one can write:

$$\int_{-z_2-\sigma\sqrt{\tau}}^{+\infty} \frac{1}{\sqrt{2\pi}} e^{-\frac{u^2}{2}} du = \int_{-\infty}^{z_2+\sigma\sqrt{\tau}} \frac{1}{\sqrt{2\pi}} e^{-\frac{u^2}{2}} du$$

and as a result:

$$\int_{ln\frac{E}{S}}^{+\infty} e^{R-r\tau} \frac{1}{\sigma\sqrt{2\pi\tau}} e^{-\frac{\left[R-\left(r-\frac{1}{2}\sigma^2\right)\tau\right]^2}{2\sigma^2\tau}} dR = \int_{-z_2-\sigma\sqrt{\tau}}^{+\infty} \frac{1}{\sqrt{2\pi}} e^{-\frac{u^2}{2}} du = \int_{-\infty}^{z_2+\sigma\sqrt{\tau}} \frac{1}{\sqrt{2\pi}} e^{-\frac{u^2}{2}} du = \Phi(z_1) \tag{28}$$

where: $z_1 = z_2 + \sigma\sqrt{\tau} = \dfrac{ln\frac{S}{E} + \left(r + \frac{1}{2}\sigma^2\right)\tau}{\sigma\sqrt{\tau}}$

(m) Substituting in expression (25) the relations (26) and (28), one can write:

$$C = S\Phi(z_1) - Ee^{-r\tau}\Phi(z_2) \tag{29}$$

The explicit solution for the Put option can be determined quite easily, knowing the explicit solution for the Call.

We know that:

$$C = V(s,t) = e^{-r(T-t)} E^Q\left[max(S_T - E, 0)|F_t)\right] = Sf\,(z_1) - Ee^{-r\tau}\Phi(z_2)$$

and whereas $P = V(S,t) = e^{-r(T-t)} E^Q\left[max(\mathrm{E} - S_T, 0)|F_t)\right]$ from the Call - Put parity Theorem $\left(C + Ee^{-r\tau} = P + S\right)$, we obtain:

$$P = Ee^{-r\tau}\Phi(-z_2) - S\Phi(-z_1) \tag{30}$$

2.3. On the use of the Feynman-Kac theorem for option pricing

The Black-Scholes equation (12) above can be solved using the Feynman-Kac Theorem, having a single probabilistic solution. The Feynman-Kac Theorem tells us that (Negrea, 2006): if we have a function *f* with positive values, *V, V`and V``* are *Lipschitzian*, then the function $V(S,t) = E^Q\left[\frac{V(S_{T,}T)}{e^{r(T-t)}}\right]$ is the unique *Lipschitzian* solution of equation (12).

This can be demonstrated as follows (Brătian, 2018; Negrea, 2006):

(a) We know that the price of the underlying asset follows a random risk-neutral evolution. Such dynamics can be determined with the Girsanov Theorem as follows:

$$dS = rSdt + \sigma SdB^* \tag{31}$$

where: $dB^* = dB + \frac{\mu - r}{\sigma}dt.$

(b) We know that the price distribution of the underlying asset is lognormal. As a result, let $F = lnS$, and the differential equation satisfying F is:

$$dF = \left(r - \frac{1}{2}\sigma^2\right)dt + \sigma Z\sqrt{dt} \tag{32}$$

where: $Z \sim N(0,1)$.

(c) Integrating expression (32) we obtain:

$$lnS(t) - lnS(0) = \left(r - \frac{1}{2}\sigma^2\right)t + \sigma Z\sqrt{t}, \tag{33}$$

and as a result, in one time step (Δt) we will have:

$$S(t+\Delta t)=S(t)+\Delta S=S(t)exp\left[\left(r-\frac{1}{2}\sigma^2\right)\Delta t+\sigma Z\sqrt{\Delta t}\right] \quad (34)$$

(d) In a risk-neutral universe, the Black-Scholes equation (12) can be written as follows:

$$\begin{cases} \mathcal{L}(V)=rV \\ V(S_T,T)=(S_T-E)^+ \ for\, Call\, or\, V(S_T,T)=(E-S_T)^+ \ for\, Put \end{cases} \quad (35)$$

where, $\mathcal{L}(V)=\frac{\partial V}{dt}+rS\frac{\partial V}{\partial S}+\frac{1}{2}\sigma^2S^2\frac{\partial^2 V}{\partial S^2}$ is the *Dynkin operator.*

(e) As a result, the stochastic differential equation that checks the option price can be written: $dV = \mathcal{L}(V)dt+\sigma S\frac{\partial V}{\partial S}dB^*$ and knowing that $\mathcal{L}(V)=rV$ then:

$$dV=rVdt+a(S,t)dB^* \quad (36)$$

where: $a(S,t)=\sigma S\frac{\partial V}{\partial S}$.

(f) Equation (36) has as its unique solution:

$$V(S,t)=e^{-r(T-t)}\left(V(S_T,T)-\int_t^T a(S,u)e^{r(T-t)}dB^*\right) \quad (37)$$

(g) Applying now, under a risk-neutral probability, the expectation operator on equation (37), we have:

$$V(S,t)=E^Q\left[\frac{V(S_T,T)}{e^{r(T-t)}}\right], \quad (38)$$

where we admit that in equation (37) the application of the expectation operator on the stochastic integral is zero.

(h) As a result, whereas $V(S_T,T)=(S_T-E)^+ \, or \, V(S_T,T)=(E-S_T)^+$, we will have:

$$\text{for Call}: E^Q\left[\frac{\max(S_T-E,0)}{e^{r(T-t)}}\right] \tag{39}$$

$$\text{for Put}: E^Q\left[\frac{\max(E-S_T,0)}{e^{r(T-t)}}\right] \tag{40}$$

3. Empirical results

In the following, we will empirically address the pricing of European Call and Put options with a representative stock market index in Germany as the underlying asset. For this purpose, we consider the DAX stock index (GDAXI) as the underlying asset. For the calculation of the drift coefficient and the diffusion coefficient of the underlying asset we consider the daily closing value of the DAX stock index (GDAXI) over the period 30 December 2021 – 21 December 2022 and the risk-free interest rate (r) as 2,585% (in December 2022 for one-year German government bonds). The data used are obtained from Thomson's Reuters' Eikon Refinitiv platform.

The price of the underlying asset is simulated for the year 2023 using the Monte Carlo method, performing 10.000 daily scenarios over 252 days (one stock market year). The strike price is considered at the money ($S = E = 14.097{,}82$ Eur, date of analysis) and the values of the European Call and Put options for one underlying asset are determined at 3 months, 6 months, 9 months and 12 months.

The results of the data analysis are presented below as follows:

(A) using the Black-Scholes methodology, a summary of the results obtained is given in Tab. 9.1;

(B) using Monte Carlo simulations for the price of the underlying stock and the application of the Feynman-Kac theorem, the summary of the results obtained are shown in Figs. 9.1–9.4.

Tab. 9.1: Call and Put price results using Black-Scholes methodology (results in Euro currency)

The Maturity in 3 Months				
z_1	z_2	τ	The value of the Call option	The value of the Put option
(0,11)	(0,00)	0,25	662,89	572,07
The maturity in 6 months				
z_1	z_2	τ	The value of the Call option	The value of the Put option
(0,16)	(0,00)	0,5	987,14	806,10
The maturity in 9 months				
z_1	z_2	τ	The value of the Call option	The value of the Put option
(0,19)	(0,00)	0,75	1197,61	926,92
The maturity in 12 months				
z_1	z_2		The value of the Call option	The value of the Put option
(0,22)	(0,00)	1	1407,23	1047,47

Source: Authors' calculations

			Time	SIM 1	SIM 2	...	SIM 9999	SIM 10000
DAX (GDAXI) close - 21.12.2022	14097,82		0	14097,82	14097,8	...	14097,82	14097,82
Drift	-0,1198218		0,00396825	14077,21	14275,4	...	13803,57	14100,83
Duffusion	0,2342583		0,00793651	13903,89	14094,6	...	13783,59	14250,35
Time step (Δt)	0,00396825		0,01190476	13673,07	13848,8	...	13729,93	14281,58
Risk-free interest rate	0,02585		0,01587302	13887,25	13440,8	...	13595,85	14254,74
Strike price (at the money)	14097,82		0,01984127	13988,97	13622,7	...	13281,79	14375,22
			...	...	...	...	...	...
			0,98809524	12937,82	13798,6	...	10876,72	18621,16
			0,99206349	13011,27	13400,6	...	10963,29	18696,54
			0,99603175	13068,65	13547,7	...	10954,88	18717,26
			1	13240,09	13430,2	...	10684,92	18418,27
		3 months	0,25	12935,38	15632,9	...	14154,41	13581,58
	Call	Payoff		0	1535,07	...	56,59093	0
	Put	Payoff		1162,445	0	...	0	516,235
	Call	Average Payoff		702,3121				
	Put	Average Payoff		610,6709				
	Confidence value of the Average Payoff Call (α=0,05)					20,8423		
	Confidence value of the Average Payoff Put (α=0,05)					16,9019		
	Call	Value of the option		697,7881				
	Put	Value of the option		606,7372				

Fig. 9.1: Price results for Call and Put (3-month maturity) using Monte Carlo simulations for the underlying asset price and Feynman-Kac Theorem (results in Euro currency)

Source: Authors' calculations

			Time	SIM 1	SIM 2	...	SIM 9999	SIM 10000
DAX (GDAXI) close - 21.12.2022	14097,82		0	14097,82	14097,82	...	14097,82	14097,82
Drift	-0,1198218		0,003968	13829,86	14367,86	...	13830,78	14338,1
Duffusion	0,2342583		0,007937	14048,9	14305,78	...	13743,47	14506,3
Time step (Δt)	0,00396825		0,011905	13780,21	14571,24	...	13551,62	14711,29
Risk-free interest rate	0,02585		0,015873	14143,7	14846,74	...	13590,07	14581,78
Strike price (at the money)	14097,82		0,019841	14256,21	14876,41	...	13755,98	15139,09
			...	...	...	...	...	...
			0,988095	20662,51	14485,32	...	9915,915	14144,12
			0,992063	20530,8	14482,18	...	9676,978	14135,5
			0,996032	20438,83	14663,31	...	9775,875	13744,46
			1	21287,21	15174,27	...	9889,457	13474,34
		6 months	0,5	20976,35	13074,55	...	14141,07	15509,11
	Call	Payoff		6878,534	0	...	43,24855	1411,286
	Put	Payoff		0	1023,267	...	0	0
	Call	Average Payoff		1032,179				
	Put	Average Payoff		854,036				
	Confidence value of the Average Payoff Call (α=0,05)					31,2496		
	Confidence value of the Average Payoff Put (α=0,05)					23,29191		
	Call	Value of the option		1018,924				
	Put	Value of the option		843,0686				

Fig. 9.2: Price results for Call and Put (6-month maturity) using Monte Carlo simulations for the underlying asset price and Feynman-Kac Theorem (results in Euro currency)

Source: Authors' calculations

			Time	SIM 1	SIM 2	...	SIM 9999	SIM 10000
DAX (GDAXI) close - 21.12.2022	14097,82		0	14097,82	14097,82	...	14097,82	14097,82
Drift	-0,119821762		0,00396825	14018,44	14491,69	...	14036,56	13826,38
Duffusion	0,2342583		0,00793651	14119,92	14491,6	...	13881,46	13953,02
Time step (Δt)	0,00396825		0,01190476	13973,22	14166,79	...	13514,28	14261,69
Risk-free interest rate	0,02585		0,01587302	13678,44	14201,5	...	13827,36	14257,75
Strike price (at the money)	14097,82		0,01984127	13855,15	14338,28	...	13281,78	14180,83
			...	...	...	...	...	...
			0,98809524	13286,11	13046,24	...	11800,44	15115,96
			0,99206349	13397,59	13125,04	...	11967,49	14991,94
			0,99603175	13569,36	13326,85	...	12129,45	14888,5
			1	13071,78	13537,48	...	11711,96	15198,5
		9 months	0,75	15827,19	16600,85	...	14091,34	13723,52
	Call	Payoff		1729,373	2503,03	...	0	0
	Put	Payoff		0	0	...	6,48118	374,2967
	Call	Average Payoff		1262,892				
	Put	Average Payoff		1025,712				
	Confidence value of the Average Payoff Call (α=0,05)					38,0148		
	Confidence value of the Average Payoff Put (α=0,05)					28,0352		
	Call	Value of the option		1238,643				
	Put	Value of the option		1006,017				

Fig. 9.3: Price results for Call and Put (9-month maturity) using Monte Carlo simulations for the underlying asset price and Feynman-Kac Theorem (results in Euro currency)

Source: Authors' calculations

			Time	SIM 1	SIM 2	...	SIM 9999	SIM 10000
DAX (GDAXI) close - 21.12.2022	14097,82		0	14097,82	14097,82	...	14097,82	14097,82
Drift	-0,11982176		0,00396825	14055,81	13892,11	...	14014,14	14081,83
Duffusion	0,2342583		0,00793651	13873	13443,12	...	13727,52	14303,61
Time step (Δt)	0,00396825		0,01190476	14041,16	13476,61	...	13728,61	14199,72
Risk-free interest rate	0,02585		0,01587302	14232,12	13386,7	...	13788,35	14020,97
Strike price (at the money)	14097,82		0,01984127	13699,05	13516,57	...	14012,45	13751,47
			...	...	...	...	...	...
			0,98809524	11686,36	18885,5	...	15216,43	17589,26
			0,99206349	11830,14	19045,38	...	15227,99	17587,13
			0,99603175	11555,31	18799,7	...	15327,91	17821,3
			1	11372,24	18639,77	...	15518,8	17866,58
	12	months	1	11372,24	18639,77	...	15518,8	17866,58
	Call	Payoff		0	4541,954	...	1420,984	3768,764
	Put	Payoff		2725,577	0	...	0	0
	Call	Average Payoff		1487,064				
	Put	Average Payoff		1178,609				
	Confidence value of the Average Payoff Call (α=0,05)					46,4101		
	Confidence value of the Average Payoff Put (α=0,05)					31,3206		
	Call	Value of the option		1449,116				
	Put	Value of the option		1148,532				

Fig. 9.4: Price results for Call and Put (12-month maturity) using Monte Carlo simulations for the underlying asset price and Feynman-Kac Theorem (results in Euro currency)

Source: Authors' calculations

4. Conclusions

Based on the preceding findings, we can summarize as follows (see Tab. 9.2):

Tab. 9.2: Summary of Call and Put prices using the two modalities described in the methodology (calculations are made for one unit of underlying asset at the date of analysis)

Call and Put Prices Using the Black-Scholes Methodology		**Call and Put Prices Using the Feynman-Kac Theorem**	
Call	**Put**	**Call**	**Put**
3 months: 4,7 % of the underlying asset on 21.12.2022	3 months: 4 % of the underlying asset on 21.12.2022	3 months: 4,9 % of the underlying asset on 21.12.2022	3 months: 4,3 % of the underlying asset on 21.12.2022
6 months: 7 % of the underlying asset on 21.12.2022	6 months: 5,7 % of the underlying asset on 21.12.2022	6 months: 7,2 % of the underlying asset on 21.12.2022	6 months: 5,9 of the underlying asset on 21.12.2022
9 months: 8,4 % of the underlying asset on 21.12.2022	9 months: 6,5 % of the underlying asset on 21.12.2022	9 months: 8,7 % of the underlying asset on 21.12.2022	9 months: 7,1 % of the underlying asset on 21.12.2022

Tab. 9.2: Continued

Call and Put Prices Using the Black-Scholes Methodology		**Call and Put Prices Using the Feynman-Kac Theorem**	
12 months: 9.9 % of the underlying asset on 21.12.2022	12 months: 7,4 % of the underlying asset on 21.12.2022	12 months: 10,2 % of the underlying asset on 21.12.2022	12 months: 8,1 % of the underlying asset on 21.12.2022

Source: Authors' calculations

As can be seen from Tab. 9.2, the prices for Call and Put options, using the two modalities described above and the related results, we can say that the Black-Scholes methodology yields similar prices compared to the Monte Carlo simulation of the underlying asset price and the use of the Feynman-Kac theorem for Call and Put, given the confidence values for the mean payoffs in the Monte Carlo simulations.

Bibliography

Black, F., & Scholes, M. (1973). The Pricing of Options and Corporate Liabilities. *The Journal of Political Economy*, *81*(3), 637–654.

Brătian, V. (2018). Evaluation of Options Using the Monte Carlo Method and the Entropy of Information. *Expert Journal of Economics*, *6*(2), 35–43.

Brătian, V. (2019). Evaluation of Options Using the Black-Scholes Methodology. *Expert Journal of Economics*, *7*(2), 59–65.

Brătian, V. (coordonator), Bucur, A., & Opreana, C. (2016). *Quantitative Finance – Securities Valuation and Portfolio Management* (in Romanian: *Finanţe Cantitative – Evaluarea Valorilor Mobiliare şi Gestiunea Portofoliului*). Sibiu: Ed. ULBS.

Copeland, T., & Weston, F. (1988). *Financial Theory and Corporate Policy*, 3rd ed. Boston: Addison-Wesley Publishing.

Haug, E., & Taleb, N. (2011). Option Treders (very) Sophisticated Heuristics, Never the Black-Scholes-Merton Formula. *Journal Behavior & Organization*, *77*, 97–106.

Karoui, N., Jeanblanc-Picqué, M., & Shreve, S. (1998). Robustness of the Black and Scholes Formula. *Mathematical Finance*, *8*(2), 93–126.

Negrea, B. (2006). *Valuation of Financial Assets -- an Introduction to the Theory of Scocastic Processes Applied in Finance* (in Romanian: *Evaluarea Activelor Financiare – o Introducere în Teoria Proceselor Scocastice Aplicate în Finanţe*). Bucharest: Ed. Economică.

Negrea, B., & Damian, V. (2015). *Stochastic Calculus Applied to Financial Engineering* (in Romanian: *Calcul Stocastic Aplicat în Ingineria Financiară*). Bucharest: Ed. Economică.

Refinitiv Eikon a Thomson Reuters` Platforms, Refinitiv Eikon. (2023). Available online: http://refinitiv.com (accessed on 10 May 2023).

Stewart, I. (2013). *17 Equations That Changed the World* (in Romanian: *17 Ecuaţii Care au Schimbat Lumea*). Bucharest: Ed. Paralela 45.

Wilmott, P. (2002). *Derivatives – Financial Engineering. Theory and Practice* (in Romanian: *Derivative – Inginerie Financiară. Teorie şi Practică*). Bucharest: Ed. Economică.

Wilmott, P. (2007). *Introduces Quantitative Finance.* Chichester, England: John Wiley & Sons.

Amelia Bucur

Chapter 10 Applications of novel fuzzy optimization methods

Abstract: The mathematical tool of the intuitionistic fuzzy relation has many advantages in dealing with uncertain information, because the parameters in the intuitionistic fuzzy relation have relations with the external effect on the decision. In this chapter, we defined and used the notion of t-intuitionistic fuzzy relations to solve decision-making problems from economic field. Also, an algorithm for using t-intuitionistic fuzzy relation to solve decision-making problems to the study of some current economic phenomena is being created, and its effectiveness was showed with an example. In current economic phenomena, it is observed that weight function defined in t-intuitionistic fuzzy relation provides better approximation to measure that effects of the intern parameters increassing.

Keywords: mathematical modeling, decision making algorithms, intuitionistic fuzzy relation, economic phenomena

1. Introduction

Uncertainty is an aspect of some economic phenomena that cannot be avoided. In almost all countries, we regularly find ourselves in a state of uncertainty. Uncertainty can be caused by a variety of parameters, including randomness. These types of data are studied with using fuzzy set theory, fuzzy logic. Mathematicians created models in conditions of uncertainty and imprecision. The specialist Zadeh introduced the idea of fuzzy set theory (Zadeh, 1965). In the year 1981, Mizumoto and Tanaka, the operations defined over fuzzy set were defined.

The membership of an element to a fuzzy set is defined as a single value between zero and one in fuzzy set theory. In a recent period, was proposed intuitionistic fuzzy set, as a generalization of fuzzy set (Atanassov, 1986, 2016; Ejegwa et al., 2014). This, included the degree of hesitation known as the hesitation limit. In the year 1994, Atanassov defined operations on intuitionistic fuzzy sets.

The fuzzy set and its generalizations are important tools for mathematical modeling in decision-making problems. Some applications in modern mathematics of the fuzzy set can be seen for example in (Alhamzi et al., 2023; Masmali et al., 2023; Faraz et al., 2023).

In economic field, challenges with decision-making are a main objective. A method to solve such circumstances is t-intuitionistic fuzzy, with offers a flexible model to combat the ambiguity and uncertainty associated with decision-making.

2. Basic concepts of intuitionistic fuzzy set

Definition 2.1. (Sharma, 2012) A t- intuitionistic fuzzy set A_t defined on a universal set U, is represented by a membership and non-membership grade value μ_{A_t} and ν_{A_t} respectively whose codomain is the closed unit interval. The t- intuitionistic fuzzy set may be written as a collection of ordered pairs provided by the equality $A_t = \left\{\left(a_1, \mu_{A_t}(a_1), \nu_{A_t}(a)\right) : a_1 \in U\right\}$.

Definition 2.2. (Sharma, 2012) Let A_t and B_t be two t- intuitionistic fuzzy set on U .We have $A_t \subseteq B_t$, if $\mu_{A_t}(a_1) \leq \mu_{B_t}(a_1)$ and $\nu_{A_t}(a_1) \geq \nu_{B_t}(a_1), \forall a_1 \in U$.

In the following, let U, V and W are three crisp sets (in the specialty literature, fuzzy set and crisp set are the part of the distinct set theories, where the fuzzy set implements infinite-valued logic while crisp set employs bi-valued logic). The advantages and disadvantages of both forms of concepts, fuzzy set and crisp set, have been discussed in the specialty literature (Schneider & Rohlfing, 2013; Rohlfing, 2019).

Crisp set is a term for a mathematical notion that does not use fuzzy logic. Fuzzy logic is a mathematical theory which attempts to approximate the ambiguity inherent to human reasoning. And, a crisp set, contains data into categories; each data point can belong to one and only one category (Thiem, 2013; Vink & Van Vliet, 2009).

Let X a universal set and $t \in \left]0,1\right]$. Let a fuzzy set A defined on the universal set X. $\mu_A(x)$ of an element x from X, is a value in the closed interval [0, 1]. According to Klir and Yuan (1995) the crisp set A_t is the set $A_t = \left\{x \in X, \mu_A(x) \geq t\right\}$.

Definition 2.4. (Khan et al., 2021) Consider two sets U and V. A intuitionistic fuzzy relation is of the form:

$$R = \left\{ \frac{\left(\mu_R(a_1,b_1), \nu_R(a_1,b_1)\right)}{(a_1,b)} : (a_1,b) \in U \times V \right\} \tag{1}$$

where $\mu_R : U \times V \rightarrow [0,1]$ and $\nu_R : U \times V \rightarrow [0,1]$ satisfy the condition $0 \leq \mu_R(a_1,b_1) + \nu_R(a_1,b_1) \leq 1, \forall (a_1,b_1) \in U \times V$.

Definition 2.5. (Burillo & Bustince, 1995) A t-intuitionistic fuzzy relation from U to V is a intuitionistic fuzzy set of the product space $U \times V$. The relation R_t is defined by the membership and non-membership function μ_{R_t} and ν_{R_t} respectively. The membership and non-membership function μ_{R_t} and ν_{R_t} lies in the closed unit interval and are of the form: $\mu_{R_t}(a,b) = min\{\mu_R(a,b),t\}$ and $\nu_{R_t}(a,b) = max\{\nu_R(a,b),1-t\}$.

The set of ordered pairs can be used to describe the t- intuitionistic fuzzy relation:

$$R_t = \left\{ \frac{\left(\mu_{R_t}(a,b), \nu_{R_t}(a,b)\right)}{(a,b)} : (a,b) \in \mathbb{U} \times \mathbb{V} \right\}. \tag{2}$$

The expression t-intuitionistic fuzzy relation $(U \times V)$ means the collection of all t-intuitionistic fuzzy relation on $U \times V$.

The following example illustrate an application of the concept of t-intuitionistic fuzzy relation $(U \times V)$.

Example 2.1. Suppose we want to examine the attractiveness of an economic service that a person is considering using. Sometimes, the selection of an economic service is dependent on the choice parameters of each person. Let $U = \{p_1, p_2, p_3\}$ be the set of three economic services and V= {costly, prepare, novelty, organization experience} be set of decision parameters. Let R be an t-intuitionistic fuzzy relation on $U \times V$which is given by:

$$R = \left\{ \begin{array}{l} \frac{(0.50,0.40)}{(e_1,\text{Costly})} + \frac{(0.60,0.40)}{(e_1,\text{Prepare})} + \frac{(0.50,0.50)}{(e_1,\text{Novelty})} + \frac{(0.70,0.30)}{(e_1,\text{Organization experience})} + \\ \frac{(0.70,0.20)}{(e_2,\text{Costly})} + \frac{(0.80,0.20)}{(e_2,\text{Prepare})} + \frac{(0.70,0.20)}{(e_2,\text{Novelty})} + \frac{(0.50,0.40)}{(e_2,\text{Organization experience})} + \\ \frac{(0.60,0.30)}{(e_3,\text{Costly})} + \frac{(0.50,0.45)}{(e_3,\text{Prepare})} + \frac{(0.70,0.20)}{(e_3,\text{Novelty})} + \frac{(0.90,0.00)}{(e_3,\text{Organization experience})} \end{array} \right\}$$

The t-intuitionistic fuzzy relation $(U \times V)$ to give the 70 % attractiveness of the economic service is given by:

$$R_{0.70} = \left\{ \begin{array}{l} \frac{(0.50,0.40)}{(e_1,\text{Costly})} + \frac{(0.60,0.40)}{(e_1,\text{Prepare})} + \frac{(0.50,0.50)}{(e_1,\text{Novelty})} + \frac{(0.70,0.30)}{(e_1,\text{Organization experience})} + \\ \frac{(0.70,0.30)}{(e_2,\text{Costly})} + \frac{(0.70,0.30)}{(e_2,\text{Prepare})} + \frac{(0.70,0.30)}{(e_2,\text{Novelty})} + \frac{(0.50,0.40)}{(e_2,\text{Organization experience})} + \\ \frac{(0.60,0.30)}{(e_3,\text{Costly})} + \frac{(0.50,0.45)}{(e_3,\text{Prepare})} + \frac{(0.70,0.30)}{(e_3,\text{Novelty})} + \frac{(0.70,0.30)}{(e_3,\text{Organization experience})} \end{array} \right\}$$

Thus, the decision is chosen to select the economic service $\boldsymbol{e}_2$.

Definition 2.6. If $L_t \in t-$ intuitionistic fuzzy relation $(U \times V)$, then the domain of t-intuitionistic fuzzy relation L_t is defined as a of t-intuitionistic fuzzy set of U whose membership and non-membership functions of domain L_t are:

$$\mu_{dom(L_t)}(a) = \max_{b \in V} \mu_{L_t}(a,b) \text{and } \nu_{dom(L_t)}(a) = \min_{b \in V} \nu_{L_t}(a,b), \forall a \in U \tag{3}$$

Definition 2.7. Let $L_t \in t-$intuitionistic fuzzy relation$(U \times V)$ and $M_t \in t-$intuitionistic fuzzy relation$(V \times W)$. Then the composition of t-intuitionistic fuzzy relation $L_t \circ M_t$ is a t- intuitionistic fuzzy relation in $U \times W$ is defined as:

$$L_t \circ \mathrm{M}_t = \left\{ \left((a,c), \mu_{L_t \circ \mathrm{M}_t}(a,c), \nu_{L_t \circ \mathrm{M}_t}(a,c) \right) : (a,c) \in U \times W \right\}, \tag{4}$$

where

$$\mu_{L_t \circ M}(a,c) = \max_{b \in V} \left\{ min(\mu_{M_t}(a,b), \mu_{L_t}(b,c)) \right\} \tag{5}$$

and

$$\nu_{L_t \circ M_t}(a,c) = \min_{b \in V} \left\{ max(\nu_{M_t}(a,b), \nu_{L_t}(b,c)) \right\}. \tag{6}$$

Example 2.2. Let $U = \{1,2,3\}, V = \{x,y,z,w\}$ and $W = \{l,m,n\}$ be three universals sets. Consider the two intuitionistic fuzzy relation L and M on $U \times V$ and $V \times W$ given by:

$$L=\left\{\begin{matrix}\frac{(0.40,0.50)}{(1,x)}+\frac{(0.50,0.40)}{(1,y)}+\frac{(0.20,0.50)}{(1,z)}+\frac{(0.50,0.35)}{(1,w)}+\frac{(0.70,0.20)}{(2,x)}+\frac{(0.60,0.25)}{(2,y)}\\ \frac{(0.60,0.30)}{(2,z)}+\frac{(0.50,0.40)}{(2,w)}+\frac{(0.60,0.30)}{(3,x)}+\frac{(0.50,0.45)}{(3,y)}+\frac{(0.50,0.20)}{(3,z)}+\frac{(0.90,0.00)}{(3,w)}\end{matrix}\right\}$$

and

$$M=\left\{\begin{matrix}\frac{(0.40,0.50)}{(x,l)}+\frac{(0.40,0.50)}{(x,m)}+\frac{(0.40,0.35)}{(x,n)}+\frac{(0.80,0.20)}{(y,l)}+\frac{(0.60,0.35)}{(y,m)}+\frac{(0.50,0.40)}{(y,n)}\\ \frac{(0.30,0.40)}{(z,l)}+\frac{(0.50,0.10)}{(z,m)}+\frac{(0.40,0.20)}{(z,n)}+\frac{(0.70,0.30)}{(w,l)}+\frac{(0.45,0.45)}{(w,m)}+\frac{(0.50,0.20)}{(w,n)}\end{matrix}\right\}.$$

The $t-$intuitionistic fuzzy relation correspond to the value $t=0.70$ is given by:

$$L_{0.70}=\left\{\begin{matrix}\frac{(0.40,0.50)}{(1,x)}+\frac{(0.50,0.40)}{(1,y)}+\frac{(0.20,0.50)}{(1,z)}+\frac{(0.50,0.35)}{(1,w)}+\frac{(0.70,0.30)}{(2,x)}+\frac{(0.60,0.30)}{(2,y)}\\ \frac{(0.60,0.30)}{(2,z)}+\frac{(0.50,0.40)}{(2,w)}+\frac{(0.60,0.30)}{(3,x)}+\frac{(0.50,0.45)}{(3,y)}+\frac{(0.50,0.30)}{(3,z)}+\frac{(0.70,0.30)}{(3,w)}\end{matrix}\right\}$$

and

$$M_{0.70}=\left\{\begin{matrix}\frac{(0.40,0.50)}{(x,l)}+\frac{(0.40,0.50)}{(x,m)}+\frac{(0.40,0.35)}{(x,n)}+\frac{(0.70,0.30)}{(y,l)}+\frac{(0.60,0.35)}{(y,m)}+\frac{(0.50,0.40)}{(y,n)}\\ \frac{(0.30,0.40)}{(z,l)}+\frac{(0.50,0.30)}{(z,m)}+\frac{(0.40,0.30)}{(z,n)}+\frac{(0.70,0.30)}{(w,l)}+\frac{(0.45,0.45)}{(w,m)}+\frac{(0.50,0.30)}{(w,n)}\end{matrix}\right\}.$$

The composition between two $t-$intuitionistic fuzzy relation $L_{0.70}$ and $M_{0.70}$ is

$$M_{0.70}\circ L_{0.70}=\left\{\begin{matrix}\frac{(0.50,0.35)}{(1,l)}+\frac{(0.50,0.40)}{(1,m)}+\frac{(0.50,0.35)}{(1,n)}+\frac{(0.60,0.30)}{(2,l)}+\frac{(0.60,0.30)}{(2,m)}\\ \frac{(0.50,0.30)}{(2,n)}+\frac{(0.70,0.30)}{(3,l)}+\frac{(0.50,0.30)}{(3,m)}+\frac{(0.50,0.30)}{(3,n)}\end{matrix}\right\}.$$

3. A *t*-intuitionistic fuzzy relation theoretic approach to decision making problem

In this section, we provide a $t-$intuitionistic fuzzy relation theoretic approach to finding a solution to the problem of decision-making. An algorithm based on $t-$intuitionistic fuzzy relation is also presented. This approach allows us to identify the type that organizations are corresponding from.

3.1. Algorithm

Step 1. A Input the set of organizations (O), set of parameters (P), and set of types (T).

Step 2. Construct *intuitionistic fuzzy relation* $L(O \to P)$ and $Q(P \to T)$.

Step 3. Construct $t-$*intuitionistic fuzzy relation* $L_t(O \to P)$ and $Q_t(P \to T)$.

Step 4. Apply composition of $t-$*intuitionistic fuzzy relation* to get $t-$*intuitionistic fuzzy relation* $C_t(O \to T)$.

Step 5. Convert each entry of $C_t(O \to T)$ into a real value by applying the following weight function:

$$w(C_t) = \frac{1+\mu_{R_t}}{2+\mu_{R_t}+\nu_{R_t}}. \tag{7}$$

Step 6. The decision is any one of the elements in m where:

$$m = \max\left[w(\mathbb{C}_t)\right]. \tag{8}$$

3.2. Application of t-intuitionistic fuzzy relation in economic phenomena

In this section, we use an example of an abstract economic phenomena to demonstrate the application of $t-$intuitionistic fuzzy relation and its weight function one can get the optimum recognition result by calculating the weight function.

Let $O=\{O_1,O_2,O_3,O_4\}$ be a set of economic organizations and $P=\{p_1,p_2,p_3,p_4,p_5,p_6,p_7,p_8,p_9\}$ be a universal set of parameters or indicators for quality characteristics which determine their profit. The set of type of this organizations is $T=$ {Poor profit, good profit}.

Our objective is to carry out the right decision of the type of organizations.

The Tab. 10.1 indicates the intuitionistic fuzzy relation $L(O \rightarrow P)$ between organizations and parameters. The values closer to one indicates highly levels of the parameters, whereas numbers closer to zero indicate small levels of the parameters.

Tab. 10.1: Intuitionistic fuzzy relation between organizations and parameters $L(0 \rightarrow P)$

L	p_1	p_2	p_3	p_4	p_5	p_6	p_7	p_8	p_9
0_1	(0.90,0.10)	(0.70,0.20)	(0.20,0.80)	(0.70,0.20)	(0.40,0.50)	(0.70,0.20)	(0.20,0.70)	(0.60,0.20)	(0.40,0.20)
0_2	(0.90,0.10)	(0.50,0.50)	(0.60,0.30)	(0.60,0.40)	(0.60,0.20)	(0.20,0.70)	(0.10,0.30)	(0,60,0.30)	(0.80,0.20)
0_3	(0.70,0.10)	(0.70,0.10)	(0.20,0.50)	(0.10,0.50)	(0.10,0.70)	(0.30,0.60)	(0.40,0.50)	(0.30,0.40)	(0.80,0.20)
0_4	(0.40,0.50)	(0.10,0.20)	(0.50,0.50)	(0.40,0.40)	(0.03,0.70)	(0.60,0.20)	(0.30,0.50)	(0.40,0.50)	(0.50,0.50)

Let $Q(O \rightarrow T)$ be intuitionistic fuzzy relation between the organizations and type profit as shown in Tab. 10.2:

Tab. 10.2: *t*-Intuitionistic fuzzy relation between organizations and type of the profit $Q(O \rightarrow T)$

Q	**Poor Profit**	**Good Profit**
p_1	(0.70,0.20)	(0.80,0.20)
p_2	(0.70,0.30)	(0.80,0.20)
p_3	(0.50,0.30)	(0.70,0.10)
p_4	(0.70,0.30)	(0.80,0.20)
p_5	(0.40,0.40)	(0.50,0.30)
p_6	(0.50,0.50)	(0.60,0.30)
p_7	(0.90,0.10)	(0.50,0.30)
p_8	(0.70,0.30)	(0.80,0.20)
p_9	(0.00,0.20)	(0.90,0.10)

Let $t = 80\,\%$ describe the big influence of each organization with each parameter. The Tab. 10.3 indicates the t −intuitionistic fuzzy relation $L_{0.8}(O \rightarrow P)$ of level of the parameters of each organization.

Tab. 10.3: 0.80-intuitionistic fuzzy relation $L_{0.80}(O \rightarrow P)$

$L_{0.80}$	p_1	p_2	p_3	p_4	p_5	p_6	p_7	p_8	p_9
O_1	(0.80,0.20)	(0.70,0.20)	(0.20,0.80)	(0.70,0.20)	(0.40,0.50)	(0.70,0.20)	(0.20,0.70)	(0.60,0.20)	(0.40,0.20)
O_2	(0.80,0.20)	(0.50,0.50)	(0.60,0.30)	(0.60,0.40)	(0.60,0.20)	(0.02,0.70)	(0.01,0.30)	(0.60,0.30)	(0.80,0.20)
O_3	(0.07,0.20)	(0.70,0.20)	(0.20,0.50)	(0.10,0.50)	(0.10,0.70)	(0.30,0.60)	(0.04,0.50)	(0.30,0.40)	(0.80,0.20)
O_4	(0.40,0.50)	(0.10,0.20)	(0.50,0.50)	(0.40,0.40)	(0.30,0.70)	(0.60,0.20)	(0.03,0.50)	(0.40,0.50)	(0.50,0.50)

Let $t = 80\,\%$ describe the big influence of each organization with each parameter. The Tab. 10.4 indicates the 0.80− intuitionistic fuzzy relation $Q_{0.80}(O \rightarrow T)$ as shown in given below:

Tab. 10.4: 0.80-intuitionistic fuzzy relation $Q_{0.80}(O \rightarrow T)$

$Q_{0.80}$	**Poor Profit**	**Good Profit**
p_1	(0.70,0.20)	(0.80,0.20)
p_2	(0.70,0.30)	(0.80,0.20)
p_3	(0.50,0.30)	(0.70,0.30)
p_4	(0.70,0.30)	(0.80,0.20)
p_5	(0.40,0.40)	(0.50,0.30)
p_6	(0.50,0.50)	(0.60,0.30)
p_7	(0.80,0.20)	(0.50,0.30)
p_8	(0.70,0.30)	(0.80,0.20)
p_9	(0.00,0.20)	(0.80,0.20)

Now, we apply the definition of composition of t −intuitionistic fuzzy relation, we get the t −intuitionistic fuzzy relation of organization-type of the profit.

The composition of 0.80 – intuitionistic fuzzy relation between organizations and types $C_{0.80}(0 \rightarrow T)$ is shown in Tab. 10.5.

Tab. 10.5: Composition of 0.80-intuitionistic fuzzy relation between parameters and types $\boldsymbol{C_{0.80}(O \rightarrow T)}$

$C_{0.80}$	**Poor Profit**	**Good Profit**
O_1	(0.70,0.20)	(0.80,0.20)
O_2	(0.80,0.20)	(0.70,0.20)
O_3	(0.70,0.20)	(0.80,0.20)
O_4	(0.50,0.30)	(0.60,0.20)

Now, we calculate the weight function (7) and m (8) as given in Tab. 10.6:

Tab. 10.6: Weight function $w(C_{0.8})$

m	**Poor Profit**	**Good Profit**
O_1	**0.41380**	0.4000
O_2	0.40000	**0.41380**
O_3	**0.43180**	0.40000
O_4	**0.46430**	0.42860

Consequently, we infer that the organizations O_1, O_3, and O_4 have poor profit and the organization O_2 have a good profit.

Bibliography

Alhamzi, G., Javaid, S., Shuaib, U., Razaq, A., Garg, H., & Razzaque, A. (2023). Enhancing Interval-valued Pythagorean Fuzzy Decision-making through Dombi-based Aggregation Operators. *Symmetry*, *15*, 765, https://doi.org/10.3390/sym15030765.

Atanassov, K. (1986). Intuitionistic Fuzzy Sets. *Fuzzy Sets Syst.*, *20*, 87–96, https://doi.org/10.1016/S0165-0114(86)80034-3.

Atanassov, K. (1994). New Operations Defined over the Intuitionistic Fuzzy Sets. *Fuzzy Sets Syst.*, *61*, 137–142. https://doi.org/10.1016/0165-0114(94)90229-1.

Atanassov, K. (2016). Intuitionistic Fuzzy Sets. *Int. J. BIO, 20*, 1–6.

Burillo, P., & Bustince, H. (1995). Intuitionistic Fuzzy Relations, Part-I. *Mathware and Soft Computing, 2*, 5–38.

Ejegwa, P.A., Akowe, S.O., Otene, P.M., & Ikyule, J.M. (2014). An Overview on Intuitionistic Fuzzy Sets. *Int J Sci Technol Res., 3*, 142–145.

Faraz, M.I., Alhamzi, G., Imtiaz, A., Masmali, I., Shuaib, U., Razaq, A., & Razzaque, A. (2023). A Decision-Making Approach to Optimize COVID-19 Treatment Strategy under a Conjunctive Complex Fuzzy Environment. *Symmetry, 15*, 1370. https://doi.org/10.3390/sym15071370.

Khan, M., Zeeshan, M., Song, S.Z., & Iqbal, S. (2021). Types of Complex Fuzzy Relations with Applications in Future Commission Market. *J. Math.*, 1–14, https://doi.org/10.1155/2021/6685977.

Klir, G., & Yuan, B. (1995). *Fuzzy Sets and Fuzzy Logic: Theory and Applications.* Upper Saddle River: Simon & Schuster.

Masmali, I., Hassan, R., Shuaib, U., Razaq, A., Razzaque, A., & Alhamzi, G. (2023). Stock Reordering Decision Making under Interval Valued Picture Fuzzy Knowledge. *Symmetry, 15*, 898. https://doi.org/10.3390/w15101907.

Mizumoto, M., & Tanaka, K. (1981). Fuzzy Sets and Their Operations. *Inf. Control., 48*, 30–48, O019 9958/81/010030-19502.00/0.

Rohlfing, I. (2019). The Choice between Crisp and Fuzzy Sets in Qualitative Comparative Analysis and the Ambiguous Consequences for Finding Consistent Set Relations. *Field Methods, 32*(1), 75–88. https://doi.org/10.1177/1525822X19896258.

Schneider, C.Q., & Rohlfing, I. (2013). Combining QCA and Process Tracing in Set Theoretic Multi-method Research. *Sociological Methods & Research, 42*, 559–597. https://doi.org/10.1177/0049124113481341.

Sharma, P.K. (2012). t-Intuitionistic Fuzzy Subgroups. *IJMS, 2*, 233–243.

Thiem, A. (2013). Clearly Crisp, and Not Fuzzy: A Reassessment of the (Putative) Pitfalls of Multi-value QCA. *Field Methods, 25*, 197–207. https://doi.org/10.1177/1525822X13478135.

Vink, M.P., & Van Vliet, O. (2009). Not Quite Crisp, Not Yet Fuzzy? Assessing the Potentials and Pitfalls of Multi-value QCA. *Field Methods*, 21(3), 265–289. https://doi.org/10.1177/1525822X09332633.

Zadeh, L.A. (1965). Fuzzy Sets. *Inf. Control, 8*, 338–353, https://doi.org/10.1016/S0019-9958(65)90241-X.

Iustina Tudor and Nicolae Ionescu

Chapter 11 New methods and models applicable in the development of co-created products

Abstract: The development of co-created products gives the client a very important role in all stages of the product design. In the specialized literature, there are multiple views regarding the development of co-created products, but most of the applied methods, tools and models are not suitable to allow a greater intervention of the customer in relation to the classic product development methodologies. In this chapter, the authors propose new or improved methods and models, applicable in the development of co-created products, such as: dividing products into seven classes according to suitability for co-creation, the involvement in the co-creation process of two groups (a group of experts and a wider group of users), the dynamic approach to customer requirements and product characteristics based on certain laws of evolution, the establishment of target values and acceptable limit values as an average of the values given by customers, a cost model for co-created products, etc.

Keywords: product, development, co-design, co-creation

1. Introduction

The development of products on scientific, methodological bases was and is one of the constant concerns of many specialists (Phal & Beitz, 2007; Ulrich & Eppinger, 2009; Vargo & Lusch, 2004; Dieter, 2000). The developed methodologies start from a need and the requirements of potential customers that are translated into product specifications. In many cases, a significant period elapses between the establishment of customer requirements to the actual realization of the product, meanwhile similar competing products appear, and customer requirements change. That is why, to anticipate customer requirements from the moment the product is launched on the market, the following laws can be used: the laws of the evolution of technical systems (Altshuller, 1997) and the laws of the evolution of requirements (Petrov, 2002; Tudor, 2022). In parallel, synchronous customer participation can be adopted in all stages of product development, not only in the initial stage of establishing requirements, so that the development process is permanently adapted to customer requirements. Given this, the concepts of co-creation and co-created product appeared (Kambil et al., 1996; O'Hern &

Rindfleisch, 2010; Pieters & Jansen, 2017; Prahalad & Ramaswamy, 2004; Tudor, 2022) which implies the support and direct involvement of the customer at all stages of product development. In the process of developing co-created products, the concept of a product with personality is used, suggesting the existence of feelings and emotions through a set of characteristics similar to human ones (Dumitrescu, 2013; Green, 2002; Norman, 2004).

Within the existing approaches, two weak points can be noted: the poor representation of effective customer intervention tools at various stages of product development and the lack of a methodological approach that can be customized for different product classes. Finally, there is the issue of changing production costs through the intervention of the client, as it is necessary to develop cost models specific to co-created products. In the desire to design a co-created product development methodology, the authors have developed several methods and tools that allow direct, synchronous, customer participation in the design, development, and realization of several product categories. This paper presents, selectively, the most important methods and tools.

2. Defining co-created products and products with personality

Considering the fact that the permanent relationship between producer and consumer is a very important factor for the success of a product, a clear definition of the concept of co-created products and the co-creation activity is required. Based on the study of numerous points of view (Kambil et al., 1996; O'Hern & Rindfleisch, 2010; Pieter & Jansen, 2017; Prahalad & Ramaswamy, 2004; Vargo & Lusch, 2004; He et al., 2017) the co-created product can be defined as the result obtained following an active collaboration between the design-research team and potential customers, which responds to the needs of the stakeholders and increases their degree of satisfaction from a functional, aesthetic and technological point of view (Tudor, 2022). Also, the co-creation activity can be defined as a process of making products, involving the contribution of consumers through ideas and solutions with the aim of synchronizing new strategies and technologies with the needs of users, thus giving uniqueness and innovation to the final product (Tudor, 2022).

In the specialized literature (O'Hern & Rindfleisch, 2010) four distinct types of co-creation are defined in which customers can intervene in the creation of the product: (1) collaborating, (2) tinkering, (3) co-designing and (4) submitting. Regardless of the type of co-creation, one can distinguish (O'Hern & Rindfleisch, 2010) two major stages of the co-creation activity: the contribution of customers with ideas/suggestions and the company's rigorous selection of the best possible solutions implemented. Several initiatives regarding co-created products can be exemplified, such as the Arduio platform that provides open-source boards for users to build and develop individually projects according to their own needs (Arduino, 2023), the annual competition organized by the Lilac winery (IQads, 2023), entitled "Label the Unlabelled", in which potential customers are invited to recreate the design of the product and other similar initiatives organized by prestigious companies such as Electrolux (Booster, 2023), Ducati Motors (O'Hern & Rindfleisch, 2010) etc.

Product personality can be defined as a set of human characteristics transferred to a product so that it stands out from other products through self-expression, evoking attachment (Tudor, 2022). Thus, to attain product personality, a process is needed that responds to the compatibility with the human self, designed to create attachment, to stand out easily and to spark feelings and emotions through a set of human characteristics. In this way, there is a tendency to create products enriched with similar human qualities and traits, which help the consumer identify with the product and treat it with care and attention (Tudor, 2022).

3. Development of models regarding co-created products

In relation to the existing models in the specialized literature (O'Hern & Rindfleisch, 2010), considering the seven classes of products defined in point 4, six categories of co-creation activities can be considered, grouped in a model that can be called the Model of the 6 COs (Fig. 11.1).

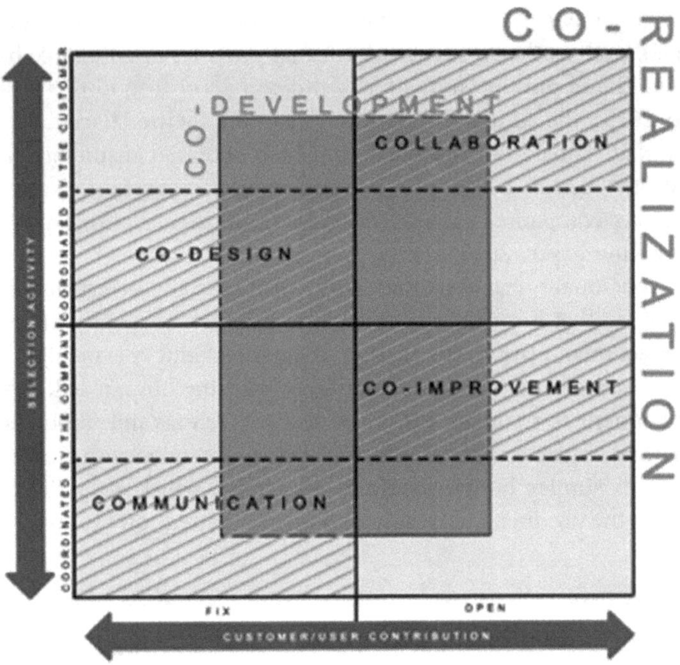

Fig. 11.1: Co-model
Source: Tudor, 2022

We define ***co-production*** as the process in which a single customer works together with the supplier to design and produce a complex, unique product. Examples: the realization of factories and/or "turnkey" workshops (GHI Smart Furnaces, 2023), the realization of construction-assembly works, etc.

For the ***concept of collaboration***, we adopt the definition from the specialized literature (O'Hern & Rindfleisch, 2010) for the term "collaborating": collaboration is defined as "the process in which customers have the collective power to develop and improve key components and the structure of new products" (O'Hern & Rindfleisch, 2010). This type of activity began in the field of open-source software (O'Hern & Rindfleisch, 2010) where customers could make fundamental changes to the underlying structure of the program, and has spread to other fields such as agriculture, pharmaceuticals, medical devices and architecture (O'Hern & Rindfleisch, 2010). An important issue that must be considered in this case is the intellectual property rights on the new product variants. Since an open-source application or product is used, it is natural that the new variants are offered to others for future improvements also in the open-source system. In this way, the concept of "Copyleft" and the concept of "Creative Commons" were born (Creative commons, 2023).

For the concept of ***co-improvement (co-modification)*** we take the definition of the term Tinkering (O'Hern & Rindfleisch, 2010): a process in which customers can make changes to a commercially available product and some of these changes are taken over by the company and incorporated in the following product releases.

To define co-design, we adapt the definition given by O'Hern and Rindfleisch (O'Hern & Rindfleisch, 2010). Thus, ***co-design*** can be defined as the process in which a group of customers submits proposals to the company for new products in various stages of design and another group of customers is asked to select solutions that will be adopted by the company in the development of new products. The proportion between the two groups can be higher or lower depending on the type of design and the type of product. Currently, this type of co-creation activity is most widespread in areas such as: clothing, television channels, household appliances, product packaging, etc.

To establish the main categories of co-design, we use the classification made by Ionescu et al. (2009) according to which there are five stages (types) of design, respectively: A – Competitive design (product planning), B – Functional design, C – Conceptual design, D – overall constructive design (architectural, embodiment design) and E – detailed constructive design. Based on this, we can formulate, by analogy, four categories of co-design, as follows.

Competitive co-design is a design phase that consists of designing a product's features and its design specifications with the active involvement of customers, considering the product's technical life cycle, according to the concept of deploying the customer's voice in the process of making products (Ionescu et al., 2009).

Functional co-design can be defined as a phase of the design in which, with the involvement of the customers, the design of the product's functions is carried out based on its design specifications and the functional implications of the requirements. In this phase, through the direct involvement of customers, the following are established: The general function of the product; Main functions; Decomposition of the main functions into secondary, tertiary functions, etc.; Critical functions. After establishing the functions, the development team establishes all the phenomena underlying the realization of each function and, using a multicriteria analysis method, determines the most appropriate phenomena.

Conceptual co-design is a design phase in which concepts are generated and the optimal concept is established, based on the functions established in the functional co-design phase, with the direct involvement of clients, using various techniques and methods to stimulate creativity. For this purpose, various techniques and methods will be adapted to allow the involvement of customers in the generation of concepts and in establishing the optimal concept. As mentioned, at this stage, numerous techniques and methods can be employed, such as: QFD, the nine windows technique, the eight laws of systems evolution, the 40 inventive principles, the QFD+TRIZ+Taguchi synergy, etc.

We define embodiment co-design as a design phase in which the preliminary structure of the product is made, and its subsystems and the links between them are highlighted, with the direct participation of customers/users. The term is known in the literature as Embodiment Design or Architectural Design (Pahl et al., 2007; French, 1971; Mirică & Cănănău, 2016; Dieter, 2000).

By adapting the definition for detail design (Ionescu et al., 2009), the detail constructive co-design can be defined as a phase of the design in which the final or detail design of the product is carried out, with the direct involvement of the customers/consumers. After this phase, the final design of the product is obtained, both from the point of view of the assembly and from the point of view of the component milestones.

4. Defining co-created product categories with personality

Among the most important existing classifications in specialized literature (Ionescu et al., 2009), we can highlight the international classification of products and services for trademark registration (the Nice classification) and the international classification of products for industrial design registration according to the Locarno arrangement. These cannot be adopted or adapted for co-created products (Tudor, 2022), although certain features could be useful at various stages of establishing specific tools to enable client intervention in product development. Thus, it is necessary to create a specific classification that facilitates the intervention of potential customers/users in the development/creation of a product to a greater or lesser extent depending on several factors such as the complexity of the product, the knowledge and experience of the customer in terms of the use and development of the product, the educational and professional training of clients, etc.

From this standpoint, seven product classes shown in Tab. 11.1 are proposed (Tudor, 2022).

Based on the seven classes of products, just as many categories of co-creation activities can be defined, as follows: Co-creation of the 1st degree, for co-created products of class 1, etc.

In future research, the seven product classes will be analyzed according to several criteria, the most important of which are: the impact of the client's intervention on production costs, the need to change manufacturing technological processes, the influence of the degree of manufacturing flexibility, the difficulty and the cost of implementing customer solutions, the production type, etc.

5. Development of methods, techniques and tools for creating co-created products and products with personality

In order to facilitate the client's intervention in the creation of co-created products, the authors have developed several methods, techniques and tools, some of which are considered more important in this paper.

Tab. 11.1: Analysis of the seven product classes

Class	Name	Description and Examples	Production Type	The Degree of Intervention of Potential Customers
Class 1	Complex factory-type products	Small factory type products in all fields of mechanical processing containing one or more sections	Unique; "Turnkey" factories	The client/ beneficiary can collaborate in the realization of the project
Class 2	Complex products of type Production Sections (Manufacturing Systems)	Products of the type of production departments, workshops, flexible cells, etc.	Unique; "turnkey" sections	The customer/ beneficiary can collaborate by choosing from several categories

(continued on next page)

Tab. 11.1: Continued

Class	Name	Description and Examples	Production Type	The Degree of Intervention of Potential Customers
Class 3	Complex equipment products	Products of the type of products of the type of complex equipment made to order: processing systems by combined processes, water jet cutting, CNC machines made in a modular way, etc..	Unique/small series	The customer/ beneficiary can select modules
Class 4	Simple equipment and devices	Relatively simple industrial equipment and device type products	Small/ medium series	The client/ beneficiary can get involved in all stages of development
Class 5	Complex consumer products	Relatively complex consumer products such as: refrigerators, washing machines, automobiles, vacuum cleaners, etc.	Medium/large series	The client/ beneficiary can get involved in all stages of development, by applying specific tools
Class 6	Simple consumer products	Wide range of simple consumer products such as: simple household products in the kitchen, in the garden, furniture, etc.	Large series/ mass	
Class 7	Service type products	This class includes all categories of services	Large series/ mass	

Source: Created by the authors

In the competitive co-design stage, after the voice of the customer is collected using one of the well-known tools (questionnaires, interviews, focus groups, etc.) and processed based on specific rules (Doicin, 2022; Ulrich & Eppinger, 2009), similar customers requirements are grouped together to obtain the so-called primary requirements. These requirements are given importance marks, on a scale from 1 to 5. In classic product development methodologies (Vişan & Ionescu, 2006; Doicin, 2022; Ulrich & Eppinger, 2009; Pahl & Beitz, 2007) the ranking of requirements primary based on relative importance scores, is done by the product development team. For the co-participation of customers part, they are asked to rank the primary requirements using an IT application (Fig. 11.2) (Tudor, 2022) which automatically averages the importance scores given by each customer for each requirement.

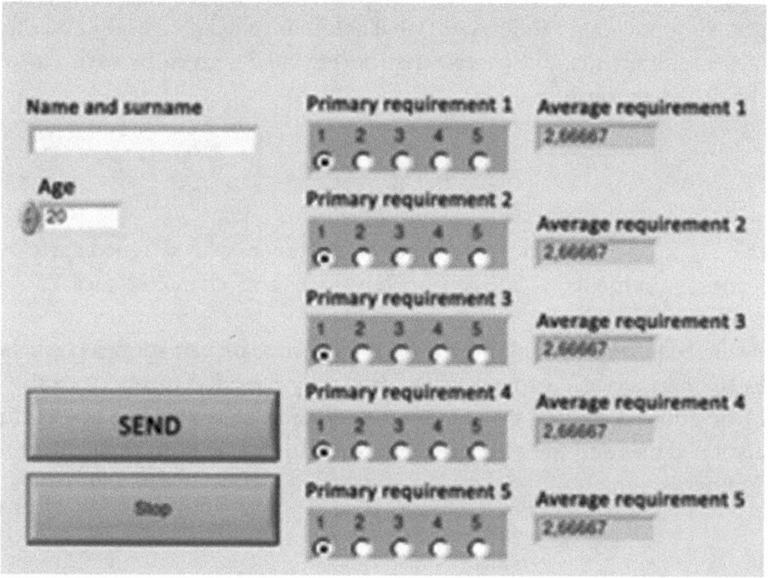

Fig. 11.2: Software application
Source: Tudor, 2022

Thus, the I_{rCi} importance score for each feature C_i will be:

$$I_{rCi} = \frac{1}{q_i} \cdot \sum_{k=1}^{q_1} C_{ik} \quad (1)$$

where $i = 1,\ldots, m$ represent the requirements and $q_1, q_2,\ldots, q_n$ – the number of customers who assigned importance marks to requirements *1, 2,…,* respectively *m*.

In order to establish correlations between customer requirements and characteristics/specifications in the specialized literature (Doicin, 2022, Ulrich & Eppinger 2009), the sizes/requirements matrix is recommended, which only allows the highlighting of qualitative correlations between the characteristics (specifications) established by the development team and customer requirements. To eliminate this disadvantage, another tool that can be used is the central part of the QFD quality house (Fehlmann, 2023) where correlations can be established by using a scale from 1 (very weak correlation) to 10 (strongest correlation), using an IT application (Tudor, 2022) that automatically averages the correlations between requirements and characteristics (Fig. 11.3), given by each customer, based on the relationship:

$$\boldsymbol{M}_{nm} = \frac{1}{q_n} \cdot \sum_{k=1}^{q_n} \boldsymbol{C}_{nmk} \quad (2)$$

where $q_1, q_2,\ldots, q_n$ represent the number of customers who assigned correlations between requirements *1, 2,….,* respectively *n* and characteristics *1, 2, ….,* respectively *m*.

As with requirement ranking, the development team can adopt as correlation values the average of customer scores (possibly rounded to the nearest whole value) or adopt an average (simple or weighted) of the average of customer correlation values and the average of the correlation values given by the product development team.

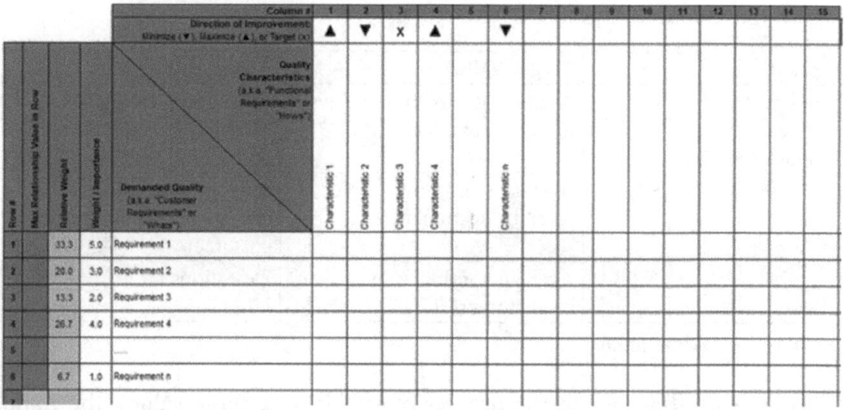

Fig. 11.3: Application for establishing the corelations between requirements and characteristics

Source: Tudor, 2022

Two strategies are commonly used to set target values. The first strategy based on the classification of product characteristics by Genichi Taguchi: *GTB* –Grater the Better, *STB* –Smaller the Better and *NTB* –Nominal the Better. This strategy has the advantage of ideal target values (infinity for *GTB*, zero for *STB* and as small deviations as possible for *NTB*), but does not offer us any solutions for establishing acceptable limit values. The second strategy allows target values to be established by reference to the best values of the competition. Thus, for *GTB* we can adopt at least the highest value of the competitors, for *STB* – at most the lowest value, and for *NTB* upper *ULD* and lower *LLD* deviations smaller than those of the competitors, in relation to a nominal value *N*. This paper proposes a third strategy (Tab. 11.2), applicable in the case of co-created products, based on the average of the values given by the customers. Obviously, in this case too, the development team can adopt the values obtained from customers or can average these values with their own, gained by applying one of the first two strategies.

Tab. 11.2: Definition of specification categories

Strategy		Target Values	Acceptable Limit Values
Strategy #3. Co-created products: average of values given by customers	GTB	Average of maximum values given by customers	Average of minimum acceptable values given by customers
	STB	Average of minimum values given by customers	Average of maximum acceptable values given by customers
	NTB	Average nominal values given by customers, N_c	Deviations $[N_c - LLD_c, N_c + ULD_c]$

Source: Created by the authors

To increase the rigor in the process of establishing these values, the Kano-Taguchi synergy can be used, where the characteristics/specifications are classified and grouped into three categories according to Kano's model: Basic characteristics (satisfactory, must be) – which reflect the quality expected, Performance characteristics (satisfactory, one dimension) – reflecting the desired quality and delightful characteristics – reflecting the exciting quality that exceeds customer expectations. If the first two categories of features, according to Kano's model, come from customer requirements, the third must be designed by the development team based on latent customer requirements through innovation and creativity.

Table 11.3 summarizes the grouping of characteristics according to Kano's model, where n_1 is number of basic characteristics, n_2 – number of performance characteristics, n_3 – number of delightful characteristics, V_a – acceptable limit value, V_t – the target value and Ca_k – the requirement associated with the characteristic Ch_k.

At the stage of Functional Co-design, when establishing the functions, the laws of the evolution of functions are taken into account (Tudor, 2022), as well as the law of evolution towards ideality (Altshuller, 1997), based on which customers are asked to indicate new functions, functions that are useless or harmful etc.

For conceptual design, for the generation of concepts through technological forecasting, the nine windows technique (Tab. 11.4) was adapted for the study of the evolution of customer requirements and the study of the evolution of features/specifications, respectively. Forecasting their future evolution can be used in gathering the voice of the customer, uncovering latent requirements,

Tab. 11.3: Co-established target values and acceptable limit values

No. Char.	Characteristic Type Conf Kano	No. Associated Requirement C_a	Char	Characteristic Type According to Taguchi	The Relative Importance of the Feature	Measure Unit	Accepted Limit Value	Target Value (Ideal Value)
1	Basic characteristics (satisfactory, must be)	$Ca_{11}, Ca_{12},\ldots Ca_{1p1}$	Ch_1	GTB/STB/NTB	$I_{rCh1} = \max\limits_{j\in[1,p1]}\{Ca_{1j}\}$	UM_1	$V_{a1} = \frac{1}{q_1}\cdot\sum_{k=1}^{q_1} V_{a1k}$	$V_{t1} = \frac{1}{q_1}\cdot\sum_{k=1}^{q_1} V_{t1k}$
2		$Ca_{21}, Ca_{22},\ldots Ca_{2p2}$	Ch_2	GTB/STB/NTB	$I_{rCh2} = \max\limits_{j\in[1,p2]}\{Ca_{2j}\}$	UM_2	$V_{a2} = \frac{1}{q_1}\cdot\sum_{k=1}^{q_1} V_{a2k}$	$V_{t2} = \frac{1}{q_1}\cdot\sum_{k=1}^{q_1} V_{t2k}$
…..			……	GTB/STB/NTB	Etc.	Etc.	Etc.	Etc.
n_1			Ch_{n1}	GTB/STB/NTB				
$n_1 + 1$	Performance characteristics (satisfactory)		Ch_{n1+1}	GTB/STB/NTB				
$n_1 + 2$			Ch_{n1+2}	GTB/STB/NTB				
….			……	GTB/STB/NTB				
n_2			Ch_{n2}	GTB/STB/NTB				
$n_2 + 1$	Delightful characteristics		Ch_{n2+1}	GTB/STB/NTB				
$n_2 + 2$	•		Ch_{n2+2}	GTB/STB/NTB				
…..	•		…….	GTB/STB/NTB				
n_3	•	8, 9	Ch_{n3}	GTB/STB/NTB				

Source: Created by the authors

Tab. 11.4: The nine-screen method applied to the study of requirements and features

		Long -term past	**Mid - term past**	**Near-term past**	**Present**	**Near-term future**	**Long - term future**
Laws of the transition from the system to the Supra-system, respectively to the sub-system	**Super-system**	• Customer **requirements** in the long-term past, at the super-system level $C_{S1}(t_l)$, $C_{S2}(t_l)$,..., $C_{Sn}(t_l)$ • Product **characteristics** in the long-term past, at the super-system level $Ch_{S1}(t_l)$, $Ch_{S2}(t_l)$,..., $Ch_{Sm}(t_l)$	• Customer **requirements** in the mid-term past, at the super-system level $C_{S1}(t_{m-})$, $C_{S2}(t_m)$,..., $C_{Sn}(t_m)$ • Product **characteristics** in the mid-term past, at the super-system level $Ch_{S1}(t_m)$, $Ch_{S2}(t_m)$,..., $Ch_{Sm}(t_m)$	• Customer **requirements** in the near-term past, at the super-system level $C_{S1}(t_a)$, $C_{S2}(t_a)$,..., $C_{Sn}(t_a)$ • Product **characteristics** in the near-term past, at the super-system level $Ch_{S1}(t_a)$, $Ch_{S2}(t_a)$,..., $Ch_{Sm}(t_a)$	• Customer **requirements** in the present, at the super-system level $C_{S1}(t_p)$, $C_{S2}(t_p)$,..., $C_{Sn}(t_p)$ • Product **characteristics** in the present, at the super-system level $Ch_{S1}(t_p)$, $Ch_{S2}(t_p)$,..., $Ch_{Sm}(t_p)$	• Customer **requirements** in the near-term future, at the super-system level $C_{S1}(t_{va})$, $C_{S2}(t_{va})$,..., $C_{Sn}(t_{va})$ • Product **characteristics** in the near-term future, at the super-system level $Ch_{S1}(t_{va})$, $Ch_{S2}(t_{va})$,..., $Ch_{Sm}(t_{va})$	• Customer **requirements** in the long-term future, at the super-system level $C_{S1}(t_{vi})$, $C_{S2}(t_{vi})$,..., $C_{Sn}(t_{vi})$ • Product **characteristics** in the long-term future, at the super-system level $Ch_{S1}(t_{vi})$, $Ch_{S2}(t_{vi})$,..., $Ch_{Sm}(t_{vi})$
	System	• Customer **requirements** in the long-term past, at the system level $C_1(t_l)$, $C_2(t_l)$,..., $C_n(t_l)$ • Product **characteristics** in the long-term past, at the system level $Ch_1(t_l)$, $Ch_2(t_l)$,..., $Ch_n(t_l)$	• Customer **requirements** in the mid-term past, at the system level $C_1(t_m)$, $C_2(t_m)$,..., $C_n(t_m)$ • Product **characteristics** in the mid-term past, at the system level $Ch_1(t_m)$, $Ch_2(t_m)$,..., $Ch_n(t_m)$	• Customer **requirements** in the near-term past, at the system level $C_1(t_a)$, $C_2(t_a)$,..., $C_n(t_a)$ • Product **characteristics** in the near-term past, at the system level $Ch_1(t_a)$, $Ch_2(t_a)$,..., $Ch_n(t_a)$	• Customer **requirements** in the present, at the system level $C_1(t_p)$, $C_2(t_p)$,..., $C_n(t_p)$ • Product **characteristics** in the present, at the system level $Ch_1(t_p)$, $Ch_2(t_p)$,..., $Ch_n(t_p)$	• Customer **requirements** in the near-term future, at the system level $C_1(t_{va})$, $C_2(t_{va})$,..., $C_n(t_{va})$ • Product **characteristics** in the near-term future, at the system level $Ch_1(t_{va})$, $Ch_2(t_{va})$,..., $Ch_n(t_{va})$	• Customer **requirements** in the long-term future, at the system level $C_1(t_{vi})$, $C_2(t_{vi})$,..., $C_n(t_{vi})$ • Product **characteristics** in the long-term future, at the system level $Ch_1(t_{vi})$, $Ch_2(t_{vi})$,..., $Ch_n(t_{vi})$
	Sub-system	• Customer **requirements** in the long-term past, at the sub-system $C_{s1}(t_l)$, $C_{s2}(t_l)$,..., $C_{sn}(t_l)$ • Product **characteristics** in the long-term past, at the sub-system level $Ch_{s1}(t_l)$, $Ch_{s2}(t_l)$,..., $Ch_{sn}(t_l)$	• Customer **requirements** in the mid-term past, at the sub-system level $C_{s1}(t_m)$, $C_{s2}(t_m)$,..., $C_{sn}(t_m)$ • Product **characteristics** in the mid-term past, at the sub-system level $Ch_{s1}(t_m)$, $Ch_{s2}(t_m)$,..., $Ch_{sm}(t_m)$	• Customer **requirements** in the near-term past, at the sub-system level $C_{s1}(t_a)$, $C_{s2}(t_a)$,..., $C_{sn}(t_a)$ • Product **characteristics** in the near-term past, at the sub-system level $Ch_{s1}(t_a)$, $Ch_{s2}(t_a)$,..., $Ch_{sm}(t_a)$	• Customer **requirements** in the present, at the sub-system level $C_{s1}(t_p)$, $C_{s2}(t_p)$,..., $C_{sn}(t_p)$ • Product **characteristics** in the present, at the sub-system level $Ch_{s1}(t_p)$, $Ch_{s2}(t_p)$,..., $Ch_{sm}(t_p)$	• Customer **requirements** in the near-term future, at the sub-system level $C_{s1}(t_{va})$, $C_{s2}(t_{va})$,..., $C_{sn}(t_{va})$ • Product **characteristics** in the near-term future, at the sub-system level $Ch_{s1}(t_{va})$, $Ch_{s2}(t_{va})$,..., $Ch_{sm}(t_{va})$	• Customer **requirements** in the long-term future, at the sub-system level $C_{s1}(t_{vi})$, $C_{s2}(t_{vi})$,..., $C_{sn}(t_{vi})$ • Product **characteristics** in the long-term future, at the sub-system level $Ch_{s1}(t_{vi})$, $Ch_{s2}(t_{vi})$,..., $Ch_{sm}(t_{vi})$
		Laws of animal evolution; Laws of the evolution of characteristics				Forecast based on the laws of the evolution of requirements and characteristics	

Source: Created by the authors

or designing exciting new features according to Kano's model. Analyzing the horizontal evolution (evolution over time) we can formulate and/or use laws of the evolution of requirements, laws of the evolution of characteristics, as well as forecasting based on these two laws. Also, within the vertical evolution (evolution in space) we can formulate and/or use laws of transition from system to supra-system, respectively to sub-system.

Also, in the conceptual design stage, the eight laws of the evolution of technical systems and the 40 inventive principles, stated by Altshuller (Altshuller, 1997; Cavalluchi, 2001) can be applied to generate a large number of concepts, in a systemic analysis. Thus, each product is analyzed in terms of how it complies with these inventive laws and principles and, depending on the differences, conceptual solutions for improvement can be proposed. In the case of conceptual co-design this activity is designed to be carried out together with customers (Tudor, 2022).

6. Elements regarding cost evaluation of co-created products

The implementation of solutions proposed by customers in the creation of the product can lead to an increase in manufacturing costs, and implicitly to an increase in the selling price of the product and/or to a decrease in the profit of the manufacturing company. One of the trends existing today is mass costuming, which aims to obtain costumed products at manufacturing costs similar to mass production. The most important factors favoring this trend are: parametric design – that allows the design of many low-cost variants, and manufacturing flexibility – that can ensure the transition from one product to another with minimal costs and in a very short time. In general, for co-created products there is a fixed part – designed by the development team and a variable part – which can be changed in a certain number of ways by the intervention of customers. In both categories, there are parts that are manufactured within the manufacturing company and parts that are delivered by various suppliers, with the company developing the product only having to assembly them.

In this context, the total manufacturing cost of the C_T product can be written:

$$C_T = C_F + C_c + C_O \tag{3}$$

where C_F represents the cost of the parts of the fixed part, C_C – the cost of the parts of the co-created part and C_O – the cost of the outsourced parts.

For the calculation of C_F and C_C, the direct cost method can be applied (Neagu et.al, 2008) in which the cost C can be expressed according to the number of products made through a linear relationship (Neagu, 2004):

$$C = A \cdot X + B \tag{4}$$

where A represents the variable costs, B – the fixed costs and X – the number of products made.

Taking into account relation (4), relation (3) becomes:

$$C_T = A_F \cdot X + B_F + A_C \cdot X + B_C + C_O \tag{5}$$

If we assume that in a product, we have n fixed parts/subsystems, m co-created parts/subsystems and p outsourced parts/subsystems, relation (5) becomes:

$$C_T = X \cdot \sum_{i=1}^{n} A_{F_i} + \sum_{i=1}^{n} B_{F_i} + X \cdot \sum_{i=1}^{m} A_{C_i} + \sum_{i=1}^{m} B_{C_i} + \sum_{i=1}^{p} C_{O_i} \tag{6}$$

Variable costs A are composed of material costs C_α, raw labor costs C_β, overhead costs C_γ and the cost of depreciation and capital repairs of equipment C_δ. For fixed subsystems, these costs do not vary from one co-created product to another, but for co-created subsystems, these costs depend on the variant chosen by the customer from a multitude of variants that we consider permanently extensible through customer intervention. Thus, the relation (6) becomes:

$$\begin{aligned} C_T = {} & X \cdot \sum_{i=1}^{n} \left(C_{\alpha F_i} + C_{\beta F_i} + C_{\gamma F_i} + C_{\delta F_i} \right) + \sum_{i=1}^{n} B_{F_i} \\ & + X \cdot \sum_{i=1}^{m} \left(C_{\alpha F_i}(v_i) + C_{\beta F_i}(v_i) + C_{\gamma F_i}(v_i) + C_{\delta F_i}(v_i) \right) \\ & + \sum_{i=1}^{m} B_{C_i}(v_i) + \sum_{i=1}^{p} C_{O_i} \end{aligned} \tag{7}$$

where v_i, $i = 1, 2, \ldots, m$, are variables that can take $q_1, q_2, \ldots, q_m$ values, respectively, depending on the contributions of the customers:

$$v_1 \in \left\{ v_{11}, v_{12}, \ldots, v_{1q_1} \right\}, v_2 \in \left\{ v_{21}, v_{22}, \ldots, v_{2q_2} \right\}, \ldots, v_m \in \left\{ v_{m1}, v_{m2}, \ldots, v_{mq_m} \right\} \tag{8}$$

This general model can be adapted for various product categories or in different contexts such as, for example, determining profit and selling price under competitive conditions using non-cooperative game theory.

7. Conclusions

The paper presents several methods and tools that allow the client to participate throughout the development of a product, which will later be brought together within a general methodology for the development of co-created products. By adapting or adopting some concepts from specialized literature, elements such as co-realization, collaboration, co-improvement, co-development, co-design (competitive co-design, functional co-design, conceptual co-design, co-design embodiment, detail co-design) are defined. Starting from the idea that co-creation depends on the type of product, seven classes of products have been shaped, that allow customer intervention to a certain extent by using specific methods and tools. Among the most important methods and tools presented in the paper, we can enumerate: making an application for averaging the scores given by customers for requirements, determining correlations between requirements and specifications based on correlation scores given by customers, setting target values by customers and the acceptable limit values of the product specifications by the double grouping of the characteristics according to Kano's model and according to the Taguchi classification, the adaptation of the nine windows technique for forecasting the evolution of requirements and characteristics, the use of the eight laws of the evolution of systems and the 40 inventive principles for co-generation of product concepts. Starting from the idea that within a product there are fixed subsystems, co-created subsystems and outsourced subsystems, a model was created for calculating the manufacturing cost of co-created products that can be adapted for various product categories and in different scenarios of market competition. The most important direction for further research is the realization of a general methodology for the development of co-created products.

Acknowledgment. This work has been funded by the European Social Fund from the Sectoral Operational Programme Human Capital 2014–2020, through the Financial Agreement with the title "Training of PhD students and postdoctoral researchers in order to acquire applied research skills – SMART", Contract no. 13530/16.06.2022 – SMIS code: 153734.

Bibliography

Altshuller, G. (1997). *40 Principles: TRIZ – Keys to Technical Innovation.* Worchester, MA: Technical Innovation Center, ISBN-13: 978-0964074033.

Arduino. *Redefining the Learning Experience One Classroom at a Time.* Available online at: https://www.arduino.cc [Accessed 28 June 2023].

Cavallucci, D. (2001). Integrating Altshuller's Development Laws for Technical Systems into the Design Process. *Annals of the CIRP*, 50(1), 113–120.

Creative Commons. *Share your work.* Available online at: https://creativecommons.org/share-your-work/ [Accessed 28 June 2023].

Dieter, G. (2000). *Engineering Design-A Materials and Processing Approach.* Bucharest, Romania: Mc Graw Hill, ISBN-13: 978-0070168961.

Doicin, C. (2022). *Product Development.* Politehnica University of Bucharest.

Dumitrescu, A. (2013). *Design Treatise* (in Romanian: *Tratat de Design).* Bucharest: Ed. Academiei Române.

Electrolux, *Booster Program*, available online at: https://open.electrolux.com/community/boosterprogram [Accessed 28 June 2023].

Fehlmann, T.M. (2023). *Do We Need a Matrix for QFD?*, available online at: https://qfdonline.com/, [Accessed 28 June 2023].

French, M. (1971). *Conceptual Design for Engineers.* Springer London Ltd., ISBN: 978-1-84996-853-9.

GHI Smart Furnaces, *Turnkey Plants*, available online at: https://www.ghihornos.com/en/turnkey-plants/, [Accessed 28 June 2023].

Green, W. (2002). *Pleasure with Products: Beyound Usablility.* Taylor & Francis.

He, L., Songb, W., Wuc, Z., & Xud, Z. (2017). Quantification and Integration of an Improved Kano Model into QFD Based on Multi-population Adaptive Genetic Algorithm. *Computers & Industrial Engineering*, 114, 183–194. https://doi.org/10.1016/j.cie.2017.10.009.

Ionescu, A., Vişan, C., & Doicin, C. (2009). *The 25 Screen Model – A Tool for Technological Innovation*, Proceedings of 6th International Conference on Management of Technological Changes, Alexandropoulis, Greece, Editor Costache Rusu, ISBN: 978-960-89832-6-7, pp. 267–270.

IQads, *LILIAC, singurul vin care se transformă în fiecare an sub inspirația artiștilor contemporani din România*, https://www.iqads.ro/articol/57287/young-liliac-singurul-vin-care-se-transforma-in-fiecare-an-sub-inspiratia, [Accessed 28 June 2023].

Kambil, A., Ginsberg, A., & Bloch, M. (1996). *Re-inventing Value Propositions*, Stern Working Paper IS-96–21, New York University, available online at: https://core.ac.uk/download/pdf/43020348.pdf, [Accessed 28 June 2023].

Mirică, R.F., & Cănănău, S. (2016). Some Aspects of Embodiment Design. *Bulletin of the Transilvania University of Brașov*, 9 (58), No. 2 – Special Issue – Series I: Engineering Sciences, 175–180.

Neagu, C. (2004). *Production Systems Engineering and Management* (in Romanian: *Ingineria si Managementul Sistemelor de Productie)*. Bucharest: Ed. Bren.

Neagu, C., Roșu, M., Mamgiridis, M., & Melnic, L. (2008). Calculation Model of Production Costs for Batch-organized Manufacturing Case. *Review of Management and Economic Engineering*, nr. 1/vol 7/2008, 169–182.

Norman, D.A. (2004). *Emotional Design: Why We Love (or Hate) Everyday Things*. New York: Basic Books.

O'Hern, M.S., & Rindfleisch, A. (2010). *Customer Co-creation: A Typology and Research Agenda. Review of Marketing Research*, 6, 84–106. https://doi.org/10.1108/S1548-6435(2009)0000006008.

Pahl, G., & Beitz, W. (2007). *Engineering Design: A Systematic Approach*, 3rd ed. Springer Verlag, London Limited.

Pahl, G., Beitz, W., Feldhusen, J., & Grote, K.H. (2007). *Engineering Design – a Systematic Approach*, 3rd ed. Springer, ISBN 978-1-84628-318-5.

Petrov, V. (2002). The Laws of System Evolution. *TRIZ Journal*, 3. Available online at: https://the-trizjournal.com/laws-system-evolution/ [Accessed 28 June 2023].

Pieters, M., & Jansen, S. (2017). *The 7 Principles of Complete Co-creation*. Amsterdam: BIS Publishers, p. 15, ISBN 978-90-6369-473-9.

Prahalad, C.K. & Ramaswamy, V. (2004). *The Future of Competition*. Harvard Business School Press. ISBN 1-57851-953-5.

Tudor, I. (2022). *Contributions Regarding the Development of Methods and Tools for the Creation of Co-created Products and Products with Personality*, Scientific Report PhD Thesis, Politehnica University of Bucharest.

Ulrich, T.K., & Eppinger, S.D. (2009). *Product Design and Development*, 5th ed. New York: McGraw Hill. ISBN 978-0-07-340477-6.

Vargo, S., & Lusch, R. (2004). The Four Service Marketing Myths: Remnants of a Goods-based Manufacturing Model. *Journal of Service Research*, 6(4), 324–335. https://doi.org/10.1177/1094670503262946.

Vișan, A., & Ionescu, N. (2006). *Tolerances. Fundamentals of Product Design and Accuracy Prescription* (in Romanian: *Toleranțe. Bazele Proiectării si Prescrierii Preciziei Produselor)*. Bucharest: Ed. Bren. ISBN 973-648-280-4.

Creative Commons, *Share your work*, available online at: https://creativecommons.org/share-your-work/ [Accessed 28 June 2023].

Arduino, *Redefining the Learning Experience One Classroom at a Time*, available online at: https://www.arduino.cc, [Accessed 28 June 2023].

Deepa Pillai and Trupti Bhosale

Chapter 12 Reconstructive mixed method for financial distress and bankruptcy prediction

Abstract: The financial system is considered as a strong pillar of the economy owing to its influence on economic growth and in sustaining financial stability. In an economic environment with developed financial markets, bankruptcy of financial institutions manifests multiple downsides. The study introduces reconstructive mixed methods as a novel method for distress and bankruptcy prediction for commercial banks. The research plan originates from the mixed research method which encompasses both quantitative and qualitative data. Integration of machine learning techniques in conjunction with the mixed research will improve the distress and bankruptcy prediction for banks. Financial statements supported with financial ratios of the banks provide the basic premise for quantitative analysis however the financial disclosures have been rarely considered in financial analysis. The primary objective of the research is to assimilate mixed research methods with machine learning techniques to devise a reconstructive mixed method to identify early warning signs of distress and to improve bankruptcy prediction accuracy. Effective integration of artificial neural networks with deep learning methods will augment the predictive power of bankruptcy based on numerical and textual data. Although there is considerable research on the use of machine learning in distress and bankruptcy prediction, however a cohesive approach of measurable and qualitative data is not extensively researched and discussed. The research intends to complement to the extant literature on the concept of financial distress which entails diverse types of financial problems in addition to bankruptcy and would add to the methodical rigour on distress prediction.

Keywords: reconstructive mixed methods, bankruptcy prediction

1. Introduction

Over the years several corporations across the globe have witnessed failures due to bankruptcy or distress. Bankruptcy is preceded by financial distress and varies significantly nationwide. Literature evidences high use of leverage in the capital structure increases the potential for default and economic distress. Financial distress is considered an unwelcome state which has a negative impact on both the firm and the economy (Rafiei et al., 2011). The United States, European and Asian economies have witnessed the aftermath of the global financial crises led by several corporate enterprises (World Bank, 2010). Financial distress prediction becomes critical as it affects the going concern and the stakeholders of the business enterprise, further it enables investors and lenders to avoid capital losses and possible defaults (Sun & Li, 2009). Studies discuss various strategies for predicting financial distress for mitigating the losses (John et al., 2013). Studies suggest a positive likelihood of ratios as predictors of bankruptcy mainly ratios measuring profitability, liquidity, and solvency were considered significant indicators. However, dichotomy exists as every study cites a different ratio (Deakin, 1972). Distress and bankruptcy prediction are considered as a critical area of research in economics and finance which can be enumerated through the growing number of studies and research subjects (Chen et al., 2016). Financial distress precedes bankruptcy exceptions being policy decisions, regulatory changes or natural disasters (Matenda et al., 2021). Thus, the question arises what are the predictable factors which determine financial distress towards bankruptcy. Moreover, recently there have been numerous innovative bankruptcy prediction models with industry relevant ratios and methodological extensions which have emerged over a period of time (Platt & Platt, 1991). There is a dearth of research in the area of financial distress prediction (Platt & Platt, 2002).

The chapter aims to convey knowledge and key insights on the aspects of financial distress, default and bankruptcy prediction models using a blended approach of quantitative and qualitative parameters. The study aims to identify the existing gaps in the current literature on the subject in terms of financial distress, its prediction, and various strategies adopted by firms to mitigate distress. The need for the study is significant as the subject of financial distress has been debated extensively across academic researchers, legal scholars and corporate enterprises. The study primarily defines the concept of financial distress and the theoretical underpinnings trailed by the latest developments in the domain of financial distress and prediction. Quantitative analysis has been an integral component for distress and bankruptcy prediction, however the qualitative reporting indicators can culminate into predictive factors for distress of corporate enterprises. The study also underlines the need for redevising the mixed research approach for predicting financial distress and bankruptcy. The primary objective of the research is to assimilate mixed research methods with machine learning techniques to devise a reconstructive mixed method to identify early warning signs of distress and to improve bankruptcy prediction accuracy. Effective integration of artificial neural networks with deep learning methods will augment the predictive power of bankruptcy based on numerical and textual data.

2. Research method

The study commences with a systematic literature analysis based on the topic of financial distress, bankruptcy and prediction models. The methodology facilitates a comprehensive evaluation to structure the research outcomes on the stated themes and to examine the important quantitative and qualitative measures (da Silva et al., 2017). This approach is beneficial as it characterizes the research gaps in the present literature and provides a basis for a mixed research approach. To address the study objectives, a systematic analysis of different journals from Scopus and Web of Science databases relating to financial distress, bankruptcy and prediction strategies by firms were examined. Initially a scientific map on the aforementioned subjects were collated from various journals listed in the databases. Data search was undertaken using keywords: "financial distress", "bankruptcy" and "prediction strategies" to retrieve the relevant literature to examine the research gaps. The structure of research method adopted consisted of: Comprehensive review of literature, Detail the research gaps, Examine the characteristics of the existing literature, applicability of mixed research design for addressing the research gaps on the stated subjects and setting direction for future research (Junior & Filho, 2010).

3. Theoretical framework

There are numerous definitions of Financial distress, however the definition lacks universality. Financially distressed firms are the business enterprises which have diminished market value due to lower performance with substantial financial leverage and liquidity crises (Chan & Chen, 1991). Further, studies describe financial distress as a situation with insufficient cash flows to cover the business obligations leading to potential damages from litigations and defaults (Wruck, 1990). The definitions also emphasize financial distress as a situation where a firm is unable to meet its current financial obligations based on Basel II principle, deferred payments for more than 90 days resulting in business defaults (Blazy et al., 2014). Depressed cash flows followed by insolvency is also a state of distress (Purnanandam, 2008) which has serious economic outcomes, thus predicting the financial failures and their trends become imperative (Hsieh et al., 2012). The characteristics of financial distress can be determined as a state of firm with liquidity crisis, lower financial performance, deferred payments and defaults. Studies have also distinguished between financial distress and bankruptcy. Distress situation depicts two states (a) probability of recovery (b) a state of reorganization and liquidation however bankruptcy is a legal status where creditors undertake a legal action against the firm in case of defaults and insolvency (Veganzones & Severin, 2020; Lukason & Vissak, 2017). The signaling theory propounded by (Ross et al., 2008) argue that there exists a presence of asymmetric information amid the investors and the management. The use of aggressive debt in the capital structure, a good signal prevails in the market which assures the ability of the administration to generate sufficient cash flows to cover the debts, concluding strong fundamentals of the company. In contrast, if a firm decreases its financial leverage then investors consider that the firm is unable to meet its interest payments, thus avoiding debts leading to negative signals in the marketplace. Hence, probability of default is a main feature of signaling theory (Raza et al., 2018). Financially distressed firms have an increased likelihood of breach on debt contracts trailed by fall in the share prices with higher equity risk premiums (Boubaker et al., 2018). Accordingly, the literature underlines the necessity to develop a competent forecast of financial distress models for corporate enterprises. Furthermore, numerous models associated with prediction of financial distress and bankruptcy prediction have been also developed by researchers (Fitzpatrick, 1932; Beaver, 1966; Altman, 1968) using financial ratios and significantly contributed in the area of financial distress prediction. These models mainly discuss only the change in capital structure, the reasons for change and other factors are not widely discussed in the previous theoretical models (Baharum et al., 2018). Univariate analysis is the traditional method used for interpreting financial statements based on firms' financial ratios which serve as explanatory variables of distress predictors, however, univariate variables are examined one after the other, these studies lack an integrated approach on financial health (Altman, 1968). The recognition of company operating and financial problems were analyzed mainly through the financial ratio analysis. Third party agencies were established for providing qualitative type of information in assessing the creditworthiness prior to quantitative analysis. The other qualitative reporting factors which have emerged due to regulatory compliances such as governance reporting and sustainability reporting measures can be used for forecasting financial distress and bankruptcy which has not been discussed in the extant literature.

4. Emerging trends in research on financial distress and bankruptcy

The study (Baldwin & Gelzen, 1992), has used quantitative modeling for predicting the insolvency and has done a comparison between the annual data models and the quarterly data that implies that quarterly models, without sacrificing the precision offered by annual models, can provide investors, creditors, and auditors with more timely bankruptcy forecasts. Studies indicate the potential issues with the usage of bankruptcy prediction models in current research. The tests conducted in the study depict the issues that can occur when bankruptcy prediction models are applied inaccurately. The time periods, industries, and financial crisis scenarios employed in this analysis were different from those used to build the (Zmijewski, 1984) and (Ohlson, 1980) models. The results (Grice & Dugan, 2001), demonstrated that, as opposed to employing the initially constructed models, the models in the earlier studies employed time period, organizations, and financial crisis circumstances. The study's results also imply that, aside from the circumstances under which Ohlson and Zmijewski developed the models, additional financial crisis scenarios are not sensitive to the models' predictions. As a result, rather than merely predicting bankruptcy, the algorithms appear to be more widely applicable for predicting financial difficulty. The study by (Agarwal & Taffler, 2008) compares the effectiveness of accounting- and market-based bankruptcy prediction models and concludes that, under the right conditions, such as differential decision error costs and a competitive pricing environment, the z-score approach significantly increases bank profitability. Literature also enumerates the use of an integrated approach by using three different methods to predict the bankruptcy, viz. case-based forecasting, neural network and discriminant analysis. The results show a higher accuracy in the prediction of the bankruptcy using the three methods together rather than only one single method (Jo & Han, 1996).

Studies discuss several models for distress and bankruptcy predictions stated by researchers which are classified as: (a) Theoretical models (b) statistical models (c) Artificial intelligence-based models. Theoretical models widely use the qualitative accounting information of default reasonings, statistical models are based on financial statements to predict the probability of default either based on univariate or multivariate analysis. With the emergence of technology and digitalization, artificial intelligence models are extensively used in forecasting the distress more accurately based on machine learning and neural networks. Multiple models have emerged post financial crisis for predicting corporate financial distress: univariate analysis, multiple discriminant analysis, Regression based models, linear probability analysis, cumulative sums methodology, decision tree methods, case based reasonings, algorithm-based models, neural networks, cash management theory and credit risk theories. Each method has its particular advantages and shortcomings. Some models are considered methodologically superior whereas others are effectual in predictions. The chapter concentrates on the technology supported models for distress and bankruptcy predictions which creates a ground for reconstructive mixed research methods.

5. Concept of mixed method

Mixed research method is defined as a method which comprises both quantitative and qualitative designs in the same research study, which are advanced in response to the practical limits of both quantitative and qualitative design (Venkatesh et al., 2013). Mixed research methods have become gradually recognized by researchers as the combination of quantitative and qualitative methods provides a greater understanding of the research problems and questions rather than limiting to one method independently (Creswell, 2012). Mixed research is considered more advanced, extensive and time-consuming which necessitates the use of a research team (Creswell, 2012). Mixed research method is a research design which combines quantitative and qualitative methods in a single study, however it has been referred to as convergent method, convergent validation, data triangulation, blended research, multi method and integrative method (Johnson et al., 2007; Bryman, 2007). The characteristic of addition between qualitative and quantitative fundamentals of a mixed method study is apparent mainly in the way interdependencies exist between the multiple components of the study which are rooted in the research design for analysis.

6. Reconstructive mixed method application in financial distress and bankruptcy

Financial statements supported with financial ratios of the banks provide the basic premise for quantitative analysis however the financial disclosures have been rarely considered in financial analysis. The primary objective of the research is to assimilate mixed research methods with machine learning techniques to devise a reconstructive mixed method to identify early warning signs of distress and to improve bankruptcy prediction accuracy. Effective integration of artificial neural networks with deep learning methods will augment the predictive power of bankruptcy based on numerical and textual data. The paper synthesizes and illustrates the application of mixed research methods in distress and bankruptcy predictions.

The paper provides a framework where Artificial neural networks (ANN) are aligned with the quantitative financial data based on various financial ratios. Qualitative factors to be evaluated based on the deep learning-based data analysis and visualizations for an all-inclusive approach. ANN is a machine learning algorithm which models complex non-linear relationships between variables. ANN is used for optimization and prediction with backpropagation algorithms which will enable in understanding the historical trends and patterns of data on the financial parameters through forward and backward learning patterns. ANN can weigh the quantitative financial data to produce accurate predictive values for financial distress prediction. Table 12.1: indicates the early warning indicators of financial distress.

Tab. 12.1: Early warning signals for financial distress based on quantitative information

Financial Parameters	Financial Ratios	Elements
Solvency	Debt to Equity Ratio	Total debt to Owners equity
	Debt to Total Assets	Long term debt to Total Assets
	Cash flows to Debt ratio	Operating cash flows / Total debt
Liquidity	Current Ratio	Current Assets / Current Liabilities
	Cash ratio	Operating cash flows to Sales
	CATL ratio	Current assets / Total liabilities
Profitability	Return on Assets	Operating profit / Total assets
	Operating profit ratio	Operating profit / Sales

Qualitative data for distress prediction will encompass the Notes to accounts, Governance reporting, Sustainability reporting, Excerpts of directors/chairman address and the new articles which are non-numeric narrative or descriptive information about the firm. Further transcripts, conversations, video and audio recordings, images and text documents, investor presentations, research reports, people's opinions, online reviews can be used for assessing the bankruptcy. Text analytics techniques can be integrated for understanding the relevance and role of qualitative data in distress prediction. A stakeholder perspective can be employed to assess the performance and reviews about the firm to gauge the early warning signals of distress. Deep learning is a machine learning program which accurately identifies the contents of an image or block of text. Embedding deep learning tools for qualitative analysis will eliminate the biases and render results with precision. Deep learning models inevitably learn pertinent features by using a network of layered "neurons" which are the biologically-inspired nodes through which data and computations flow. Algorithms detect various aspects of an image or text at different levels of complexity which allows for increased precision and the analysis of more diverse information. Financial data is heterogeneous and imbalanced due to its various sources of initiation. The heterogeneity of financial data depends on the multi-source nature, and they are closely interrelated. Additionally, deep learning permits processing of extreme data and manages heterogeneity. Natural language processing can be applied to extract information for events such as inclination score, attention index and risk volatility which are retrieved from social media (Antweiler & Frank, 2004). Financial sentiment analysis is applied to analyze the stock market price prediction which can also be applied for bankruptcy prediction (Ahmadi, 2018). Sentiment analysis can be applied to filter data which can determine a company's failure from a large amount of unstructured text based on research reports, financial news, social media tweets and analyst reports. Textual financial data is comprehensive and difficult to quantify thus, companies hardly contemplate on these data for formulating growth strategies. An effective integration of qualitative data with quantitative data in distress and bankruptcy prediction models needs further investigation. The conceptual framework of the reconstructive mixed research is indicated in Fig. 12.1.

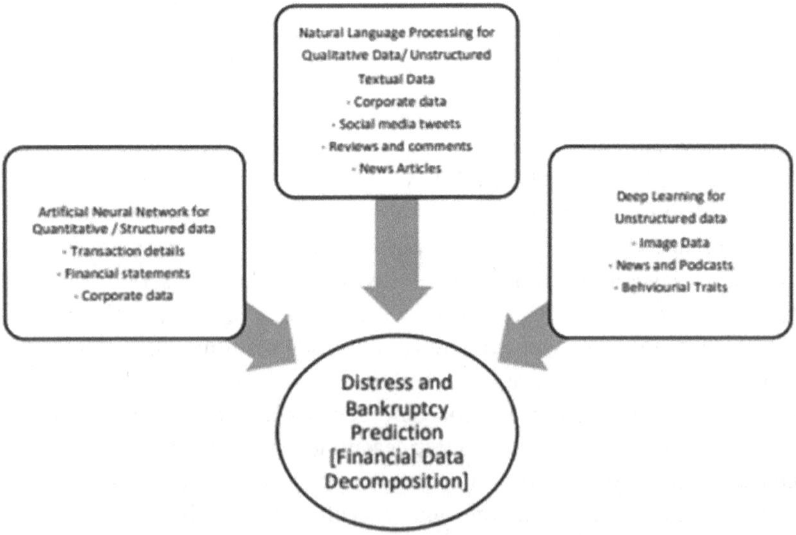

Fig. 12.1: The conceptual framework of the reconstructive mixed research

Source: Authors compilation

7. Conclusions

Financial distress and bankruptcy have global implications and is one of the significant problems for the corporate enterprises. Thus, a better understanding of the origin of financial distress is obligatory to decrease the financial and managerial consequences. The study provides a comprehensive discussion on a different perspective of bankruptcy prediction based on qualitative and quantitative data. The study contributes to the accounting and artificial intelligence literature, as it attempts to integrate the twofold for addressing a global concern of financial distress. The study reviews the applications of deep learning for financial distress prediction based on the categorization of financial data characteristics as multisource, heterogeneity and imbalance. ANNs are a promising alternative tool as compared to the statistical tools as it provides consideration for addressing real problems. From a continuing perspective, it seems more forthright and less time consuming for stakeholders to predict a company's financial distress than to analyze the financial statements published by the company. The study contributes to the applicability of machine learning in a mixed research method on financial distress and bankruptcy which provides a deeper insight on the factors and variables on the subject. The research in the area of Artificial Intelligence and Machine Learning in distress prediction is emerging and requires attention and investigation, thus, the study sets the direction for future research opening to strengthen and deepen the work on this theme of financial distress and bankruptcy.

Bibliography

Agarwal, V., & Taffler, R. (2008). Comparing the performance of market-based and accounting-based bankruptcy prediction models. *Journal of Banking Finance, 32*(8), 1541–1551.

Ahmadi, D. M. R. (2018). The use of technology in English language learning: A literature review. *International Journal of Research in English Education, 3*(2), 115–125.

Altman, E. I. (1968). Financial ratios, discriminant analysis and the prediction of corporate bankruptcy. *The Journal of Finance, 23*(4), 589–609.

Antweiler, W., & Frank, M. Z. (2004). Is all that talk just noise? The information content of internet stock message boards. *The Journal of Finance, 59*(3), 1259–1294.

Baharum, Z., Venkatesan, Y. R., Raidzuan, S. N. M., & Qureshi, M. I. (2018). The development of simulation model on environmental uncertainty factors for interval project completion. *International Journal of Engineering Technology, 7*(2.29), 62–66.

Baldwin, J., & Glezen, G. W. (1992). Bankruptcy prediction using quarterly financial statement data. *Journal of Accounting, Auditing Finance, 7*(3), 269–285.

Beaver, W. H. (1966). Financial ratios as predictors of failure. *Journal of Accounting Research*, 71–111.

Blazy, R., Martel, J., & Nigam, N. (2014). The choice between informal and formal restructuring: The case of French banks facing distressed SMEs. *Journal of Banking Finance, 44*, 248–263.

Boubaker, S., Saffar, W., & Sassi, S. (2018). Product market competition and debt choice. *Journal of Corporate Finance, 49*, 204–224.

Bryman, A. (2007). Barriers to integrating quantitative and qualitative research. *Journal of Mixed Methods Research, 1*(1), 8–22.

Chan, K. C., & Chen, N. F. (1991). Structural and return characteristics of small and large firms. *The Journal of Finance, 46*(4), 1467–1484.

Chava, S., & Jarrow, R. A. (2004). Bankruptcy prediction with industry effects. *Review of Finance, 8*(4), 537–569.

Chen, N., Ribeiro, B., & Chen, A. (2016). Financial credit risk assessment: A recent review. *Artificial Intelligence Review, 45*, 1–23.

Creswell, J. W. (2012). *Educational research: Planning, conducting, and evaluating quantitative and qualitative research*. Pearson Education, Inc.

da Silva, R. F. B., Batistella, M., & Moran, E. F. (2017). Socioeconomic changes and environmental policies as dimensions of regional land transitions in the Atlantic Forest, Brazil. *Environmental Science Policy, 74*, 14–22.

Deakin, E. B. (1972). A discriminant analysis of predictors of business failure. *Journal of Accounting Research*, 167–179.

Farooq, U., Jibran Qamar, M. A., & Haque, A. (2018). A three-stage dynamic model of financial distress. *Managerial Finance, 44*(9), 1101–1116.

FitzPatrick, P. (1932). A comparison of ratios of successful industrial enterprises with those of failed companies. The Certified Public Accountant (October, November, December): 598–605, 656–662, and 727–731, respectively.

Grice, J. S., & Dugan, M. T. (2001). The limitations of bankruptcy prediction models: Some cautions for the researcher. *Review of Quantitative Finance and Accounting, 17*, 151–166.

Hsieh, T. J., Hsiao, H. F., & Yeh, W. C. (2012). Mining financial distress trend data using penalty guided support vector machines based on hybrid of particle swarm optimization and artificial bee colony algorithm. *Neurocomputing, 82*, 196–206.

Jo, H., & Han, I. (1996). Integration of case-based forecasting, neural network, and discriminant analysis for bankruptcy prediction. *Expert Systems with Applications, 11*(4), 415–422.

John, K., Mateti, R. S., & Vasudevan, G. (2013). Resolution of financial distress: A theory of the choice between Chapter 11 and workouts. *Journal of Financial Stability, 9*(2), 196–209.

Johnson, R. B., Onwuegbuzie, A. J., & Turner, L. A. (2007). Toward a definition of mixed methods research. *Journal of Mixed Methods Research, 1*(2), 112–133.

Junior, M. L., & Filho, G. M. (2010). Variations of the kanban system: Literature review and classification. *International Journal of Production Economics, 125*(1), 13–21.

Lukason, O., & Vissak, T. (2017). Failure processes of exporting firms: Evidence from France. *Review of International Business and Strategy, 27*(3), 322–334.

Matenda, F. R., Sibanda, M., Chikodza, E., & Gumbo, V. (2021). Bankruptcy prediction for private firms in developing economies: A scoping review and guidance for future research. *Management Review Quarterly*, 72, 927–966.

Ohlson, J. A. (1980). Financial ratios and the probabilistic prediction of bankruptcy. *Journal of Accounting Research*, 18(1), 109–131.

Platt, H. D., & Platt, M. B. (1991). A note on the use of industry-relative ratios in bankruptcy prediction. *Journal of Banking Finance, 15*(6), 1183–1194.

Platt, H. D., & Platt, M. B. (2002). Predicting corporate financial distress: Reflections on choice-based sample bias. *Journal of Economics and Finance, 26*(2), 184–199.

Purnanandam, A. (2008). Financial distress and corporate risk management: Theory and evidence. *Journal of Financial Economics, 87*(3), 706–739.

Rafiei, F. M., Manzari, S. M., & Bostanian, S. (2011). Financial health prediction models using artificial neural networks, genetic algorithm and multivariate discriminant analysis: Iranian evidence. *Expert Systems with Applications, 38*(8), 10210–10217.

Raza, H., Ramakrishnan, S., Gillani, S. M. A. H., & Ahmad, H. (2018). The effect of dividend policy on share price: A conceptual review. *International Journal of Engineering Technology, 7*(4.28), 34–39.

Ross, S. A., Westerfield, R. W., Jaffe, J. F., & Jordan, B. D. (2008). *Modern financial management*. McGraw-Hill/Irwin.

Sun, J., & Li, H. (2009). Financial distress prediction based on serial combination of multiple classifiers. *Expert Systems with Applications*, *36*(4), 8659–8666.

Veganzones, D., & Séverin, E. (2020). On the Influence of Banking Relationships on French SMEs Failure. http://hdl.handle.net/20.500.12188/9674.

Veganzones, D., & Severin, E. (2021). Corporate failure prediction models in the twenty-first century: A review. *European Business Review*, *33*(2), 204–226.

Venkatesh, V., Brown, S. A., & Bala, H. (2013). Bridging the qualitative-quantitative divide: Guidelines for conducting mixed methods research in information systems. MIS Quarterly, 37(1), 21–54.

World Bank. (2010). *Global economic prospects 2010: Crisis, finance, and growth*. The World Bank.

Wruck, K. H. (1990). Financial distress, reorganization, and organizational efficiency. *Journal of Financial Economics*, *27*(2), 419–444.

Zmijewski, M. E. (1984). Methodological issues related to the estimation of financial distress prediction models. *Journal of Accounting Research*, 22, 59–82.

Printed by
CPI books GmbH, Leck